There I Was... Sea Stories, Tall Tales and other True Lies

Capt. Clifford Babson
PO Box 33
Lansing NY, 14882
607.280.8818
cliffordbabson@yahoo.com

THERE I WAS

"The sea, once it casts its spell, holds one in its net of wonder forever."
Jacques Yves Cousteau

THERE I WAS

THERE I WAS

Contents

THERE I WAS

THERE I WAS

Acknowledgements

I would like to thank my brilliant and beautiful wife Eileen for her endless support and encouragement. To my wonderful daughter, the real writer in the family, thank you for the joy you bring. To my beta readers and dear friends Jimmy Bell, and Casey Mastro thanks for the feedback. To my magnificent editor, grammarian extraordinaire, and old friend, Neil Brady, thank you for your brutal honesty, attention to detail, and your appreciation of good stories and fine whiskey. To Nancy Holzner, my writing mentor, thanks for all the great advice and patience. To all my old shipmates, fair winds and following seas. To my mom, thanks for everything, especially the work ethic, and teaching me to never quit. Mostly, thank you readers.

vi

The Big Step

It's all about the Story

"There is nothing - absolutely nothing - half so much worth doing as simply messing about in boats."— Kenneth Grahame

I was eighty feet in the air; standing at the top of the mast in a modern day version of a crow's nest. No railings, nothing to hold onto, just a few square feet of open deck high in the sky. Every instinct in my body begged me to lay down and cling for dear life, but I had work to do, and it required standing. So I stood there, precariously atop a tiny open platform, surrounded by nothing but empty space in every direction. The wind howled as it whipped past, pushing me, urging me to the edge. The mast and rigging stretched out below me, the massive gear shrinking in perspective as it receded to the point where the people below looked like ants crawling on a toy ship.

The last thought before I stepped off the mast into space was about the story. Surviving to tell the story is the most important part. I had climbed to the top of the crane tower up the long rusty vertical ladder that was welded to the side of the mast. Standing on deck, at the base of the mast looking up, the ladder stretched up and away so far I couldn't see where it ended, the mast and ladder just tapered off into the grey sky. I had learned long ago to grip the vertical rails and not the rungs, which can be rusted down to nothing. A hand gripping a loose rung can send you toppling backwards into space, but stepping on a bad rung will likely just send your foot back to the rung below, insulting your shin or knee in the process. By the time I made it to the top, my arms ached and my hands were raw, even through the thick work gloves. Death gripping is a mighty workout.

The ladder ended just below the top of the masthead, where there was a small open platform, about eight feet long, and three feet wide, with no rails. There was just a small steel bar that circled around the edge, three inches off the deck that served as a hand hold. The masthead was T-shaped, and I was standing on top of the T. The location served as a point to access the massive pulleys, called topping leads, which were there to direct the wires that raised and lowered the cargo crane booms.

The crane wires were led from a winch to the boom tip, and up through the air to the topping leads, back and forth a few times. The mast, the boom and the wire scribed a giant triangle, with the wire as the long aerial hypotenuse. My job was to grease that wire, from one end to the other.

I was looking down that long wire at the Bosun' s chair that dangled in empty space high above the deck an endless four or five feet away from me. It was windy as I stood there contemplating my next move, with dark gray clouds rolling across the sky. Those wires needed greasing, and that was why I was up there. I was an Able Bodied Seaman (an AB) and climbing the mast was a part of my job. This was a crane rigged freighter and it was up to the deck seaman to care for the cranes.

I had arrived to this ship that very day, and was being put to the test. The Captain needed deck seamen who could tend to his cranes, and he was not going to leave the dock until he was convinced that I had the skills he required. I was quite certain that he was standing in the wheelhouse at that moment, looking down the length of the ship at me, as I stood there, high atop the cross tree, clinging to the giant topping lead, staring at that ancient throwback of a climbing apparatus that dangled in space just a few feet away. Between me and that chair, nothing but air, all the way down to the deck, eighty feet below.

A Bosun' s chair is a flat piece of wood, with rope coming up through the corners like a swing, the ropes come together a few feet above the chair in a loop that was run through a shackle. When you are sitting in the chair, the ropes and chair form a small triangle in front of your midsection, where your feet pass through. The deck seaman riding the chair ties a special knot to the chair and by slacking that rope through the knot, the Bosun chair will slide carefully, backwards down the wire. It was an ancient technology, and would never pass OSHA standards, but OSHA didn't have any jurisdiction on ships at sea; regulations on ships were older, and looser.

The chair had a five gallon bucket full of grease, tied off and dangling below it with a long handled brush sticking out of it, because it wasn't dangerous enough until you and the entire chair were covered in a gooey slippery film of industrial grade lubricant. I was an AB alright, but truth be told, I had precious little time under my belt on freighters and hadn't spent nearly enough time on the mast to do what I was about to do. But I really needed this job and if I didn't take that next step onto the chair, I would be heading home within an hour.

I was damn certain everyone on deck was looking at me now and placing bets. I had taken a few of those bets before I climbed that long rusty ladder to the top, so I had that much more motivation to move. There was more than just a job at stake, there was cash money on long odds, bragging rights, and the all-important privilege of rubbing my success in the face of those random assholes who had foolishly bet against me.

Getting into that chair meant stepping across a vast four feet of empty space eighty feet above the hard steel decks below me, with nothing to hold on to but a greasy crane wire, and managing to get both feet through the small triangular opening that the ropes in the chair made, and somehow manage to land my ass on that greasy slippery seat, immediately arrest my motion precisely there and not continue into the wild blue yonder where gravity would take its toll. This was one of those moments that Mariners live for, on top of the world looking down, completely free from mundane normality, and forced to take stock, master yourself and conquer your fear. Like my dad always used to tell me: "Just fucking do it."

So there I was, perched on the flat peak of the mast surrounded by open air in every direction as far as the eye could see, the wind screaming in my ears, with nothing substantial to hold on to. The tiny people below looking up and betting on whether or not I would gather up the balls to do it, and all I can think of is… "If I survive this, it's going to make a hell of a sea story".

THERE I WAS

The art of the Sea Story

There I was

> *"A little bit of one story joins onto an idea from another... not old tales but new ones. Nothing comes from nothing... no story comes from nowhere; new stories are born from old--it is the new combinations that make them new." – Salmon Rushdie*

This book is a collection of sea stories loosely woven together as a single story through the eyes of a lone career Mariner. It is a story about sea stories. What is a sea story? A myth? A memoir? A legend? Is it a perfectly factual representation of some Mariner's experience or a complete fabrication created to entertain? Or is it some careful mix of each? It is all those things and more. They are rich, intriguing and terrifying stories told to delight and entertain. They come from an experience so vastly alien to most listeners that they have the ability to transport the audience to fantastic new places.

Whether they originate from an exact recounting of some salty recollection, or straight from the imagination of some grizzled swab, they are all gifts from the sea. *They are all true, and they are all lies.* They are often amalgams of experience, lovingly pieced together from treasured memories, and stories shared, then seasoned heartily with artistic license. (For the record, the following stories are complete fiction any resemblance or similarity to real persons or events is entirely coincidental.)

They are told in the first person, and like blessed whiskey and fine wine, they improve with age. In each telling they grow and evolve, gaining rich new nuance and depth, and achieving new heights of truth in their deepening embellishment. The fine art of telling sea stories can challenge all the senses. They are deeply enhanced by the accompaniment of a fermented beverage.

When delivered in the vicinity of Mother Ocean, their effect is multiplied, the salt air and scent of the tide acting like fuel for the vehicle of the listener's journey. Told over a meal, they are like an exquisite inter-mezzo to cleanse the palate between courses. Whether they are told with a moral in mind, or simply to entertain, they help the seagoing storyteller share their magnificent adventures, and unveil their unique experience to both their land bound and seafaring brethren.

These are my sea stories, many of them are my own experiences, while some are the experiences of others. Many are nothing more than flights of pure fancy. They are there for the telling, and nothing else. It is my hope to entertain, and share a view of the watery part of the world so familiar to me, and so foreign to others.

THERE I WAS

It might be appropriate to warn the faint of heart, the easily offended, those who have led deeply sheltered lives, or anyone else with a fear, distaste, or lack of exposure to the harshest realities that humanity has to offer. Mariners are a profoundly diverse lot, ranging from highborn Lords of the Admiralty, to the lowest dregs of society. They live in a world that brings them intimately close with war, poverty, violence, depravity, crime and the full catalog of the darkest aspects of the human condition on a scale most people can't even imagine.

There are Mariners who revel in that grittier side, and live the Mariners' life specifically for its darker aspect. Many Mariners are unfit for any other role, and live there in the Maritime nether regions somewhere between prison and marginally productive member of society. It has long been a haven for those too violent or anti-social for decent society, yet not quite criminal enough for incarceration. The advent of women in the Merchant Marine and 9/11 are changing that, but most of these tales happened long before that epoch.

It should also be noted, that the people who make up these stories, are usually featured because they are doing something 'colorful', odd, outlandish, or perfectly awful. The stories were chosen for the distance they stand from the normal experience of normal people. It is safe to assume that most people who would chose the life of a Mariner have elected to be different and have chosen a road less travelled. Among the odd lot of non-standard individuals we call Mariners, the ones that stand apart from that crowd of misfits and shine for how unique they are among the unique, are the people most likely to be included in these stories.

If this book appears to reflect on any particular group unfavorably, be they Mariners in general, women, or any specific ethnic or cultural group, it is due to the fact that this book, by design, is filled with tales of bad behavior. The typical, sane, well behaved, hardworking people of the Maritime world are less likely to have acted in a manner that would merit their addition to this catalogue of recalcitrant, reprobate, and deviant maritime misfits. To the hard working men and women of the Merchant Marine, Navy and other Maritime professions, I apologize for your lack of representation in this chronicle of sin.

For those of you completely unfamiliar with even the basics of shipboard life, please refer to Appendix A where a detailed description of the Maritime world can be found.

THERE I WAS

1000 Ways to pass the time on a long ocean voyage
1000 Words

"How do I love thee, let me count the ways" – *Elizabeth Barret Browning*

We did occasionally hear of the world back home and the things that were happening there. At one point, there was a Broadway show titled the "Vagina Monologues". Now, a million Broadway shows could come and go and nary would a merchant seaman take notice, but you go ahead and name it "Vagina" anything and suddenly Broadway is on the RADAR.

No one I knew ever saw the show or had any direct experiences, but it came up as a topic of conversation, as Vaginas so often did, and it was said that the Vagina was referenced over 100 times, a hundred different ways. We had no actual knowledge of this, of course, but that led the discussion to the comparison of the play to your typical merchant seaman, who also might use the word vagina 100 times, in a 100 different contexts in the course of a two hour discourse.

We all wholeheartedly believed that no merchant seamen were involved in the writing of said monologues, if the full tally of vaginal references was merely 100. We challenged ourselves to find a thousand different ways to say vagina. It was a pursuit perfectly suited to prolonged days of uneventful watchstanding on the long run across the sub-equatorial Pacific.

This particular watch team was perfectly suited to the endeavor. The group was comprised mostly of that special breed of Merchant Marine who dedicates his life to the pursuit of sexual adventure. Mariners come in many varieties, there are lovers, and fighters, oddballs, academics, adventurers, and there are those like me who seem to be a little of each. This team had three members, myself, Lyn Abel, and Bobby Jones. His first name was Bobby, but his last name wasn't really Jones, it was some marginally pronounceable Greek name ending in ...opolis, but Bobby idolized Tom Jones. He would walk around the ship singing "whoa, whoa, whoa" and between that, the shiny nightclubbing clothes, and his constant, focused, unrelenting desire for one thing, and one thing only, he became Jones.

He had once been in an extremely swank hotel in Tokyo, and had seen Tom Jones in person in the bar, dancing up a storm with three super-models. The sight of a man past his fifties, capturing the full attention of every woman in the club and then spending the entire evening dancing with the three finest of them had been a religious experience for Bobby, and speaking ill of Tom Jones in his presence was an act of pure blasphemy. Bobby dreamed that one day he too would have women hurling their panties at him.

Bobby was by all accounts, and even his own admission, a pervert. He loved sex, he spent every waking moment thinking about sex, pursuing sex, or thinking about pursuing sex. His appetite was legendary, and he constantly told stories of his deviant adventures. He had many disgusting sexual appetites, and had an encyclopedic knowledge of sexual practices learned in his relentless pursuit of procreative adventure.

He was descended from Greek immigrants and often used the word "Malaka" which is the Greek word for asshole. It is by pure coincidence... or not, that the busiest waterway on earth, a narrow strait between Indonesia and the Asian mainland that connects the Indian Ocean to the Pacific, is named the Straits of Malacca. He found that to be profoundly amusing, and in his never ending accounts of his Charnel escapades, he would refer to a person's back end as "the straits of Malacca".He referenced many of his preferred amorous techniques by name, as players are prone to do. His favorite was in fact "The Straits of Malacca", which was a technique of his own devising (so he claimed), and he considered it his trademark. It consisted of him standing or kneeling behind his bent over partner, punctuating his rhythmic performance by slapping the girl on the rump as loudly as possible while shouting "STRAITS OF MALACCA" at the top of his voice. Bobby was not, by anyone's measure, a role model. He did have a strange internal version of ethics, insofar as a whore mongering deviant can, but there were in fact lines he would not cross.

He believed firmly in adult consent, which in the world of sex crazed Mariners who ply the Pacific trades is not always the case. There are Asian countries that are known cater to pedophiles, and Bobby had a healthy respect for children, and made a point to avoid even visiting those places. For Bobby also, as much as the physical act, he enjoyed the pursuit and the seduction. Informed consent was important to him, and it was also important that his quarry be sober. Respect was not exactly his attitude towards women though, rather much the opposite.

His attitude towards the fairer sex can be summed up by something he said during one of my first experiences with him. Prior to leaving Long Beach California, we all went out for some dinner and few drinks. Hooters of course, at his suggestion. He stepped through the door into the bar and slowly scanned the landscape, eyeing all the beautiful women in their scanty outfits, admiring their gorgeous cleavage and tight clothes, and he turned to us with a smug look, smirking slightly, and said:

"I bet every woman in this place has had a dick in her mouth at some point". That statement summed him up. He did manage to harness his evil powers that night to add "Hooters waitress" to his list of conquests.

7

THERE I WAS

My other watch partner was Lyn Abel, and while the focus of his life, and his every endeavor was nearly identical to Bobby's, they couldn't have been more different. You see, Lyn loved women. He loved everything about them, adored the ground they walked on, and wanted nothing more than be close enough to them to worship them properly. Lyn's sexual exploits were legendary, I had heard stories about him long before I ever met him. He had girlfriends all over the world, and wives in dozens of countries, and according to him, they were all aware of one another.

He received copious amounts of mail, sweet smelling letters in pink or lavender envelopes, or packages with gifts, even money arrived on a regular basis. It was rumored around the world that Lyn could satisfy any woman. Frustrated women came to him from far and wide with their sexual frustrations. Lyn was happy to help. There was a vast network of women across the world in near constant communication, keeping tabs on his whereabouts, and there were usually women waiting for him when he arrived in port.

It was this team of miscreants that began discussing vaginas' that fateful night, as the sun settled down on the horizon, dead on the bow, two days out of Long Beach enroute to Hong Kong and Singapore.

"We could easily come up with a thousand words for *Pussy* (1)*" Bobby ventured.

"*Piece of cake* (2)" Lyn added,

"*Piece of ass* (3)" Bobby countered. "Are you keeping track" Bobby asked me, "That is three already".

So began the quest for 1000 words. Bobby began rattling off words without interruption even faster than I could write. Lyn had a more thoughtful approach, concentrating hard, with an intent expression on his face and occasionally blurting out something. His aim was far loftier than Bobby's, trying to lend poetic justice, in his simple way, to the *sacred object of his desire* (4). As Bobby rambled off a litany of disgusting pejoratives, Lyn interjected excitedly from time to time with a "*Consummation devoutly to be wished!*"(5) or "*Promised Land*" (6).

Lyn, of course, became consumed with his vaginal musings over the course of the long voyage, and would be sit lost in thought in the mess hall, or the lounge and suddenly shout out "*ALTER OF VENUS!*"(7) Excitedly. As the official recorder of the event, it was my responsibility to keep the tally. One night my phone rang at 2AM, and Lyn simply shouted "*Amazon Forest!*"(8) Into the phone and then hung up.

The next morning is when we decided that maybe he should start keeping a notebook with him, and writing his thoughts down to avoid seriously angering his watch officer. Legend has it that from that day forward, Lyn kept a small notebook with him every day for the rest of his life. He titled his little memoir "Ode to *the Love Garden* (9)."

THERE I WAS

That first watch we came up with about 100 words:

Each watch would began with both the excitement of knowing that the next four hours would be filled with discussions on our favorite topic, as well as the trepidation of knowing that we were far from our quota, and that a 1000 words was more of a challenge than we had first imagined. Lyn was always well prepared, of course, no doubt having focused his full concentration on the matter every second since leaving the Bridge the watch prior.

Lyn's contributions were smaller, but more thoughtful and respectful. The tally grew longer each day. As the voyage progressed, and it became more difficult to make the list grow, themes began to emerge, some colorful and benign, others grotesque and vulgar, but we were on a mission. Entire watches would be devoted to exploring names that contained the word "Pink" like *Pink Turtleneck* (10) and *Pink Muffin* (11), or the word "Baby" like *Baby Cannon* (12) and *Baby Cave* (13). Days were spent musing on variations of "Meat" or "Seafood" references.

As the list grew, and it became more and more difficult to think of new words, we enlisted the help of other crewmembers. Ships are typically *melting pots* (14) of international ethnic diversity. Our galley crew alone had people originating from no less than three continents. Our deck department had a similar mix of global humanity, and all told the crew represented the Philippines, Australia, Poland, Puerto Rico, Brazil, Cape Verde, New England, Texas, Brooklyn, and Boston. They each contributed with bon mots in their own native vernacular. As time passed, and new words became harder to find, everything started to sound like a vaginal reference. (As the numbers in parentheses throughout the book demonstrate)

One day, late in the game, when the list was topping 900, after a long few hours with not a single new word, it was decided that vaginal hairstyles qualified for the list, and "*Buckwheat in a headlock* (15), *the Philosopher* (16), *Bear trappers hat* (17) and several others made the list, sparking that last stretch of creativity that we so desperately needed to finish our disgusting tribute to the female anatomy. We felt all at once, triumphant, relieved, ashamed, and a little unclean when it was all said and done, much like we would all feel after our port visit in Hong Kong in a few days. Our list was complete, and is presented in appendix A for your enjoyment.

*The running tally of words is noted throughout the book by the numbers in the parentheses as the words are added to the list.

THERE I WAS

Part 1 – Voyage End

>*"Some went down to sea in ships, they were the merchants on the mighty waters. They saw the works of the Lord, his magnificent deeds in the deep."* Psalm 107

To End Where We Started

"...And know that place for the first time." (TS Eliot)

"And how have I lived? Frankly and openly, though crudely. I have not been afraid of life. I have not shrunk from it. I have taken it for what it was at its own valuation. And I have not been ashamed of it. Just as it was, it was mine." Jack London

Normally, stepping off of a ship into Olongapo City in the Philippines is a *joyous occasion* (18), the start of a *lavish tropical adventure* (19), but on this day it was less festive than usual. The papers had been signed, the ship turned over to the oncoming Captain, and travel back to the states had been booked. I was about to take the first step on my Journey home to Ithaca, where my wife and 18 month old child awaited.

This was likely the last time I would walk down a gangway with my seabag slung across my back. I was sure I would never see this ship again, and for a Captain that is like losing an *old friend* (20).

I knew it was time. I knew I was ready. This ship had been conducting Oceanographic Surveys in the San Bernardino Straits in the Philippine Archipelago for the past few months, and spent seven out of every 30 days in Olongopo City on Subic Bay just outside of Manila. Manila is like an amusement park for Mariners, and one might wait ones entire career to land a gig like this. But each month when the crew excitedly lined up to storm ashore and enjoy the Fantastic San Miguel Beer, delicious food, gorgeous women, and a full catalog of sin at ridiculously low prices, all I could think about was going home. That alone made it perfectly clear. The sin of Sin City no longer interested me.

I stood at the bottom of the gangway looking back, and realized that I would never again stand on the weather deck and stow a gangway for sea. Never again feel the unparalleled joy of casting that last line off as the tug pulls us off the dock, away from the cares and troubles of the world. That feeling of forging on to places unknown, the pure peace of open ocean and big skies, would forever just be memories. I remembered the first time I lugged my seabag up a gangway, 25 years before and suddenly realized that on that day I was greeted by the very same person who I was planning to see today. The voyage of my life travelling a full circle would, in a manner of speaking, end where it started.

THERE I WAS

This being my last time in the Philippines, and Manila being such an old *treasured friend* (21), I felt the need to say a proper goodbye. I had an old shipmate who owned a small beach resort close by and I was heading out to pay him a visit. The odds of him being there were long, but this resort had been an important crossroad in my life and I wanted to revisit it one last time. There was damn fine blessed whiskey to be had there, and it was a fitting farewell to this country, this continent, this entire hemisphere and the *life of a Mariner* (22) in general.

I had hired a car for the day, which finally arrived, as I stood ruminating at the base of the gangway. The young driver smiled broadly at me when I told him my destination. As we drove through the busy streets of Olongapo City and Manila, at the end of this 25 year long voyage, it got me thinking about how this trip had started.

Saquish Point

The Turning Point

> *"Rich and happy as I was after my third voyage, I could not make up my mind to stay at home altogether. My love of trading, and the pleasure I took in anything that was new and strange, made me set my affairs in order, and begin my journey through some of the Persian provinces." The Seven Voyages of Sinbad the Sailor: the fourth voyage"*

"The mess hall was filled with an acrid blue smoke and the deck was starting to feel hot. This wasn't a drill, the space below us was burning. The fire was in Auxiliary Machine Room Number two, which was the *main fuel transfer station* (23). The space was filled with pumps and valves and manifolds all sitting on top of fuel tanks with more than 50,000 gallons of Fuel. It was the worst possible place for my first real fire. It was my job to lead the hose teams into that space. The fire was below us, which meant we would have make a vertical descent into a burning fuel fire... and that my friend... was not how I wanted to die."

I paused a moment, poking the campfire for effect, making it pop, and releasing a cascade of sparks up into the clear October sky. This was one of my favorite sea stories, and this was no ordinary audience, this was Matthew, the Ancient Mariner. Telling a sea story to landsmen is one thing, but telling a story of ocean adventure to a man who had spent more time riding the waves than I had spent on God's blue Earth was a different matter altogether. Matthew had asked me "What's the bravest thing you ever done?" This was the story that came to mind. It was the perfect time and place for a good sea story.

The sun was setting placidly into the bay behind us as the crisp ocean breeze on our faces described the impending change in season. We were three different men, from three different generations, there on Saquish beach that October evening, overlooking Plymouth Harbor and Cape Cod bay, all sitting around a warm fire and passing a bottle of 150 year old Dominican Private Stock Rum. Saquish point was a long spit of beach that angled off of the elbow of Gurnet point overlooking Plymouth Harbor. Saquish, together with Duxbury Beach was part of the barrier beach that formed Duxbury bay, and the shelter for Plymouth Harbor.

It was a pure New England Evening, right down to the cast of characters. Matthew was as crusty an old salt as any that ever left land, safety and common sense behind to chase a distant horizon. He had retired out of the Navy as a Chief Boatswain's Mate, and continued his seagoing career in the Merchant Marine,

THERE I WAS

working commercial freighters and tankers, and whatever other paying berths that suited his fancy. He retired again from that career and lived now out there on Saquish point, down 10 miles of sand beach with no utility services, no paved roads, and no excuses.

Matthew was now a lobsterman, living in a magnificently simple beach shack, weathered gray by the constant assault of salt air and New England Weather. His leathery skin was deeply tanned, and his tangled mop of hair and bushy beard were shocking white. The gray eyes that sparkled out from under the brim of his hat were as deep as the oceans that he had been working for over 40 years. We sat there between the beach and his home, adorned with the same color coded buoys that marked his lobster pots, several of which were retired decoratively nearby in his garden.

My father and I had come to visit Matthew to ask some advice. I was 24 years old and had spent the last two years in college studying aviation after a four year enlistment in the Navy. We were from an old New England family, directly descended from one of the early settlers of Gloucester. I spent my youth reading the stories of my seafaring ancestors, 16 generations of Gloucester fishermen, Merchantmen, and Whalers. Their ranks included Privateers in Washington's Navy, and veterans of naval service in every US War. The family history had logged hundreds of thousands of long ocean miles, and a few thousand of them were my very own. I continued with my story.

"When I finally got to the repair locker it was like a funeral, people walking around too dazed or afraid to think straight. Guys who could normally slap on the oxygen kits blindfolded in less than a minute during a drill where just staring dumbly at it, or trying to put it on upside down. They knew that they had to get up close to a fuel fire, and they were scared. I was the On Scene Leader, this was my team, and I had to do something fast, so I just did what they taught me... I yelled. They don't call us On Scream Leaders for nothing."

"I started barking orders at people, especially the dazed ones. There were people just walking in circles, but the second you gave them something to do they snapped out of it. "GO GRAB AS MANY FIRE EXTINGUISHERS AS YOU CAN FIND AND BRING THEM HERE, YOU– GO SET UP A PHONE LINE, YOU– GRAB GARCIA AND JONES AND GO SET UP THE PORTABLE PUMPS - USE THE DISCHARGE BY THE MESS LINE" The more I yelled, the more purpose they had, and the calmer they got."

That's when I learned that calm spreads just as easily as panic, maybe more easily, since people resist panic"

"The good ones do anyway" Matthew commented, a smile painting itself across his weathered face, etching itself into the deep creases at the side of his eyes. I nodded silently, exuberant that I had engaged such a formidable listener to my tale.

THERE I WAS

"So I got everybody dressed out in the turnout gear, got us all to the top of the ladder, and when we opened that hatch it was like opening a chimncy, all hot air and smoke, but it was blue smoke, not black smoke and that was good" I paused to take a sip of the molasses thick Rum.

"Why was that good?" My dad chipped in. Matthew answered for me "Black Smoke would be the fuel burning, that's a nasty hot fire that's hard to put out, blue smoke is an electrical fire, once you shut down the power, it just leaves a smoldering mess to clean up." Matthews's speech was slow and deliberate, and his New England accent was as thick as a Cape Cod fog on a summer evening. He wasn't actually wearing a 'Sou'wester rain hat like the Gloucester fisherman, but it felt as if he should have been. I moved on:

"Exactly. Not a 'class B' fire, but a fire nonetheless, and a fire on top of a giant fuel tank, which meant it could turn into a 'Bravo' fire at any minute. So there I was... standing next to that oven door with the smoke rolling out so thick that I could barely see the guys in front of me whose shoulders my hands were resting on. We had to enter that space to fight the fire" I paused a moment, tossing some driftwood onto the fire, continuing slowly, "On a ship you have no choice, you fight fire or you die, there is no walking home from there"

"A hatch is just a *hole in the deck* (24), this one was three feet wide, maybe five feet long, with a ladder leading down into the space. It wasn't a vertical ladder, but it was steep enough when you weren't in full turnout gear with an Oxygen kit on your back, lugging fire extinguishers, and a hose.

"I was pretty sure none of us would get out of there alive, but if we didn't go in, everyone on that ship was likely to die, so I took that first step down into that smoky, burning space... and that, is the bravest thing I have ever done."

Matthew nodded his approval. He had likely walked through a door into a burning steel room at least once in his long career, with no plans of ever coming out. His career had started in WWII, and like most Mariners of that era, he had survived more than one U-boat attack. He handed the bottle of rum over to me with his knobby calloused hands, scarred and crooked, with at least two fingers clipped short. Matthew was as hard as steel, toughened from decades of working outdoors on steel decks, in any weather, in every conceivable climate, but under that grizzled shell, Matthew was as playful as an elf. He always had a joke at the ready, and was a master of straight-faced delivery.

The rum just kept tasting better the lower the sun got. "Better than Bilge Wine any day" I offered. Matthew nodded.

"Bilge Wine?" my father quipped, curiously.

THERE I WAS

"Booze is illegal on US Flagged ships," Matthew replied, "Especially Navy ships, you can get in a lot of trouble just having a bottle of rum, but if you happen to have some apple cider..."

"That maybe you added some raisins or sugar to, and left in a dark place" I added.

"Nature might enhance that elixir with blessed fermentation, not a crime at all, just...... spoiled fruit juice" Matthew continued.

"Bilge wine... the next best thing." Tonight we were drinking something decidedly better than blessed bilge wine.

I looked out across the bay at Plymouth Harbor, where it had all started for me. 15 years before, a friend and I had rented a small boat and spent an entire day motoring about the Bay. That day was like no other day. That was the day that the sea gods first spoke to me and invited me to live in their world. As we motored back into the Marina just ahead of the setting sun, after 12 full hours of maritime adventures, the owner of the boat, after informing me that he was starting to get worried and was preparing to go out looking for us, upon hearing that we simply were having too much fun to come back, spoke those fateful words "If you like it that much, you should be working on boats."... Someone will pay me to do this? That day, I decided to go to sea (to see what I could sea).

When I left the Navy, I believed that I had satisfied my seagoing desires. Four years of military creases, polished brass, and "yes sir, no sir" (you bloated arrogant Annapolis history major who couldn't navigate your way out of a paper bag with a flashlight a road map and ten months of preparing for the event) led me back ashore. Like my dad always used to tell me: "Get out." It had, actually, been the best four years of my life, had straightened me out, rescued me from myself, and opened the entire world up to me, but most of that realization came later, in hindsight.

There had been a nasty eight months in the Persian Gulf, smack dab in the middle of the Iran/Iraq shooting war, watching ships burn, and people die. It was there I watched my sister ship, the USS Stark, burning on the horizon, while my shipmates fought and died saving their ship. The experience led me to think that four years at sea was enough and I should move on to something safer... Like flying airplanes.

I had spent the last two years in flight school, buzzing about the skies of northeast Massachusetts, southern Maine and New Hampshire. I did well in college, but flying is expensive, and even with the scholarships, loans, grants, and holding no less than two jobs at any given time, I was broke. Worse, I was in debt.

I came to a crossroads when my personal life collided head on with my professional life on a worn mat in a small Martial Arts Gym that reeked of sweat, perseverance and over achievement.

THERE I WAS

I had been studying martial arts since high school, but got serious about it in the military. In college, it kept me fit, healthy, and offered me the opportunity to work out my frustrations by pummeling some poor helpless bastard every Thursday at the open Spar. One fateful Thursday, I was the poor helpless bastard getting pummeled. I am told it was as fine a match as ever I had fought, though I remember little. I took a well-aimed foot to the face which left me less than conscious and with a big black eye.

The damage was a tiny loss of peripheral vision that the flight surgeon said might heal, or might get worse. If it got worse, and he felt it would, (mistakenly it turns out), then I would have a difficult time passing an FAA class one physical. The class one physical is the physical that a professional pilot must pass to work in Commercial Aviation, the precise specific purpose of all of my collegiate endeavors.

So there I was, broke, training for a career that the Doctor was telling me that I likely would not be fit to practice, and starting again to hear the Sirens sweetly singing. Which brings us back to that picturesque New England beach, with the sun setting, the tide ebbing and that fine, fine liquor flowing. I had decided to return to sea, this time in the Merchant Marine, which actually had been the original plan before my brief dalliance with aviation. I had gotten my Mariners Document, the vaunted "Z-card", done all the homework, joined a union; I had even packed my sea bag.

My dad knew of Matthew, the ancient Mariner, and liked to visit him from time to time out there on lonely Saquish, and thought he might have some advice to give. There were maybe 20-30 homes on Saquish, and another 20-30 on Gurnet Point, but mostly just seasonal cottages, and my father and Matthew were amongst the small handful of taciturn hard core New England malcontents that weathered the place year round. The tourists had mostly gone back to the suburbs by now, and Saquish was left to the seagulls, terns, and pariahs.

We had been there since the sun was high, keeping company with the clams, lobsters, and corn on the cob that were nestled nearby in a *bed of seaweed* (25); steaming happily away in the *fire pit* (26) in a delicious brew of seawater, beer and their own juices. We feasted as skies darkened, and drank. Matthew spoke little, mostly just an occasional "ayuh", and a few brief, but impressive sea stories. A lot of very clever one-liners, delivered perfectly deadpan, the only indication that it was meant to be a joke was the sparkle in his eyes, like the sun glittering off the water.

Eventually, as the end of the evening approached, Matthew mustered his formidable gravitas and broached the topic:

"So how did you fella's fare in that fire, once you stepped through that door?" Matthew asked

THERE I WAS

"We were incinerated to fine ash every one of us, and our remains are at the bottom of the Sargasso Sea"

"I figured that's how it would end, good thing you ain't considering getting into firefightin'," He cracked the claw off of a Lobster that he had no doubt just recently removed from the ocean himself"

"A hero, I am not."

"Ayuh, I hear your thinking about joining up in the Mahchant Marine eh?"

"Yes Sir."

"One bit of advice… (Long pause)" The moment we had all been waiting for…. "Nevah… sail… with Greeks."

Leaving the dock

Anchors Aweigh

> *"If your ship doesn't come in, swim out and meet it." - Jonathan Winters*

A good story is much like a sea voyage. It has a beginning, a middle, and an end, and it takes you somewhere. My story, like so many other good sea stories, began at age 18, with the sweet lies and sea stories of a Navy recruiter. I should have suspected something when I first met him. He was a tall rotund bald man with a porn star moustache, and looked nothing like one would expect a career military non-comm to look like. I bragged of my maritime lineage, and told him I wanted a technical job, and he assured me that the Naval Quartermasters were the technicians that kept the complicated gyrocompasses and navigational equipment tuned and running. It was, of course, a complete fabrication, as Naval Quartermasters are pure Mariners, navigating, manning the helm, running the Bridge and wheelhouse and would only pick up a screwdriver or multimeter if they were handing it to a tech.

It was all for the best of course, as navigation and ship handling are in my blood. I like to think that maybe that inaugural sea story was told as a result of that recruiter's keen insight to my maritime destiny, or at the behest of the sea gods, but most likely there was a shortage of Quartermasters, and he was aiming at a quota. But the sea gods in their wisdom, led me to the path of the professional Mariner, and I have walked it proudly ever since. That they chose an overgrown bald version of Ron Jeremy to lead me towards it shows that they have a sense of humor.

The recruiters office was followed by the requisite humiliating entry physical, where a long line of young men in their underwear are marched from station to station... proceed to room A, wait 20 minutes for your blood pressure to be taken, proceed to room B wait 30 minutes and have your balls manhandled... "Turn your head and cough", proceed to the next station, wait 20 minutes for the next personal violation, and so on. It is the most efficient way to turn a 60 minute physical into an all-day affair. From there, after filling out tens of thousands of very similar forms, I was put on a plane and flown to the *Recruit in-processing facility* (27) at the Naval Training Center in Orlando Florida... Boot Camp.

I awoke from my 2 hours of sleep to the thunder of batons on trash cans and the maniacal screaming of the rabid Drill Instructors as they over turned beds with still dozing and dazed recruits, while striving so hard to live up to the stereotype. They herded us down to the street and corralled us into our first formation and then left us there, in ranks, in the pre-dawn darkness for what seemed like hours. The recruit training center is a bustling place at 4AM, filled with the sounds of hundreds of marching, stomping boots in groups of 50 or so, pounding in perfect military unison, providing the necessary backbeat for the rhythmic song of the marching cadences... left righta left.

Naval cadences are sung lustily like sea chanties, the callers carefully chosen for the rich depth and clarity of their voices. I stood there with 69 other mesmerized recruits, as the daylight slowly emerged through the Florida morning haze, listening to the dozens of marching companies stomping and singing, near and far, and knew that I had entered a new world.

As we stood there, in the twilight colored fog of that Orlando winter morning, the silhouette of a seasoned company of nearly graduated recruits emerged from *the foggy darkness* (28)... crisp, uniform and precise. They marched straight towards us, and we watched fascinated, certain that they would collide and mow us down, when with one swift command "Left oblique march," and the distinctive stomp/grind/step sound of a flanking maneuver, 60 men turned on a dime in perfect unison, twice, neatly sidestepping us, and then flanking back to the right side of the road and their original path, before marching off into the rising sun. The maneuver was executed, not with robotic straight backed army perfection, nor the fierce precision of the Marines, it was done with swagger, naval swashbuckling swagger.

The next week was a carefully orchestrated miasma of sleep deprivation and rapid fire degradations designed to rip down even the sturdiest recruit into a raw state from which they can be either built up into a military stalwart, or easily discarded. Recruits are rushed from place to place and hurried through the task at hand, from the one minute haircut to the disturbing uniform issuing process where people with no training, skill or understanding of how to fit clothes, randomly assign ill-fitting garments to throngs of sleepless, dazed, and confused recruits.

"This shirt is three sizes too big"

"Don't worry you'll lose weight"

"But..."

"Shut up and move along recruit"

At the end of that day, back in the barracks, as we sat around stenciling our uniforms, and shining our shoes, one of the funnier looking recruits sat mesmerized staring at the pile of newly issued gear. What few teeth he still had were crooked, and his shaved head was covered with scars, and dents, and other evidence of a hard life. His normally big goofy smile was replaced with a look of confused awe:

THERE I WAS

"Two pairs of shoes" he kept repeating "two pairs of shoes". I had witnessed a grown man receive his first pair of shoes, something that coming to age in the hills of Tennessee had apparently denied him. It was at that moment I realized how different we all were. How my firm belief that I knew every damn thing, was a mistaken belief, and that at best, all I had was the very narrow perspective of a middle class white kid from the suburbs of Boston. This was my initiation into the small club of fortunate people allowed to step out of their world and look back in. This perspective widened and deepened over the ensuing years of my maritime career, further opening the gulf between me and the life I left behind.

My awareness broadened further one day when the recruit in the bunk next to mine, a proud confederate citizen of the Deep South, heard me speak the word theatre, which in my native Boston patois is pronounced "Theedah". He took that opportunity to mount the Deep South soapbox and lecture us Yankees on the correct pronunciation, Thhee-ATE-er, with a strong sibilant Thhhh. There are an E and A, and he was quite certain that one should show them the proper respect and enunciate them both, Yankees were always in too much of damn hurry to do anything properly including speaking proper "American" .

As I listened silently with rapt interest to his Redneck tirade on proper pronunciation; he continued to rant on about the three different types of Yankees. There are Yankees- people who live in the north, Damn Yankees- people from the north who come to visit the south, and Goddam Yankees- people from the north who come to live in the south, and how none of us had the common sense to speak properly. He finished with a knowing smirk on face, and his chin held overly high, one shoulder dropped low, and the opposite elbow kicked out slightly, in that classic trailer park prelude to a strut, waiting for my response. I let the moment linger briefly before responding simply with just one word

"Reee ALE lee? (Really)". The look on his face screwed up slightly, his eyebrows furrowing and slow dawning that he may have spoken too soon. From that moment forward I called him See-AY-man (seaman) Diphthong (diphthong: noun, a sound formed by the combination of two vowels in a single syllable, in which the sound begins as one vowel and moves toward another.), the meaning of which I am sure he misinterpreted. I never missed the opportunity to correct his speech where an E and A resided in the same syllable.

"Hey See AY man Diphthong, it's 'To the Reee AYER (rear) March".

"That's pronounced Wee-AYER and Tee AYER (wear and tear)"

"Take your SEE-ate (seat) See AY man Diphthong" etc. Boot camp is an unpleasant place by most accounts, but my interactions with See AY man Diphthong were some of the few pleasant moments I enjoyed during those nine long weeks. He was good natured about it, and decided from his experience with me that yet another category, beyond Goddamned Yankee, was required.

The Orlando Recruit Training Center was, at that time, the only one of the three naval boot camps where women trained. So we were blessed with a 'sister' company; a sordid collection of some of the ugliest women ever assembled in one place. We trained together at times, meaning we sat at opposite ends of the same classroom, or field lab. As we watched them from across those rooms each day, they grew less and less hideous. Then one day in the chow hall as we lined up at the scullery window, near the tables where they sat eating; one tall broad shouldered blond girl fellated an entire banana for our viewing pleasure. At that instant they all miraculously transformed from the cast of Deliverance, into a troupe of *gorgeous flowers* (29), and the *objects of our every desire* (30).

As the weeks passed, and we endured our eight mile runs, the tear gas house, burning buildings, 'motivational' training, and endless pushups, we began to firm up into a well-trained, cohesive, military unit of American Fighting Men. Nine short weeks passed quickly, and the great day finally came where we "passed in review" before the admiral, and graduated into the proud ranks of the US Navy.

The Naval base in Orlando, was a training facility, and my next assignment, like most of the recruits in my company, was right there on that same base outside the fenced in boot camp, just a few blocks and an entire world away. We marched out of Boot Camp on Friday morning, reported to our school, were assigned a barracks and told to report Monday AM at 0600. An entire weekend off? An entire two days without a screaming maniac telling me to sit down, or stand up, or drop and rifle off 50 pushups. There was a club on base known as "The Mariner's Club" and there we all found each other, the remnants of Company 59, on the cusp of their first night on the town as sailors on liberty.

We found our way, as sailors will, to the nearest strip club, in Orlando's "Orange Blossom Trail" district. We drank hard, and laughed loudly, and most likely made an annoying spectacle of ourselves. For many of us, it was our first legal visit to a bar. Inevitably, when uniformed sailors go adrinkin' in public, someone will feel the need to call them a "dumb squid". There are other pejoratives, but that is one most often heard, and the one most often resulting in bloodshed.

Apparently, in this fine establishment, rich with naked women and drunken sailors, there were Marines. Marines don't generally need an excuse to call a sailor a dumb squid. That is to say, a sailor could be praying at church, or helping an old lady across the street, and a Marine will still feel the need to vocalize that belief. This is not a criticism of Marines. There is no group of fighting men that I respect more. Sailors feel the same compulsion to treat Marines like aspiring village idiots. It is that mutual love that makes ships such gentle happy places.

THERE I WAS

These Marines were a group of about the same size as ours, and we all adjourned to the alley to add swollen knuckles and the smell of blood to the evening's festivities. A large crowd of civilians followed us out there to add to the spectacle and began cheering on the Marines. The Marines were not in uniform as we were. Orlando was home to a Navy base, and so most of the civilians had experience with sailors and not all of those experiences were pleasant. So as the fight progressed, the locals became more and more involved and at one point they decided to participate.

Marines are perfectly happy to fight sailors, more than happy really, but these Marines were downright offended that mere civilians would involve themselves in a Marine Corps melee. Suddenly it was civilian vs. military, and Marines and Sailors were now brothers in arms fighting the infidel civilians of Orlando's Orange Blossom Trail.

Soon our small crowd of America's finest were completely surrounded by what was fast becoming a raging mob. We began to realize that this was getting serious, and only the steely faced determination of the Marines preparing to die fighting kept us from panicking. We stood our ground, fighting the tide of angry civilians when suddenly, into the alley emerged what appeared to be the US Navy Weight lifting team. No less than a dozen gigantic Sailors, clean cut in civilian clothes, but easily identifiable by their distinctive tattooing and military haircuts.

They waded in and quickly turned the tide, tossing the tiny civilians aside like rag dolls, and before long it was over. We adjourned to the next bar together, Marines, boot camp Sailors, and freakishly large fleet sailors recently returned from a long stint at sea. We learned that long sea voyages on Navy ships involve an inordinate amount of weightlifting, hence the gigantism. We drank together, and regaled the events of the past hour, and my very first naval sea story was born. Soon we all went our separate ways, we "Boots" wandered off to the "ABC" lounge in pursuit of feminine companionship. I don't know whether it was the sharp uniforms, the swaggering good looks, the black eyes, the excessive alcohol or the blessings of the sea gods, but many of us were successful in that endeavor.

We proceeded to the fine accommodations of the "Pink Flamingo" (31) Motel, and electing not to employ the hourly rates option, pooled enough money for a few rooms. We spent the rest of the weekend there, lolling about the pool, drinking cheap beer, eating fried chicken, and enjoying that auspicious beginning to our maritime careers. It was the first of many such weekends.

Class 'A' school was followed a brief week of 'leave' which is the military word for vacation. I travelled home less than five short months after leaving, and little had changed, except everything. I spent just enough time at home to realize that, while the lives of my family and friends were very much the same, mine was forever altered. I left Boston and reported to my first ship, the USS MyFirstNavyShip.

THERE I WAS

As I stood on the pier, looking up that long Gangway at my very first ship, I remember thinking how that narrow plank led to a whole new world. Then I heard a voice that I would hear again many time over the years.

"What the fuck are you waiting for, a fucking invitation?" but it was in a Philipino accent so thick that it come out as

"Wat da puck are you baiting por, a pucking inbitation?"

"No, I was waiting for a random asshole to talk shit and give me a hard time, are you here to carry my bags?"

"Ha, puck you, obviously I am here to teach the new recruit how to walk up a gangway, it's very simple, just put one foot in front of the other. (Eets bery simple, just one put one poot in front ob de odder")

"Do you have a name, or should I just call you asshole?"

"Only my father (Pahder) can call me asshole, my name is Santo"

"That is funny, it's like my father always used to tell me, 'You are an asshole'".

"Good wise men the both of them I am sure, to honor their offspring so"

That was the beginning of a long friendship that lasted decades. Santo took me aboard and got me signed on.

The MyFirstNavyShip was a recently built Oliver Hazard Perry Class Guided Missile Frigate whose *home-port* (32) was in Mayport Florida, just outside Jacksonville. The first thing that struck me, stepping onto that Navy ship, was *the shine* (33). Every square inch had been worked to a high polish, and was perfectly clean. The air was thick with the scent of industrial pine oil. Sailors were everywhere, crawling in corners with tiny *scrub brushes* (34), standing on ladders polishing drain pipes, waxing floors, shining brass and making that ship a glaring, reflective paragon of Naval busywork. It was relentless, and any time of day of night there would be someone, somewhere on that ship, polishing brass. Naval ships require constant vigilance to remain shiny.

I was assigned a bunk in the "Ship Control" Berthing, where 60 or so enlisted men below the rank of E6 were packed in like sardines, in coffin bunks stacked three high, facing each other about two and half feet apart. My bunk, a top bunk of course, was mere inches from an enormous loud ventilation fan. It was like sleeping next to a jet engine. I remember weeks later, looking at the fan that I no longer heard and remembering that thunderously loud first night.

The first week aboard your first ship will always be a memorable experience. I was inundated by an assault of new sights, sounds, smells, words, people and experiences. There was so much to learn in a short time it was like drinking from a fire hose. Like most newbies, I spent the first week getting lost, pranked, yelled at and tested. I got into three fights that week, and no less than a dozen 'altercations', which Santo assured me is more than average, but not uncommon for a person who wins the first few fights.

New arrivals must have their mettle tested, as the life of a Sailor can be dangerous, and crews must know if the new arrivals are made of stern enough stuff. Everything that a new recruit does... is wrong, every action will draw a criticism. The intent, I later deduced, is to provoke the sailor to rise to the challenge and take extreme care in all the details, which on a ship can save lives, or failing at that, to be identified as a weak link. It was also considered good sport to bait the newbies. Those practices, I am told, are no longer tolerated or cherished as they were in those days, the Navy is a much more sensitive and caring place in modern times, but in those days, the expression was that the surface Navy "eats it young".

The high stress environment of a ship, any ship, can cause even the stoutest of hearts to falter, and any person who has elected to follow *the siren song* (35) has at least one, and typically many, stories of someone succumbing to the pressure and flying off the handle. I saw my first episode of a Mariner going off *the deep end* (36) during my first week aboard ship. A baby faced, crazy-eyed, southern boy, who looked like more of a lover than a fighter, had simply had enough. He took a stand in the wheel-house as the ship lay at dock, screaming with a southern accent so deep it was almost a caricature. "Fuck the Navy", "You can kiss my Goddam Ass", and "Fuck You, you can kiss my Goddam Ass", over and over again while he swung a length of pipe to keep the watch at bay. He was later subdued, straitjacketed and removed, never to be seen on the USS MyFirstNavyShip again. It was as interesting a welcome to shipboard life as one could ask for.

Santo and I watched the shore patrol drag him ashore.

"Probably you next" Santo commented.

"Could be, to add injury to insult, I hear in addition to assaulting the watch and disobeying a direct order, they are going write him up because the straight jacket wasn't pressed."

"Even crazy people need to maintain their military bearing."

It was a few months before we put to sea, and when we did, it was a short jaunt to escort the USS Iowa and a few patrol boats down to the Panama Canal. President Reagan had embarked on a mission to revive the Navy, and had floated three old WWII era Battleships out of mothballs to parade about the planet. It was pure joy to watch that magnificent ship project power, history and a massive ball of fire across the ocean as she blasted her enormous guns in a glorious broadside, lobbing shells as heavy as Volkswagens across the horizon. Nothing says "Fuck you, I am an American" like rapid fire, long range, heavy Naval gunfire.

The cruise took us from Jacksonville Florida, to Key West, St Thomas USVI, Grand Cayman Island, Colon Panama, Honduras and Guatemala. I spent the beginning of

THERE I WAS

the cruise doing my obligatory kitchen duty ("Mess cranking") but I managed to make it up to the Bridge in the evenings to learn my trade. My first port visit was to Key West Fl. on Halloween 1984, then the US Virgin Islands, which are stories that come later, but since this particular sea story is about the birth of my seagoing career, it ends with my baptism.

I was a Navy Quartermaster, one of the oldest ratings in the Navy, dating back to the days of sail and the Mother Royal Navy. Quartermasters man the Bridge. They are expert helmsmen, Navigators, deck seaman and just pure Mariners. On US Navy ships, they stand Quartermaster of the watch (QMOW) and are responsible for the safe navigation of the vessel. They fix and plot the ships position, do all the voyage planning, assist the Officer Of the Deck (OOD) in all matters navigational. It is a position of high trust, as the OOD and Captain are ultimately responsible for navigation, yet typically assign most of that responsibility to the QMOW. It takes weeks to qualify to stand the watch solo, and I had only had a few weeks of spare time instruction between meals during my mess cranking tour. I had been standing QMOW watches under instruction with a qualified QM for only a few weeks when we pulled into the Grand Cayman Islands.

We anchored on a *sandy bottom* (37) on the south side of the island. Once the anchor was set, the entire watch started to proceed down to the quarterdeck. I was told that I was ready to stand QMOW alone on the Bridge. Anchor watch is generally much simpler than an underway watch, as your job is simply to ensure that the ship does not drag anchor. You take fixes and plot them and all is fine so long as you stay inside the carefully plotted "drag circle", a radius essentially equal in length to the amount of chain deployed, around the position where the anchor was dropped. Nice and easy, no course changes, speed calculations, no ETA's, no "time to turn", just 30 minute fixes, and a close eye on the anchor chain. A chain that on that evening, was under a heavy strain. Santo was the last to leave the Bridge.

"Don't fuck (puck) it up, everyone (ebryone) is watching"

"Your confidence is underwhelming"

"All you have to do, is not fuck (puck) it up... simple (seemple)"

Plotting a fix that close to land, especially in those days before GPS, consisted of taking visual bearings and RADAR ranges to charted objects and features on land. Squinting through the sight vanes of a bearing circle mounted on the bridgewing compasses, at various blinking lights, to get 'lines of bearing', then plotting the lines on the chart, and where they all intersect is where you are. My fixes that day, some of my first ever, were plotting suspiciously close to the edge of the drag circle. On an anchor watch, the QMOW is alone on the Bridge, the rest of the watch moves below to man the "Quarterdeck" or embarkation deck below. I called a senior

THERE I WAS

Quartermaster and told him that I thought we might be dragging anchor, and he told me "The person to call is the OOD, and you better KNOW you are dragging anchor."

Fortunately for my reputation, we were indeed dragging anchor, though most were inclined to believe that the new guy was just nervous. Not only were we dragging anchor, we could not get the anchor to set up, despite repeated attempts. So my first solo watch ended prematurely, due to my vigilance and navigational prowess. Santo welcomed me to the real Navy, where only those elite "who don't fuck up" are allowed membership. The other QM's started treating me differently that night, and the navigational Bridge became my home. It remained my home for the next 20 years.

CREWING MERCHANT SHIPS IN WARTIME

The House of the Rising Sun

> *"When a man comes to like a sea life, he is not fit to live on land."*—
> Dr. Samuel Johnson

Just a few short days following my beach barbeque with Matthew and that magnificent old rum, several years and three oceans beyond that first lone Bridge watch, I found my first merchant ship. The gulf war (episode One) was now fully warmed up, and plugging along, and like all wars it had created a sudden and drastic shortage of merchant seamen. It was this shortage that had inspired me to return to sea, as getting a foot in the door of the Merchant Marine, in those days, was no easy task.

I wandered into the union hall with the credentials of an Able Bodied Seaman (AB) and was assigned a 'fly out' job later that very day. Boston had once been a mighty shipping port, but those days had waned, and precious few ships plied the Boston waterfronts anymore. Its former glory, combined with its long maritime tradition and a disproportionately high population of Merchant Mariners, meant that not only were there still hiring halls, (which the trade did not support) but the union official running that hall was very influential within the union. Boston got a lot of 'fly outs'. Union rules are a complex maze of draconian and often disturbing edicts that are built on the abusive heritage of the world's most dangerous work environment, and the time honored maritime tradition of indentured servitude. The rules that governed the treatment of Mariners by their employers echoed of historical mistreatments, mandating that employers feed Mariners thrice daily, and outline precisely how much flour, butter, and water each Mariner should be allotted daily, guaranteeing the Mariner carefully defined clean linen, soap, and access to bathing facilities (38).

There were also more internal rules about how jobs were awarded, seniority, who could hold what type of job, etc. The purpose of these rules was to ensure that jobs were awarded fairly with respect to seniority, geography, etc. These rules were often not carefully enforced, especially on the less popular ships, and most especially not during wartime manpower shortages. So it often happened that permanent berths were occasionally held by members not senior enough to be allowed a permanent berth. Often a Mariner who had taken the job on a four month shipping ticket might still be there seven or eight months later, against the union rules. On the better paying ships, and the better runs (The vaunted *banana run* (39) from Rio to

THERE I WAS

Capetown for example) the governing port office would send out a "Patrolman" to visit the ships and chase away the job squatters who were violating the various union job rules. These visits usually ended up with the patrolman 'firing' several people creating open berths for his port hiring hall to fill.

So there I was... sitting on the plane, fresh from college, a yellowing black eye still twitching slightly, surrounded by a raucous group of highly scarred, tattooed, possibly bloodthirsty Mariners. I was excited and not a little nervous about the complete unknown that lay before me. That nervousness was both exacerbated, and somewhat alleviated when the meanest looking scar faced, marginally sober, thug of them all, a Viet Nam vet named Sean O'Grady leaned over and said "Don't worry rookie, we got your back".

My only Maritime experience at that point had been the Navy, which did indeed lead me into some nasty, dangerous situations, where I had learned the value of having a crew of tough bastards watching your back, but arriving to a new ship had never before qualified as one of those situations.

I had met Sean briefly at a bar near the Union Hall in Southie the night before, where a local had harassed me mildly and Sean had been thoroughly amused at my response of just laughing at him and walking away. Amusing Sean had apparently won me enough regard that he deemed my back fit to watch.

The ship was the MV MyFirstMerchant. The MV stood for Motor Vessel, as opposed to SS meaning Steam Ship. It was a crane rigged "Break-bulk" freighter of moderate size and vintage. Break-bulk freighters have their own *cargo handling equipment* (40) and are capable of loading and unloading themselves, without requiring *special port facilities* (41). They can handle most every type of cargo and are extremely versatile. Once the most common type of Merchant ship, the practices of the modern day shipping industry have largely replaced them with specialized ships and containerized cargoes that require special ports to load and unload. This ship was under charter to the National Science Foundation and the US Navy to service the US Mission at McMurdo Station Antarctica. I was quite excited to hear that I was going to the bottom of the world. The far flung fringes of the known world were always my favorite places.

My first impression of a Merchant Ship was precisely the opposite of my first impression of a Navy ship. It was the dirt that captured my attention as I stepped aboard my first Merchantman. Oil, grime, and rust.... lots and lots of rust. The second impression was the difference in size and scale, beamier and deeper than the sleek warship I had served on previously. Larger with cavernous spaces instead of the tight honeycombed confines of the war-ready frigate of my past.

It was my first Cargo ship and at that time, I was also only vaguely aware of the often bitter rivalry between Mariners and Longshoremen. Longshoremen are the

THERE I WAS

dock workers who load and unload ships. Longshore unions have long been known to be criminal enterprises with close ties to organized crime (as have some maritime unions it turns out). When ships enter a port, the waterfront is generally an enormous acreage of securely fenced cargo lots and warehouses. These areas are vigorously patrolled, not by the police, but by private longshore security forces who, as mentioned, tend to be closely affiliated to the local crime lord. The 'security' patrolmen, presumably having purchased the job from some criminal intermediate functionary, were then required to furnish part of the money they received in the shaking down of Mariners back to said crime lord. These Longshoremen and Mariners then often spend their days in port working alongside each other on the ship. This can make ships, especially freighters, where there is the most interaction, quite interesting places. Violence and harsh language are not unheard of.

This is true of any freighter. Also unbeknownst to me at the time, the wartime shortage of Merchant Seaman had made ships inordinately difficult to crew. This was particularly true of low paying ships on dangerous scientific missions to remote places. No ammo bonus, no hazardous cargo pay, no hostile fire bonus, very little overtime, a famously mean Captain and bad food made this ship damn problematic. Hence the green light for the Boston fly out, with the clueless rookie and his thug companions, but even that was not enough to get this ship fully manned. This ship had picked up crew in New Orleans not long previously and, again unbeknownst to me, in a drastic effort to fill the jobs, the New Orleans Port Agent had apparently worked a deal with a local prison release program and furnished an abundance of crewmen who were thrilled at the option of serving their remaining time on a ship instead of a chain gang. So there I was...in the House of the Rising Sun, having witnessed in my first three days aboard, well over a dozen bloody altercations of criminal magnitude, and no one seeming to think anything of it. I thought, "Wow... the Merchant Marine is a bit rough."

Sean always seemed to be involved in these bloody altercations, and would thump his chest and raise his arms like Winged Victory after vanquishing some poor Longshoreman or shipmate foolish enough to tangle with him. He was always sporting some minor bruise or cut on his face, and he always smelled of fresh blood.

Watching a Mariner savagely beat a longshoreman nearly to death with a pipe-wrench for the crime of pissing in the bilge, while no less than a dozen people went on about their business as if it happened all the time, was a new and somewhat unsettling experience for me, but having a handful of South Boston toughs watching my back, and being young, strong and composed of a careful mix of stupidity and bravery, I elected to rise to the challenge.

There were on this fine vessel (for I did indeed grow to love her) two crewman of note. The first, known to his shipmates as "The Turk" was a corpulent dangerous

THERE I WAS

man who worked as a machinist in the engine department. He spent his spare time crafting any scrap of metal he could find into elaborate, ornate, fiendishly evil looking edged weapons that appeared to have originated in Middle Earth somewhere. He hailed from Turkmenistan, and had the eyes of a stone cold killer. It was a generally accepted notion by both crew and longshoremen alike, not to mess with him. He and Sean seemed to be old friends, and the Turk loved his Boston shipmates, referring to them as "Maskarachusetts men". He would sing when one entered a room, in the melody of a Muezzin calling the faithful to pray "Massscaaaraaaachuuusetts maaaan... like maaaan of Turrrrkmeeeenistaaaan". It was presumably a compliment. Sean, who feared nothing, had a healthy respect for the Turk, and advised anyone willing to listen not to cross him.

The second crewman of note, was a young, brash and very foolish Philipino deck seaman whose was ostensibly named Jun. Often times, when a Philipino feels that you won't be able to pronounce his name, or perhaps is bothered by the sound of Westerners mispronouncing it, he will simply introduce himself as Jun. Living on a ship with many Philipinos an observant person will notice that the other Philipino's never address him as Jun. Jun's actual name likely had an overabundance of syllables, and probably rhymed with adlangbayanganyanbo.

One day in the chow hall, Jun was yammering at full volume while standing at the table where Turk was eating, and a dialog was opened. Turk sat there at the table, slowly skinning an apple with a delicately curved blade, shaped like the letter S, edged on the inner side, and toothed on the outer, crafted from a discarded circular sawblade, while Jun prattled on in a loud and disruptive way that obviously (to everyone but Jun) disturbed the Turks digestion.

The Turk calmly told the young fellow to mind his manners, lower his voice and stop behaving like a monkey. Now it should be mentioned here that Philipino's are a prodigiously seafaring people. They are a strong presence on ships of every flag all over the world, and most Mariners have had the privilege of living and working with dozens of Philipino shipmates. They are justifiably and rightfully proud of their maritime and cultural heritage. Calling a Philipino a monkey is akin to, or perhaps even worse than, using the N-word to a person of color. Turk knew this, and young Jun was understandably upset.

Jun was young and brash, and just didn't quite understand the depth of the danger he was now facing. Quiet fell over the mess hall as the bystanders focused in on the pending event of dinner entertainment. Sean was generous enough to suggest to Jun "Let it go shorty, Turk will eat you alive and spit you back out dead. But Jun was not in the mood for good advice. Jun, like all deck seaman, carried a knife and like many of his countrymen, it was type of knife called a Balisong. A Balisong, also known as a butterfly knife, houses the blade within the two halves of the split handle that fold back away from either side of the blade (like the wings of a butterfly) to form the handle. Owners of such knives tend to become very proficient at flipping the knife open rapidly in a stylized, flowery display of high speed knifemanship. Jun, decided that it was time to display his knife opening prowess in a show of pure dexterous bravado.

Turk, was decidedly less showy, and far more to the point, seeing the display of a lethal weapon as a mortal challenge (A reasonable assertion) he launched himself over the table, his dinner fork still in hand, and promptly stabbed poor Jun in the face.

Fortunately Jun was nimble and quick, and the fork missed his eye, lodging firmly in his cheek. Several people removed the Turk before he could stab again, and Jun was wise enough to keep his mouth shut (save for some bewildered sputtering) and leave quietly. No one ever spoke of it again, though in the following months Sean would often tell Jun not to get "cheeky". Welcome to the US Merchant Marine, this is just another day. Like my dad always used to tell me, "Keep your mouth shut Boy."

So there I was... travelling this Maritime path after my recent visit to the crossroads. Returning to my original voyage plan down nautical roads. It was still in my head that I might return one day to college, but the next waypoint on that journey would be the South Pole, via New Zealand.

THERE I WAS

Changes in Latitude

Fire and Ice

> *"The wind and the waves are always on the side of the ablest navigator." – Edmund Gibbon*

We had just loaded 100,000 tons of Number Two Oil in Montreal and were headed outbound up the St. Lawrence River enroute to St. Johns New Brunswick. It was unseasonably cold for November, which meant it was frigid. I was standing lookout on the morning watch, about 6AM, under perfectly clear skies and a brisk arctic breeze. The frigid air didn't bother me, enveloped as I was in my expensive winter gear in addition to every other piece of clothing in my possession.

I was standing perfectly still when the Kestrel, a small falcon, landed on the rail next to me, not two feet away. He stared at me, cocking his head, as if he were unsure. He turned and looked at me sideways, keeping his focus on me, but I stood motionless and watched him. It went on for a while, several minutes at least, until I moved, and he suddenly realized that I was *a living creature* (42). He spread his wings, puffed out his chest, screamed at me and flew off in a huff. I could have stayed still for much longer, allowing the moment to linger, but the fact was that the little Kestrel was the least interesting wildlife to observe that morning.

We were approaching Gulf of St. Lawrence at the point where the river starts to widen near Port Cartier. The shores were still visible to either side of us about fifteen miles away to port and starboard, receding farther every hour. The waters were so thick with wildlife that one could have walked across the estuary on their backs. There were pods of Orcas racing about at speeds that baffled the mind, and the strange white Beluga whales with their odd bulbous heads. They seemed to like the ship, and would swim lazily down the side, looking up at me, reminding me of my first up close encounter with a whale.

The deck of a heavily loaded ship might be as low as just a few feet off the water. I was walking down the well deck of a deeply laden freighter one day, when the loud explosion of a whale blowing just a few feet away startled me. It smelled of *fish and brine* (43), and was close enough that I was covered in the spray. I looked over the side to see that an enormous sperm whale was leisurely swimming alongside us. He seemed to take notice of me and sort of rolled over to get a better look, giving me the opportunity to stare into *the deep dark eye* (44) of this fifteen ton animal. I assured him that I had no use for lamp oil, and that were no harpoons on this ship, but warned him that had this been a Japanese ship, he would be dangling by his tail over *the processing hatch* (45) to be rendered into jerky and cooking oil. He seemed

33

unconcerned, and with a flap of his *mighty tail* (46) sounded to the great depths below.

"Send my respects to King Neptune!"

Whales are a common sight at sea. If you pay attention, you can learn to identify them by when and where you see them, how they present and behave, and of course the degree of enormity. The elusive Sperms and Blues are rarer than the almost common Humpbacks and Orca's, but they are unmistakable. There are *'whale grounds'* (47), areas where they feed, mate, or migrate along with predictable regularity. There are several such places off the Coast of my home state Massachusetts, and I would often bring friends or customers out to Stellwagon bank to watch whales. Many recreational boaters are hesitant to leave sight of land, and there always seemed to be someone willing to pay me to bring them out there.

Back in the St. Lawrence, in addition to the Orcas, Belugas and Humpbacks, there were huge fish boils everywhere. Entire schools of baitfish would rise to the top, churning the water in the characteristic 'boil', much to the delight of the herds of seals that were porposing about in droves, and the flocks of excited sea birds cashing in on the easy food. Fish boils are always *hotbeds of marine wildlife activity* (48), and you can typically see the birds before you see the boils.

Fish boils can range in size from a few yards across, as big as a small boat, or from horizon to horizon. Tuna will hunt in groups, swimming in circles to herd the entire school into a smaller and smaller area driving them to the surface. Gannets, Boobies, and Gulls will fill the sky, dive bombing the boil and coming up with kicking fish in their mouths or talons. Every now and again 500 pounds of Bluefin *Tuna* (49) will come rocketing out of the water just behind a terrified fish. Sharks, Dolphins, *Barracudas* (50) and other predators, will hover around the edges of the boil taking the fish that escape the circling Tuna. Now and again one will get too close and provoke a Tuna to attack, scattering the sharks and 'cudas as if they themselves were mere baitfish.

Tuna fishing ships will see all this activity and they will start circling the entire event, streaming a long net called a Purse Seine astern of them. They will eventually come full circle back to the tail end of the Seine, now miles long, and connect the two ends, entrapping the entire boil. They then draw the top and bottom of the Seine in tighter, closing the circle, and bringing the lower part of the net in, cinching it like a giant Bowl. As the boil gets constrained ever tighter, the activity gets more concentrated, and surface becomes a *turbulent frenzy of wildlife* (51).

The Tuna fisher will put small speed boats in the water called "Dolphin Wranglers" to herd the terrified Dolphins out through the carefully tended opening. The wrangler must contend with not only the scared Dolphins, millions of panicked baitfish, and dive bombing birds, but also the lightning fast, hard as stone, 500

34

pound Tuna that are at this point, angry as hell and aggressive enough to scare a frenzy of Bull Sharks off a bloody carcass.

If the Tuna get spooked enough, or smart enough, they will sound, or dive. They are powerful enough to take the net down and any vessel connected to it with them. I once saw a tiny 25 foot herring boat using a much smaller seine, maybe a few hundred feet across, suddenly stand up vertical like a fishing bobber with a trophy striking it. The Herring had sounded and were taking the boat down with it. We watched as the crew frantically started hacking at the nets with axes, hammers and crowbars to get the nets free and save the boat, finally freeing the net and launching the boat back out of the water like a torpedo.

Back in Canada, the skies were starting to cloud up, and rumor had it there was a nasty storm headed our way. We were enroute to St. Johns New Brunswick, which was just a few days run from where we were. The storm kicked up that very night, and lasted for more than a day. The winds were steady and strong, and *the funnel* (52) shape of the gulf, seemed to drive the wind and seas straight at us. We pitched headlong into them. Loaded tankers are low to the water, low enough that most of the ship was underwater at any given time, which is just as unnerving as it sounds.

Looking out from the Bridge, down the length of the ship, we watched the bow ride up a wave and then plunge down, crashing into *the trough* (53) as the oncoming wave buried the ship in green water. Then the sickening feeling of the ship straining under the weight of all that water, was enough to bring religion to the most ardent atheist. We could even see the ship flexing and bending under the strain, which is what it was designed to do, but it is no less disturbing for that knowledge. When a thousand foot ship bends like pencil right before it snaps, it brings home how powerful the oceans can be, and how powerless the Mariners who travel them are.

The constant spray, and sub-arctic temperatures caused a lot of ice to build up on the superstructure. The entire bow of the ship was covered in ice. The bow was raised above the main deck, which had its share of ice as well, but all the equipment up on the bow had gathered more ice, and it looked like an enormous amorphous frozen blob. We were just twelve hours away from St. Johns before the seas calmed enough that you didn't need to hold on. We would need every minute of that time to chip a path in the ice up to the bow, and hammer the anchors and other equipment free enough to operate.

The storm had subsided, but it was still rough. The seas were still occasionally breaking the bow, which would make life exciting. I was sent out with the rest of the deck department to clear the ice. There is nothing quite so bracing as a constant 20 knot wind of icy sub-zero air blasting across your face, through your clothes and into your very soul. Better than coffee for a sleep deprived watchstander. We were armed with sledge hammers, wrecking bars, and ice scrapers, and the going was

THERE I WAS

slow and rough, with the entire bow being one giant solid ice cube. We worked for twelve hours straight, hammering and pounding away at the ice.

Oil tankers have steam lines running through the cargo to keep it liquid, which meant that there were steam lines available on deck. The Chief Engineer took pity on us, and fashioned a rig that looked like an oversized flame thrower, but shot steam instead. It made life a lot easier, and we finally got the bow clear enough to tie up. Just in time too. We had barely time enough to get a hot meal and get back out on deck to tie up.

St John is a well sheltered harbor, in the Bay of Fundy, known for its extreme tidal range. The harbor entrance is *a small opening* (54) in a coast that faces the full fury of the North Atlantic. The seas were rough. No sheltered approach, or slow easy transition from full ocean exposure to safe harbor, but rather an abrupt entrance from a heavy seas mid-ocean passage to the *calm inner harbor* (55).

The ship had not yet made that transition, and was turning north now to approach the harbor. The winds had been dead on the bow, and the seas slightly to starboard, which left them both now abeam to starboard, coming at us directly from the side. This resulted in a heavy roll, and caused lots of sea and spray to visit the deck, making life more than a little exciting, and even colder. We were now soaked from head to toe in what seemed to be liquid ice.

The cold was a brutal, bone chilling misery like nothing I had ever encountered before, and I had already been to both poles, and spent an entire year of my life in the Arctic. It made everything more difficult, my hands were so numb that I could barely hold a tool. My nose was constantly running, even my eyes hurt. The cold of the steel deck, travelled through my numb feet into my legs, causing them to ache. The numb eventually gave way to throbbing aching pain, then burning itching hell.

We finally got tied up and had to rig *the gangway* (56). Saint Johns has an extreme tidal range of over 20 feet. The tide was low, and the ship was loaded down, so the dock towered more than 20 feet above us, which made the gangway difficult to rig. The Bosun on this ship was a drunken fool who had spent most of his career on passenger ferries and knew virtually nothing about operating a boom or crane. The crew of mostly tankermen were also ill prepared to make the complicated lift required to put the 40 foot gangway in a near vertical posture from the deck all the way up to the pier. I had spent most of the past three years on freighters making complicated lifts, and while this lift was tricky, it should never have been the cluster fuck that this Bosun was making of it.

We were into our second hour of the Bosun lining up everyone to man-haul the guy lines to spot the boom into place, and the boom not cooperating. He seemed perfectly unaware that the Naval architects had conveniently put winches and pulleys all over the deck to make the job of moving the boom, and lifting the loads easier. I had been cold and wet long enough. Normally I would never disrespect my supervisor publicly, but I needed to get into the warmth, and I could have had this lift finished over an hour ago, and 90 minutes into this we were no closer to having the gangway rigged than we were when we started.

I just took charge and started yelling, pointing to the leads on deck, and grabbing the lines from people's hands and running them through the leads and pulleys to the capstan head on the winch, and singlehandedly slewing the boom where the entire team had been failing for the past hour and a half. The deck crew saw that I knew how to get it done and started to listen to me. The Bosun sputtered and cussed a bit, but no one paid any attention. I climbed up the mast to get a better view and directed the now grateful and compliant crew, and we had the boom spotted and the gangway lifted and rigged in its nearly vertical state in just 15 minutes. I had never been so happy to finish a shift and get indoors as I was that afternoon.

We had been expecting a replacement AB to arrive in this port, and I had seen him standing on the dock watching us as we fumbled about. He was long and lean, and stood there motionless, oblivious to the freezing cold, with his seabag at his feet. He was the first person down the gangway, acting as if walking down a near vertical plank was easy and normal. He gave me nod as he came aboard. His name was Henrik and he was well known throughout the union as perhaps the most skilled and knowledgeable AB in the industry. He had retired out of the Coast Guard 20 years before, and had been working as a deck seaman in the Merchant Marine ever since.

The Captain had been so upset at the Bosun for botching up the gangway that he fired him. Which left us sailing shorthanded. He had offered the job to Henrik, but to his surprise and chagrin, Henrik had declined. Henrik's ambition in life was to be the best possible AB that he could be, maybe even be the best possible AB that anyone could be, but he had no desire to become a supervisor, and be accountable for others.

Unbeknownst to me, Henrik had been impressed with how I got the gangway rigged, and recommended to the Captain that he offer the job to me. He promised to watch over me to ensure that I not screw it up. The Captain was leery to put someone so young, and with so little tanker experience in the 'Bosun' s role, so again, unbeknownst to me, he arranged for Henrik to put me through a series of tests, to show that I was up to the task. It started by having me stow the gangway. The tide was now at its peak high, and the ship having unloaded, was now standing 20 feet out of the water, so now instead of the gangway standing vertically up to the dock above us, it stood vertically down to the dock below. This was no more difficult than getting it rigged, but it proved to the Captain that my previous effort wasn't just luck.

We put to sea headed for Baton Rouge, a trip of roughly two weeks. The crew was excited, as the ship would be getting a new cook and steward in Baton Rouge. The

THERE I WAS

New Orleans union hall would be providing the new cooks, and that likely meant Cajun food for the foreseeable future.

The voyage would take about two weeks, and as each day passed on the southerly course, the weather got milder and we were wearing fewer and fewer clothes on deck until, within the space of a week, I went from wearing six layers composed of every piece of clothing in my kit, down to just cutoff shorts, boots and a bandanna on my head. Nothing will put the song "Changes in Latitude", by the great Mariner troubadour Jimmy Buffet, into perspective like spending fifteen straight hours in sub-zero temperatures, hacking at an ice cube the size of an apartment building, and five days later your boot soles are melting on steel decks baked in the hot equatorial sun. "Changes in Latitude, changes in attitude..."

Henrik's next task for me was more challenging, and more tanker specific, not to mention far more dangerous. There had been a problem during the offload with a stripping pump in one of the tanks and someone needed to go down into the tank to investigate. I was, of course, selected for this horrible chore. A cargo tank on an oil tanker is about the size of a small warehouse. It is a massive steel cavern, 30 feet deep, ninety feet wide and maybe a hundred or more feet long. There is only one way in, through the tank top, where a long narrow ladder, without a climbing cage, descends down into the murky, greasy depths below. Everything is covered in thick black oil, slick and slippery. The walls and floors are a web of structural components, steel beams and webbing that crisscross across the floors and walls. Knee high beams, a few feet apart create troughs, filled with opaque black oil, as thick as mud.

The unfortunate tank diver must wear a Self-Contained Breathing Apparatus, which is a bottle of compressed air like firefighters wear. The SCBA should provide about 30 minutes of air, but 30 minutes is optimistic, since climbing down a narrow, fully greased, 30 foot ladder into a terrifying dark abyss and conducting heavy manual labor can lead to heavy breathing, which uses up your air faster. I knew that for me, I had about 20 minutes to get down that long greasy ladder, all the way to the other end of the lengthy dark obstacle strewn jungle gym to find the pump, and clear whatever garbage had clogged it. Knowing that if I slipped on the slick surface, and hit my head, I would fall into a thick opaque soup of heavy black oil just deep enough to cover my unconscious body and destroy any chance of rescue. Fun stuff.

Descending any long vertical ladder into darkness is a challenge, but when the ladder is covered from top to bottom with a viscous layer of slippery black oil thicker than tar, it is a nightmare. By the time I got the bottom, my hands were cramped from 'death gripping' the verticals, and my shins and knees were battered and abused from my feet repeatedly slipping off of the rungs. Each time that happened, my heart would stop, and I would have to take a moment to recollect myself. As I

38

dismounted the ladder, I looked back up at the four foot wide round opening I had just climbed through, and it was now just a tiny dot of light seemingly miles above me. I banged on the ladder with my flashlight to let everyone know I was down safely, and to signal them to lower a small bag filled with a few tools, and started my long trip into the murky darkness to find the basket strainer that was the likely culprit.

I managed to navigate to the pump suction, the tiny point of light that was my only way out, my sole point of reference and my one beacon, was getting smaller and smaller. By the time I got to the pump, I was twelve minutes in, and had been breathing heavy the entire time. The strainer was indeed clogged up with what appeared to be a hoodie sweatshirt. I pulled out the oil soaked garment and noticed the classic NY, of the Yankees logo. It figures, some damn Yankees fan had put me in harm's way. Like my dad always used to tell me: "Fuck the Yankees!"

About halfway back to the ladder, the low air alarm started sounding, 18 minutes in. The trick here is to not panic. I knew that I still had a few minutes, so I keep plodding along at a normal pace, knowing that hurrying was the best way to fall or increase my breathing rate and use up what precious little air remained. I was about halfway up the ladder when I ran out of air. The alarm still beeping furiously in my ears, I somehow managed to climb the last 15 feet of oil slicked ladder while holding my breath. Henrik and a few others grabbed me and hoisted me out off the ladder as I franticly pulled my mask off and gasped for that delicious salt air. Just another day. Now we were ready for loading in Baton Rouge. Though apparently, I was still not yet ready for the role of Bosun.

This was my first trip up the Mississippi and I was excited. The Mississippi is *its own little Maritime World* (57) with a unique and special way of doing things. They even have their own set of particular navigation rules that don't apply anywhere else on earth. Like most voyages through navigationally constrained waters, the deck crew mans the anchors in case of emergency. Even anchoring in the Mississippi is different, with the currents so strong, and anchorages so limited, the custom is to drop both anchors, which is a whole different ball game.

We picked up the first Pilot in the Gulf of Mexico and the plan was to run up the river to just north of New Orleans, anchor overnight, take on fuel from a bunkering barge, and finish the run to Baton Rouge the next day. Henrik had other plans that I didn't know about. Running up the Mississippi is an experience you always remember. The river has been carefully engineered, with levees and revetments and various other forms of environmentally unsound engineered machinations that stabilize the banks. What I remembered most was the levees. Levees are giant earth berms that contain the river. The effect, especially from the deck looking down, is that the river is literally higher than the land surrounding it.

THERE I WAS

What made it even more surreal to me, was that the land below the levees was populated, and looking across the water at the levee, what you see are the rooftops of the homes below the levee. I remember thinking how crazy you would have to be to live there, the levee was just dirt. What if it ever broke? My fears were not unjustified as Hurricane Katrina proved.

The anchoring went off without a hitch, and like every other maritime operation, rare or otherwise, Henrik seemed to be an expert. The chains had to be scoped out to two very different and precise lengths to hold the bow steady into the current, and prevent the jerky 'horsing' movements that can happen when using both anchors.

Having left all of our oil in St. Johns, we were 'in Ballast', which means our main tanks were empty and the ship was standing high out of the water. The bow of most, if not all, ships are designed to flare out. That is, the bows all come together at the foremost point in the ship in a V-shaped confluence of structure. They rise vertically out of the water, and then flare out and away from the deck like a funnel. The name of the ship is typically written on bow where the flare is at its steepest. Normally painting the name is a task left for the shipyard, when the ship is in a drydock, or at least tied up to a pier where a staged barge can come up alongside. That is the sensible way to do it, but that method doesn't require acts of supreme, Bosun testing, seamanship.

Henrik informed me that it was my job to paint the name. When I simply stared at him blankly, confused, as Henrik was known to be extremely serious and not prone to joking around where deck seamanship was concerned, he explained the Captain's plan to test my mettle for the Bosun's job. Henrik informed me that he would not assist me in planning the rig, unless I suggested or did something remarkably foolish, in which case he would step in and I would have failed.

Normally, when painting the hull, you would simply drop a Bosun' s chair or stage down the side and do your business, but that was only appropriate on the vertical parts of the hull, and wouldn't work on the bow where it flared. A Bosun's chair dropped above the name would plumb down vertically, and the name and the rest of the hull would be flared in 10-15 feet away from you. Like trying to paint the bottom of a roof by hanging from the peak ridge in the attic. Henrik left it to me to solve that little problem. Fortunately for me, I had been constructing complicated rigs in the daily care and maintenance of my freighter cranes and booms for the past three years, and this was not nearly as daunting as this tanker Captain seemed to imagine. Henrik knew this, and had another more interesting test planned, but for now my problem was to somehow get close enough to the name, from above, to get it painted.

There are *openings in the hull* (58), just above the deck, called chocks, where lines are passed through when tying up, or working tugs etc. My strategy was to run a bit of line from the bullnose chock at the very front of the ship, back to another chock located just aft of the area on the hull where the name was painted. This would form a giant loop or bight. I would then rig the Bosun chair within the bight, lowering myself inside the bight, with the line rigged right onto the Bosun chair. When Henrik heaved on the line, tightening the bight, it would carry the Bosun chair in towards the hull, close enough to paint the name. It worked like a charm, for the most part.

We used a similar technique to move me right and left like a pendulum to avoid having to come up and re-rig the Bosun chair, and when you start tugging, pulling and levering a free hanging body in space, you can find yourself out of vertical pretty quickly, sitting in a backless chair that is getting squeezed up and in, putting you in a face up posture, with gravity not exactly working in your favor. It was more exciting than frightening, and when it was over I thought that I had won the prize, but Henrik had something else in mind.

As the sun settled into the western horizon, we sat together on the bow, disassembling and cleaning the gear. All the rigging equipment had to be cleaned and stowed, so we had another hour or two of mindless work to do. Henrik's lined face, normally stoic and reserved, was showing just a hint of amusement. There was a tiny sparkle in his grey eyes, as if he might actually be capable of good humor.

"Lots of deck seamen can rig, and it's easy enough for a freighter hand to impress a tankerman with a fancy rig, but you and I both know that painting the name wasn't even difficult for you." I nodded, starting to suspect that the test wasn't over.

"A good Bosun, has to know how to tell a good sea story." Now I understood. The real test was at hand. Henrik didn't tell stories often, but like everything else he did, he did it well, giving it his best effort and showing it the respect it deserved. Henrik was committed to honoring Maritime traditions and craft, and he would be expecting a great story. I thought carefully, Henrik was former Coast Guard, and I would do well to honor that tradition in the story. Coast Guardsmen spent a lot of time on smaller craft, and are some of the best boat handlers in the world. I had worked smaller craft in my career, not all blue water Mariners had, so demonstrating that my experience included the fine art of boat handling and small craftsmanship would also score points. I had just the story.

"So it's a story you need, ay? I have stories I do, and I have just the story for you Mr. Thorvaldsen, just the story." Henrik simply nodded and stood up. He had been sitting on the hatch to the forepeak, the forward most space in the ship, traditionally used to store deck equipment and lines. He started spinning the large wingnuts on the hatch dogs, undogging the hatch.

"Well, the story won't tell itself boy, let's get to the telling part."

THERE I WAS

"Aye, Aye Chief. I call this one 'The Bubble Gum Beanie', and it is a story of an experiment in Maritime Law enforcement gone wrong." I caught the slightest hint of a smile on Henrik's face. No subject is closer to the heart of a former Coast Guardsman as Maritime Law Enforcement. I was sure that a good portion of Henrik's own stories involved that very same subject.

"I was working as Captain of a 100 Ton charter boat in Boston Harbor. She was a magnificent 70' luxury yacht for hire that chartered out for weddings, dinner parties, tours and the leisure of the obscenely wealthy. Mostly four hour trips for dinner, with the occasional day trip or weekend charter."

"Got your Hundred Ton License do ya?" Henrik asked.

"I have an unlimited Third Mates license, but I figured I needed more time boat handling if I was ever going to consider myself a professional Mariner" Henrik actually cracked a smile, a small approving grin. This man had dedicated his life to perfecting the skills of a Professional Mariner, and had done so by practicing the exact same skills I was referring to in my tale. I had scored an important point with Henrik, connecting with him. I continued:

"This particular weekend was the fourth of July, which is a big event in Boston, especially with the charter boat operators. There is a traditional outdoor concert performance of the Boston Pops at an outdoor venue called the Hatch shell on the banks of the Charles River every year that culminates in a grand fireworks display as the Pops launch into *John Phillip Sousa's "1812 Overture."* (59)

We worked on getting the lines ready to stow, both of us working together without having to communicate. I fed Henrik the 'gantline' that had supported me and the Bosun chair during the previous test. Henrik stood at the hatch–combing, lowering the line into the Bosun's locker. The typical deck seaman would have climbed into the locker, and coiled the line carefully at his feet on deck, but Henrik was not typical and was able to stack the line into a perfect working coil from 15 feet above. This was no simple task, even a skilled hand would have had trouble laying such a perfect coil on the deck at his own feet, much less fifteen feet below. Henrik kept both of his hands on the line, twisting it into its natural 'lay', the direction of the wound fibers. He would coax the line to bend and arc in the air, holding tension in it as it coiled down through space seeming to want to lay into a perfect coil. I went on with my story.

"The fireworks are launched from a barge on the river, and the river is the best place to see and hear both the concert and the fireworks. Every drunken pleasure boater for hundreds of miles would journey out into the river that night to see the show." I saw Henrik nod slightly, still focused on coiling the line below. I had been to dozens of events like the one I was describing, and knew that there was not a single Coast Guard small boat operator alive who hadn't been there, in some crowded harbor, filled from horizon to horizon with drunk pleasure boaters.

"For the charter boats, and sight-seeing tours it was the biggest night of the year. We left Boston Harbor the day before and headed up river, to stake out a position within sight of the barge and Hatch shell, dropping our anchor before the mob of drunken amateurs arrived in their open boats with coolers full of canned beer and soggy tuna fish sandwiches."

"We had arranged for a water taxi to bring on our passengers for the night's festivities, and to bring them ashore later that night. This particular charter boat was a top end luxury yacht with room for 60 passengers. There was a full service bar, world class catering, and uniformed staff and crew attending to the guests every need."

"As Captain, my job was simply to man the Bridge and ensure that the anchor held, monitor the radio, keep lookout, and of course chat with the passengers. The passengers showed up in the afternoon, enjoyed their surf and turf dinner and spent the early evening drinking and watching the riff raff in the pleasure boats as they steadily covered every square inch of open water."

"Now of course the US Coast Guard was there in force, buzzing about professionally in their crisp blue uniforms and sharp white boats with those comforting orange stripes, but this being an inland waterway, and within the jurisdiction of various state and local entities, there were also other less salty law enforcement agencies present."

"Massachusetts in those days, and perhaps still, was famous for sheer number of law enforcement agencies with overlapping jurisdictions. The Boston and Cambridge Police Departments were present, the Metropolitan District Commission (whatever the hell that is) had their police boats out there, various state agencies, including the Parks department, Fish and Wildlife, and State troopers were all represented in various small watercraft."

"One such agency, who will remain nameless, had decided that marine law enforcement needed some innovation, and thought that that a jet ski would be the perfect vehicle for a waterborne cop. Sounds good on paper doesn't it?"

"I am sure that you are familiar with jet-skis, those small single person craft like a water borne motorcycle, lightning fast and maneuverable. The operator sits astride the seat holding handlebars like a motorcycle, and as one can imagine, with all that speed and sharp turning, one cannot avoid becoming completely, bone soaking wet." Henrik was nodding, it was is if he were there on the River Charles with me.

"So this intrepid peace officer was adorned in a surfer like wet suit, neoprene shorts and top, with of course the requisite cop gun belt and a helmet... but this was no ordinary helmet mind you, this was a very special marine law enforcement helmet. This helmet had the obligatory cop flashing blue bubble gum light perched atop in a comic caricature of legal authority.”

“When I first saw him, in the official looking blue and white crotch rocket with the rotating bubble gum light on his head, I thought it was a joke. Some rich clown making a spectacle of himself, but it became obvious by his interaction with the other law enforcement boats that he was one of them. I watched him buzzing about the ever growing crowd of increasingly inebriated revelers and just waited with anxious anticipation for the inevitable entertainment.”

“I had spent many a long day of my life working on a small boat and like you Henrik, I was keenly aware of the challenges one faced in that environment. I was anxious to see how an actual law enforcement action might play out on an ocean skidoo with a soaking wet cop in a wet suit, and lucky for me, I didn’t have to wait long. A group of thoroughly intoxicated concert goers decided to heave anchor and move closer to the launch barge.

“Apparently they decided that the well-marked *exclusion zone* (60) was not intended for them. This aroused the high speed reaction of our hero in blue... drippy wet blue. Undoubtedly the moment he had been waiting for, he came rocketing across the water at high speed towards the offenders.

“The jet-ski garnered its name from its innovative water jet propulsion system. A stream of water is pumped out through an underwater nozzle at very high velocity thrusting the vessel through the water at breakneck speeds. This type of propulsion, unique among watercraft, has the ability to reverse direction rapidly by re-directing the vector of the thrust with a diverter that hooks abruptly into the path of the jetstream, reversing it. This allows the craft to “brake” or stop rapidly from its top speed, down to a dead stop in just seconds. It was just such a maneuver that our hero attempted. As he raced across the water towards his prey, I, being a dutiful Charter Boat Captain, announced to my guests via the PA system that there were interesting goings on close aboard on the starboard bow.”

“The speeding cop came up on the boisterous barge squatters quickly, stopping in an impressively short distance. He immediately captured the attention of the four less than sober gentlemen in the 20 foot speedboat. One thing about stopping abruptly in a watercraft, unlike land based transportation, is the influence of the wake. The marvel of jet propulsion can stop the boat on a dime, but as you know Henrik, the wake continues to travel along at high speed, and this wake did just that.”

“Right as the officer was announcing his presence, just a short moment after his dramatic arrival, the wake caught up to him, and slammed into the back of the jet-ski sending the officer, who had risen to his feet, unceremoniously back on his ass as it spun the craft around facing the cop away from the boaters. The pratfall and the

44

ridiculous helmet proved too much for the drunks to bear, and they broke out in a fit of uncontrollable laughing. They pointed and laughed, doubled over with glee, and the more this poor hapless cop tried to recover his dignity, the more they laughed and ignored him. No partner there on the jet ski to call for back-up, just one lone, dripping wet, recently humiliated constable who was becoming very obviously agitated."

"By now the cop was gesticulating wildly, away from the barge, indicating to his tormentors that they needed to move, but to no avail. They soon went from laughing at him, to ignoring him completely, which was straw that broke the camel's back. The cop gunned his engine, bringing the jet-ski close aboard to the target, and reached for his weapon."

"He reached for that weapon with soggy wet hands that had been clutching for dear life to the vibrating handles of a bucking banging stallion of a watercraft as it thundered about in the hot July sun all afternoon. The weapon did make it out of the holster and was brought to bear, but in that place where the cops arm stopped, the gun didn't. The gun continued to travel up and along in a lazy arc till it landed at the feet of the prime offender in the small boat that was causing this poor cop so much trouble. The drunken thug at that point, picked up the gun and pointed it back at the cop." Henrik paused from his work now and looked at me. This story had just changed tone, especially in the eyes of a retired water cop.

"It was here that I decided to elevate my status from that of amused bystander to active participant, and I reached for my VHF mike.

"MAYDAY, MAYDAY, MAYDAY... Officer in need of assistance at the southwest corner of the exclusion zone approximately 100 yards astern of the barge, assailants are armed and threatening MAYDAY, MAYDAY, MAYDAY". Even in the context of a sea story, Henrik tensed up as I spoke the word 'MAYDAY'. Henrik had the air of an oak tree under the best of circumstances, garnering him the nickname "The Mighty Henrik", but now, fully engaged in the story, with a Marine Law Enforcement officer in peril, he seemed to grow. His already lanky tall frame, coiled up like a Lion ready to pounce.

"Nothing gets the attention of Coast Guard like the word Mayday, and from the speed of their response, they must have been enroute already. The Whaler came speeding up from behind with three Guardsmen onboard, one driving the quite serious looking craft neatly between the thugs and the outmatched cop, one with an assault rifle trained perfectly on the thugs, his weapon tracking as the Whaler approached, and one with a loudhailer instructing the fool to put down the weapon."

"The 'Coasties' had the situation in hand in no time, as 'Coasties' will, and soon they had all four of the drunk idiots face down in hand cuffs, and the small boat under tow with offenders on board. The land based cop in a lifeguard watercraft experiment had failed, and the poor miserable jet-ski patrolman puttered away forlornly as the sun set over Cambridge." Henrik obviously approved, he had calmed back down to his easy relaxed state, and had a big grin on his creased weathered face. His beloved Coast Guard had saved the day, yet again, besting the provincial neophytes and demonstrating to the Maritime world the proper way to conduct Maritime Law Enforcement operations.

He said nothing as he climbed down into the Bosun' s locker, gathering up his perfect coil onto his shoulder, and shouting up to me:

"So where do you want me to stow this line Bosun?"

The Comeback

What a Difference a Decade Makes

> *"'Wouldst thou,' so the Helmsman answered, 'learn the secret of the sea? Only those who brave its dangers comprehend its mystery!" - Henry Wadsworth Longfellow*

I was approaching Norfolk, VA via commuter air from the north, above the infinitely familiar entrance to Chesapeake Bay. Looking down at the York River, Norfolk Harbor and Newport News from this altitude was like looking at the navigational chart that I had practically memorized, so often had I worked on it. Cape Henry is an old friend, and it had been too long since I had visited him.

I saw that we were just east of Little Creek, the Marine Base at the southern end of the entrance to the bay. The perfectly arrayed ships looked like toys from up here. The Marine base was impeccably neat and well ordered, which surprised me not at all. Modern Marine landing hovercraft flitted about the bays entrance, as usual, as if to say "Welcome to Chesapeake Bay". Welcome indeed.

The flight had been long and wearisome, and I was glad it was over. I lugged my ridiculously heavy baggage to the cab stand and anticipated with joy the end of this leg of the journey, and the new beginning it signaled. Next to my hotel, as if the Sea Gods had been listening, was a Texas Steakhouse. The perfectly frosted mug was delivered at the same time as the exquisitely cooked steak. I let the beer chill as I sampled the fine blackened beef, warm and pink on the inside, like so many of life's finer things.

When the head of the beer was sufficiently frozen, I washed down my *ambrosia* (61), allowing the tastes to mingle perfectly. The impossibly perky waitress arrived, smiling and seemed genuinely concerned with how my meal was. Magnificent, I assured her, meaning it, magnificent in every respect. The day ended appropriately sharing a fine cigar, a glass of blessed whiskey of the highest caliber, with that very same waitress, all beneath the clear starry Virginia sky. A fitting start to this new chapter in my life.

After a brief and unsuccessful attempt at living a normal life ashore, I was going back to sea where I belonged. I was here in Virginia to attend the requisite training required for employment with Military Sealift Command. This was a government organization that operated or oversaw the operation of all the government ships that weren't warships. There were hundreds, maybe even thousands of these ships, from

THERE I WAS

the government owned ships, to the leased and chartered ships, some operated by contractors, some operated by Civil Service Mariners.

Mariners make good money, and in order for the government to attract Mariners to work for them, they had to pay industry wages. So there I was, taking a job with all the security and benefits of government work, but with Merchant Marine pay. I spent the next six weeks in training, learning everything from the proper way to file a leave request in triplicate, to how to fight an aircraft fire, or get out from under a life raft that has flipped over onto you. That was an exciting day in the pool. It finally ended with me getting assigned to a Naval Auxiliary stores ship in Guam.

There is a large Navy base on Guam that had been there since the US had appropriated the Island following the Spanish American War. Guam is a small Island in the middle of the Pacific, and is part of the Marianas chain. It is a *hot delicious mix* (62) of *tropical paradise* (63) and ghetto. Guam is fairly large by south pacific standards, about 30 miles long, and 12 miles wide. Contrary to congressional opinion, it is in no danger of capsizing.

The Japanese took and occupied the Island in the opening days of WWII, as they had nearby Saipan, and still some of the wounds remain open. Guam was the Island where as late as the early seventies, a Japanese soldier had been found in the dense jungle hiding, imagining that the war was still raging. One could still happen upon an old pillbox, or the battle scarred rusting hulk of a tank here and there, out in the boondocks.

The Japanese had been brutal overlords to the local Chamorro people, and there were still old timers in the bars and at the parks who would tell stories of Japanese cruelty and the degradations that they had suffered. It made it all that much more ironic that Guam had now become a major tourist destination for the Japanese. They arrived by the planeload every day, and filled the tall hotels clustered in Tumon, at the northern end of the island.

It was my first ship with Military Sealift Command (MSC), and I was happy to be returning to sea. My nostalgia for both the Navy and the Merchant Marine had led me to the place where they met, and I was returning to an organization that was an unholy mix of the two. I had left the Navy well over a decade prior, and spent most that interim in the more pirate like corners of the Merchant Marine. I had squandered the past three years living ashore in a foolish dalliance with normality, but the sweet song of the sirens had lured me back to mother ocean, and I couldn't have been happier about it.

So there I was... surrounded by Ocean for thousands of miles in every direction, stepping aboard a big grey ship that was Navy-like without being too military, crewed by ragged masses of swaggering, tattooed, long haired, bandanna clad civilians. It made me want to say Arrr.

48

THERE I WAS

The ship was a fleet auxiliary stores ship. Military Sealift Command's main mission was to supply the Navy while they were at sea. These ships, which had once been crewed by the Navy, were designed to replenish fleet warships while they were at sea. Which is as an amazing maritime operation as ever graced the waves, and the ability to do it is just one of the many reasons that the US Navy is the envy of the world. These ships come in various flavors: oilers for refueling, ammo ships, stores ships, and various types of hybrids. They were all designed to maneuver close enough to a Navy ship to connect a clothesline rig and pass pallets of supplies across, while pounding through ten foot seas at 15 knots. This is an act of supreme seamanship, and there are plenty of Navies in the world that are incapable of such dexterous ship handling.

The act of bringing two 40,000 ton ships, each as big as a floating skyscraper, within 50 yards of one another at fifteen knots and connecting a rig is akin to maneuvering two semi-trucks within two inches of one another at 60 mph with enough precision to pass a full glass of water from one to the next without spilling any. The act of underway replenishment, or in Navy parlance, UNREP, was an act of supreme seamanship and I was now officially a Military Sealift Command ship handling deck officer.

I had just flown across half the planet, and was now arriving at my new ship. These ships were unlike merchant cargo ships that would move cargo from point A to point B. They were more like floating warehouses, where the cargo was not packed into a hold and left there until it was unloaded, but was stocked onto shelves and racks where it could be picked, palletized, and delivered while at sea.

Not all the deliveries were made by UNREP, in fact most of them nowadays were made by helicopters, vertical replenishment or VERTREP. No less an amazing business, helicopters bouncing from ship to ship with netted pallets dangling beneath them.

Typically an entire squadron of Navy ships would meet and surround the replenishment ship. Two Navy warships would come alongside close aboard of the supply ship, unrepping from both the port and starboard side while a constant flow of helicopters picked pallets off of the flight deck and delivered them to the other ships in the formation. It was an amazing business. I had seen my share of at sea replenishment while in the Navy, but aside from delivering fuel to a few patrol boats, most of my experience was on the receiving end.

I walked up the gangway with my heavy seabags, and watched the fork trucks skirting about in the cramped shipboard environment. The ships were crewed by civilians, but the Navy still owned them, and there was always a contingent of Navy sailors on board. The Radiomen, some storekeepers, a few officers and maybe an administrative person or two. When the ships deployed, there would also be a naval

THERE I WAS

aviation detachment attached to the ship, with a pair of helicopters. The normal crew was about 180-190 people, 20 to 30 of which were Navy, and with the 'Air Detachment' (AirDet), an additional 20 to 30 Navy airmen.

Placing civilians and military together on one ship did create some problems, but in general everyone worked and played well together. The two groups mostly kept to themselves, the civilians averaging about 40 years old, and the naval contingent being composed mostly of older teen-agers. In the old days, before women could serve in combat roles, the auxiliary ships were the only sea duty a woman could get. So these groups of Navy sailors attached to these ships were traditionally mostly female. At this point in history, the combat ships were opening up to women, but that process was still underway, so these ships were still known for being crewed by an odd mix of 40 year old men, and teenage girls.

The Captain was there to meet me on the gangway, which was a *rare honor* (64), or fortunate coincidence. He was an easy going, good natured, seasoned professional who could drive a ninety four foot wide ship through a ninety five foot wide *canal* (65) at full speed in the dark while servicing a dozen helicopters off his flight deck.

He introduced himself and we stood there and chatted as the tropical sun lowered and the temps started to cool. One of the young Navy girls, a particularly pretty one, ambled up to us, stood a little too close to the Captain, and giggled at everything he said. He politely engaged, keeping his distance and being careful not flirt back. She eventually sauntered back off to work, or whatever it was the Navy kids did all day. We both stood there and watched her wiggle away. The Captain, muttering

"I love my job, I love my wife, I love my job, I love my wife" to himself.

Women had come a long way in the Maritime in my short career and had driven, and were still driving, immense changes in the maritime world. When I started, women on ships were rare. The Captain of my first ship summed up the old school Navy philosophy of women by declaring that there were only two types of women in the Navy, those who wanted to be men, and those who wanted to be surrounded by men. Times were changing and now doors were opening for that third type of women to join the club, women who wanted the same opportunity as men to work and serve and be treated fairly.

There were still plenty of the first two types of women, but the second you put any type of women into a traditionally all male environment everything changes dramatically, and changes that profound can be difficult. Ships filled with men are hard, course places, smelly and filled with grunting and farting, with regular episodes of physical violence. Differences were settled on the stern, physically. Black eyes and *fat lips* (66) were common, and simple strict hierarchies are formed based on rank and how tough, hardworking, or mean you are. No one EVER even acknowledged that they had feelings, much less discussed them.

THERE I WAS

When women started showing up, the world changed. Things started to get more civilized, there was less cussing, and fighting, but things also got more complicated. Not all Mariners embraced the changes, in fact to the surprise of no one, many resented it. In those days there were numerous socially handicapped malcontents who were unfit for normal society and they understandably resented the changes. If the maritime world were given the polish of feminine civility, then all that would be left for those poor marginal bastards would be prison.

I remember in the early days of the female invasion, watching the entire gender communication gap summed up neatly in a single interaction between two mates on a Tanker. This ship had a female Second Mate. She was an intelligent, emotional, free spirited redhead whose name was probably Becky. She was as pale as a ghost except for the sprinkle of brown freckles on her face, and presumably elsewhere. She wore her hair in a single waist long, thick braid. She had thick horn rimmed glasses, and seemed better suited to academia, or organic farming than the harsh ocean shipping trades.

The Chief Mate on this ship was a precise, by the book, all business, short tempered Kings Pointer whose name was probably Atherton. He didn't like people, and was not prone to small talk, but if you did your job, and didn't screw things up or make his life difficult, he was easy enough to be around. He was an open book, and there was never any guessing, if he was mad at you, it was never a secret, if he was content it was obvious to see.

I stood watch with him on the Bridge four hours at time, twice each day, and she was his relief. Turning over a navigational watch involves what can be a significant transfer of information. The textbook approach, which every man on board knew is how this Chief Mate would want to proceed, was to pass along the significant information in a clear effective manner, addressing only facts and items pertinent to the watch, and to keep all discussion related to the turnover. No chatting, no small talk, no interpretive dance, just the facts ma'am.

Becky was chatty. Becky believed that everyone was concerned with whatever one of the ten billion emotions in her repertoire that she happened to be feeling at that moment. Becky herself, to her credit, was in fact very concerned with how others were feeling and would constantly ask people how they felt. "How did that make you feel?" To her great consternation, her perpetual concern for the emotional wellbeing of her shipmates did not endear her to the crew.

It is my personal belief that, in general, men have a much narrower range of emotions than women, orders of magnitude really. I believe that a typical woman can experience more emotions in a minute than a typical man will feel in his entire life. Your average Mariner had an even narrower emotional range than your normal male, with rage, disgust and exhilaration being the predominant states of mind, and really very little departure from there.

Becky was blissfully unaware of this, for some reason, and twice each day she would come up to the Bridge and instead of asking what our speed over ground was, or the time to the next turn, or if the engineers were shifting tanks, she would ask if the Mate was nervous about the upcoming *strait transit* (67), or if he missed his wife. The Mate tried his hardest to be civil, gritting his teeth and steering the discussion back to the turnover, but at best he was curt, and as the days rolled on he became less and less patient.

Becky began to sense his irritation, and instead of backing off, she pressed harder, trying to get to the root of his discontent. Trying to compliment him, or engage him, or affect his mood positively. I would listen and watch, seeing the set in the Mate's jaw, and see his shoulders tense, and hear the tone of his voice strain as he tried desperately to complete the turnover and escape the Bridge and his nemesis with her useless chatter.

One fateful day, Becky decided that she needed to call the Mate out, and open a lengthy, gooey conversation about Atherton's feelings towards her. She was completely oblivious to the fact that this was the worst possible approach, and was in fact Atherton's worst nightmare. She expressed that she felt Atherton didn't like her, and she was feeling some hostility from him. She thought that it was important that they talk about it. She was persistent and demanded to know why the Mate was so distant and unfriendly to her.

I watched the Mate's color rise and felt his resistance fall. I could see his clenched jaw grinding, and his grip on the chart table edge tighten and I sensed him losing his self-control. It was a monumental personal struggle I was witnessing, and it was fascinating. I could almost hear the voices in his head "Don't scream at her, don't lose your cool, don't let her get to you." Yet she persisted

"Why won't you talk to me?" she whined. In an instant his resolve melted and he exploded, leaning his tall slender frame down to her level just inches from her face and screaming at the top of his voice

"BECAUSE I FUCKING HATE YOU!"

A painful, graphic example of the profound communicative challenges that the new paradigm posed. Military Sealift Command ships were ahead of the curve in these matters, having been dealing with these issues longer than other segments of the industry. I had been witness to some of these issues in the Merchant Marine, but my memories of the Navy were decidedly masculine.

On this ship, a big grey naval vessel with a hull number painted on the bow, I was again, after ten long years, in a naval environment. I wandered about the ship taking in the familiar 'Merchant Marine' qualities of the ship, and enjoying the

THERE I WAS

juxtaposed naval aspects. Numbered spaces and neatly labeled pipes and wires, but instead of young techs in neat blue uniforms, there were grizzled salty crusts in tattered jeans and greasy work shirts. Merchant quality food, with naval quality cleanliness. It was like the perfect melding of two disparate worlds.

I wandered up to the Bridge, which would become my home for the foreseeable future, to visit the electronics. The Bridge was filled with top of the line commercial quality gear, with the spare no expense naval redundancy attitude. A small group of Navy personnel were gathered up there, having a meeting of some type when I wandered in. I was lost in my nostalgic reverie as I stepped onto the Bridge, and stopped short when I realized that I was interrupting a meeting. In that brief moment when I stopped and snapped out of my daydream, the message being delivered by the young green naval officer running the meeting sank in.

He was informing everyone that they needed to take care, when addressing a coworker, especially a lower ranking coworker, that the tone of their communication be modulated to prevent them from potentially hurting someone's feelings. He droned on in that vein, about how easily someone's feelings can be inadvertently hurt etc. and how damaging that can be.

Now, in most workplaces, or other milieu's, this is not an unreasonable discussion, but to me at that moment, the sight of a US Navy officer speaking those words so contrasted with my memory of the US Navy that it hit me like a brick in the face. In the Navy that I had served in, when a person arrived at a ship, he was assaulted from every direction: physically, mentally, and emotionally. Every infinitesimal little mistake you made was noticed, announced, and made available for public ridicule. The tiniest slip of the tongue, undotted i, or uncrossed t, would garner you a vicious "Stupid fucking recruit." Everyone tested the new guy with a relentless barrage of unforgiving challenges.

I was in Navigation, a Quartermaster, and every Quartermaster on that ship was trying his hardest to out navigate every other Quartermaster. I lived in fear that my plotted fixes would be a fraction of a millimeter out of place, earning me the scorn and ridicule of my peers. Emerging from the forge of that baptism of fire, were hardened, seasoned salts, capable of engaging the fiercest enemy, even in face of potentially hurt feelings and negativity.

Standing behind the baby faced ensign as he delivered his sensitive message, was the senior petty officer in the group. An older first class petty officer, about my age, with the grizzled leathery face of a man who had spent a career covered in salt spray in heavy weather.

He saw the look on my face in that moment, when I stepped through the looking glass into what only appeared to be a naval Bridge, and I could see the pain in his face, the shame. He knew what I was thinking as if I had spoken the thoughts out loud. He knew the Navy I was remembering, and the Navy I was seeing now, and he looked down, unable to meet my eyes, as if I would blame him. He realized that I was learning in that very moment of the death of the Navy I had known. He had likely joined the same Navy that I had joined, and then lived through its slow transformation, and saw his worst fears confirmed in my reaction. Like looking in a mirror and finally seeing the wrinkles and gray realizing that you are no longer a young man. That your past is forever behind you.

I apologized to the group for interrupting their meeting and expressed my sincerest hopes that no one's self-esteem had been damaged by the interruption and departed, my nostalgic journey through the past now ended firmly in the future. The times they were a changing. I was left to ponder the odd duality of a ship filled with the raw machismo of unparalleled ship handlers, helicopter Pilots, and pirates with their long traditions and old fashioned ways, alongside a team of HR savvy, world changing pioneers, constantly on the lookout for a hostile work environment, ocean hostility notwithstanding.

It didn't make it easier that there were those three different types' of women out there, and that one type in particular made it extremely difficult for everyone. That newest third type of hard working women who just wanted a fair shot, and the older traditional group of women who themselves simply adopted the male attitude and became one of the boys, both forged ahead together, changing people's attitudes and chiseling away at centuries of prejudice and bias.

The wrench in the machinery of change was that young pretty that flirted with the Captain, and those like her, who wanted nothing more than to be surrounded by men. They were the women who added the element of romance to shipboard life, filling a century's old vacuum and adding a dimension to shipboard living, previously unheard of. It was a perfectly natural reaction, boys and girls will be boys and girls, but it added a profound new level of social complexity to ships, and created a fundamental change in the fabric of the Maritime society.

In those days, the ratio of women to men was very low. On that ship with nearly two hundred people, there were maybe 20 females. Many of those women had elected not to cleave tightly to the Navy's "No fraternizing rules", nor did they chose to adopt the highly professional "I am here to work" attitude. As was the norm in these situations there was a contingency of women in the group who were looking for love. Some few, were focused more on variety and quantity, liberated as they were, but others were more in the market for a single partner.

There is an odd dynamic, that is more common than not, that I noticed many times over the years. A woman in search of a mate on a ship, will often, either consciously or not, seek the highest ranking male she can attain. With the tiny crews of Merchant ships, it isn't uncommon for the lone female to be paired with a much

54

higher ranking officer. You can often see them in their pursuit, working their way down until they find a willing partner and become a 'ship wife'. The main problem with this, is that these women now often believe that they have the rank and status as their mate, and depending on the partner, they just may.

There was a crusty old Boatswain on one ship, who was forced to deal with this issue head on. He was a grizzled old salt, adept at both deck seamanship and storytelling, whose name was probably Brutus. The Boatswain (Bosun) is an 'unlicensed' officer, and since this ship had an automated Engine Room, there were no senior Engine Room trades in the unlicensed mess, this made him the senior unlicensed person on the ship. A 'mess' is the nautical term for the food service area, but also refers to the group of people who eat there together. There is typically an officer's mess and an unlicensed mess. The ancient shipboard tradition, holds that the senior person in the mess often has a special status. This is truer in the officer's mess, and in the Navy, but these traditions still exist to some extent in the Merchant Marine.

There was a female cook on this ship. Not even a cook really, but a galley lackey, an entry level food handler, which is the lowest position on any ship except maybe a cruise ship. She was an insufferable whiner, constantly complaining, and worse she was a know-it-all. Her name was probably Amy.

She lectured everyone constantly about everything, manners, dress, how they should eat, behave, speak etc. Mostly it was mildly irritating, but being the person who served the food, she was unavoidable. This ship was making a long run from Jacksonville, FL all the way to Toyo Japan, and that was about six weeks of whining and lecturing three times each day, without relief. In her defense, I think that it may have been the rising hostility of the crew that drove her to seek the protection of an alpha male, or in her case a high ranking Beta.

So she wound up finding solace in the arms of the Chief Engineer. He was a graduate of California Maritime Academy, and was a very stereotypical 'hey dude' southern Californian who was probably named Keanu. Chief Engineers are equal in rank to the Captain, and can wield considerable clout on a ship, but this ship was brand new, with an automated Engine Room, which rendered his department small. It was a low paying ship, which meant that it was not a desirable job, so he was a young and inexperienced Chief Engineer. He was by nature, an easy going good natured person and not a strong leader.

He was also married, which meant that his public affair with the galley wench, cost him some respect, in addition to creating a liability for him. So once she and he were established in their liaison, she decided that she now was the equivalent of the second highest ranking person on the ship and she went from insufferable, to intolerable in a very short while. She took to nagging.

THERE I WAS

Her job was to keep the mess clean. After each meal she would wash the tables, sweep the floors, clean up the beverage machines etc. She began to interpret her job as preventing the messdecks from ever becoming dirty to begin with and would nag at the crew to stop making such a mess, and clean up that spill, or be more careful about getting crumbs on the table. As the senior unlicensed person on the ship, this was traditionally the Boatswains mess. Any rules in the mess were his to make and she was starting to behave like it was her mess.

In an all-male environment, this would be considered a challenge, and a very inappropriate one. An entry level cook challenging a Boatswain, is like a Beverly Hills lap Chihuahua challenging an Alpha wolf. Much leeway had already been given, and by now she had used up what little slack the Boatswain was willing to offer. One night, Brutus the Boatswain, after a long day of hard physical labor in the hot tropical sun, gathered up his tray after a fine dinner, and neglected to add a used crumpled napkin to his tray, leaving it on the table behind. Amy snapped

"Don't you leave that on the table, clean up after yourself." That was the last straw for Brutus, who hurled his tray across the room, splattering it across the floor and wall. He then snatched another empty tray from the hands of a shipmate and sent that flying at the beverage line.

"Your fucking job is clean up the mess, not prevent it from getting dirty in the first place, this is MY mess, and don't you ever tell me how to act in my mess, or anyplace else ever again, you are the Goddamn galley ape, and you have no business telling the Ship's Bosun how to act, now clean up this fucking mess, and shut your damn mouth for once in your miserable life." Extreme, yes, but you must remember, that her behavior for the past five weeks, had consistently violated what was considered acceptable, and Brutus was not exactly socially adept. He was in fact a fairly dangerous man, and she was too foolish to realize it.

She looked to the Steward, another unlicensed officer, the senior officer in her department, but not senior to the Boatswain by any stretch, and he was likely relieved that Bosun had stepped up, he himself not willing to challenge the Chief Engineer, who was by proxy now involved. He simply stared at her, and nodded toward the mess, offering no support and everyone just left the room leaving her to her thoughts and the spattered food.

Now had the Chief Engineer been smart, he would have stayed out of it, but smart men don't cheat on their wives, at least not publicly. He not only foolishly stepped into a fight with a formidable opponent, but chose a poor battle to fight, and then selected the worst possible strategy. He must have imagined that his high rank would carry the day, so he marched right into the crew's mess during a meal and challenged Brutus.

THERE I WAS

Officers have no business in the crew's mess, or involving themselves in the affairs of the crew. It is a breach of etiquette for a licensed officer to even enter the crew's mess without an invitation. Brutus being the senior unlicensed was also the senior union member and the ships official union rep. Keanu stepped into the mess with a confident easy stride, completely unaware that he was strolling into a lion's den. The mess immediately fell silent as he walked in, and when he called the Bosun out about how he had treated Amy, you could feel the anger in the room rise.

Brutus didn't even bother to get up.

"What the hell makes you think you can come into our mess, interrupt our union meeting, and address how we deal with an insubordinate applicant who was derelict in her duties and disrespectful to the ship senior unlicensed officer in his own mess!" Keanu went white, 'union meeting?' It was not a union meeting of course, it was just another dinner like any other dinner, but Keanu didn't know that, and it became a union meeting the moment the Union Rep said it was union meeting. Amy had heard her 'applicant' status called out, and realized with horror that her extremely low standing in the union was now jeopardized. Brutus pressed on

"I move that we file an official complaint with the union and with the Captain immediately that a senior manager of the company is interfering with the right of organized labor to lawfully gather." The entire mess responded nearly in unison:

"Seconded!"

"I am not... I wasn't... Union Meeting? I didn't mean..." He sputtered and back-pedaled. Brutus had anticipated that Amy's sugar daddy would come and had already bribed the radio officer to provide the "In Case of Emergency" contact list, and Keanu's in case of emergency name was Jeannie, presumably his wife.

"What do you think Jeannie would say if we told her the massive union investigation that is about to disrupt your world was the result of you deciding to elevate your whore to lord of the unlicensed mess? How do you think the company would feel if they heard that you had decided that you are in charge of the Stewards Department and had entered the unlicensed mess uninvited to dictate how the lowest ranking person on the ship was directed by her appointed supervisors, nowhere near your department?"

Keanu had gone pale, and quiet, which likely the smartest thing he had done all day.

"Get out of my mess, never come back here, never speak to me again, and never involve yourself in our internal union matters again." Again, extreme reactions, but these types of pissing contests were quite common in those days, and often females just added fuel to those fires without even realizing it.

On the larger ships, with bigger crews, it was more complicated, and it was harder for the 'social climbers'. The wiser officers at Military Sealift Command were

THERE I WAS

smart enough to avoid the pitfalls of shipboard romance, and the Navy dets often had female officers in charge who were generally smart, high powered military officers who had no tolerance for such shenanigans and were uniquely empowered to deal with it. Still it happened, and the obstacles didn't stop the more determined social climbers.

Towards the end of my career I saw the tables turn a little, and saw higher ranking women selecting lower ranking men, and they seemed to follow that same penchant for the extreme, generally selecting the lowest ranking partner they could find, right there at the bottom of the barrel, which is where the young studs would likely be anyway so it all seemed to work out.

The other type of romance seeking women were more of the fun-loving type, and were not looking for relationship per se. These women were beloved by the men, and often despised by the other women. The taboo and stigma of this behavior seemed to be wearing off a little by the time I left, with people being less judgmental, but it was still dangerous territory. I recall one young pretty Navy girl who was in fact wise enough to keep from fraternizing with her shipmates, but was very open about her social life and sexual exploits outside the ship. One night, in some seedy bar, in some foreign country, after a few beers, she confided to a rather large group of her shipmates, that she enjoyed anal sex. Then and there, a nickname was born, and she was forever after known as 'Up the Butt Girl' or UTBG for short.

It may surprise the reader that I am not good at remembering names, but even now, decades later, if I were to bump into this girl (no pun intended), she would immediately register to me as 'UTBG Girl'. Note to self, be careful what you share.

There was one girl on this very MSC ship, who had identified a particular Third Mate as the object of her desire. He was freshly graduated from Cal Maritime and was a dashingly handsome surfer boy with a perfect tan and a chiseled six pack that he was proud to display every chance he got. He was smart enough to steer clear of romantic entanglements with shipmates, but she was quite determined. She loved to openly pursue him, and reveled in his discomfiture. She would go out of her way to make openly suggestive comments in public just to see him squirm. She had a fantastic sense of humor and transformed her pursuit into a magnificent comedic performance.

He stood a navigational watch, and she knew that he was tied to the Bridge, unable to escape her advances, for four hours at a time, twice each day. She would come up to the wheelhouse during his watches to press her case. One day she arrived in the pilothouse after dinner, with a small plate of desert to offer the Mate, and she entertained the entire Bridge expounding to the poor embarrassed Third Mate the virtues of her *pie* (68), and how she would dearly love it if he would sample some of her pie. She took it up a notch when she said that she too loved pie, and that her

THERE I WAS

friend also had wonderful pie, and they should all go out for pie together sometime. She was kind enough to relent eventually, before it became too uncomfortable. It was never a problem that I had to deal with, sometimes it pays not to be a totally rad, handsome, six pack surfer boy.

Uncomfortable sexual tension, hostile workplace environments, misogyny, and promiscuity weren't exactly a prominent part of the tableau, they were more of a persistent undercurrent. Like background music, always there, rarely in the forefront. Mostly it was a fun and interesting place to work and people got along well, as much as people from every corner of the earth, and every walk of life can get along when confined together in close quarters, under stressful conditions, and with several differing sets of standards governing the various groups differently, either fairly or unfairly.

Most people were just too busy trying not get run over by the ever present fork trucks that incessantly buzzed about the decks to get into trouble. Many of the older traditions were dying, modern society had brought the internet, TV, phone access and all the consequences of connectivity, and gone were the days of leaving the world behind when you cast off the lines. With that connection, and women, came civilization. For the small, but potent, sub-class of recalcitrant, vagabond, drunken sailors the writing was on the wall.

Tolerance for drunken idiocy was waning. There were still a few hardcore inebriates clinging to their sodden lifestyle, but they were fewer and further between. A few stalwarts, entrenched within the old boy network were tolerated, even coddled, as relics of the past. There remained a stubborn contingent of old school Chief Mates, whose bacchanalian ways would forever prevent them from being promoted to Captain. They still wore their hair long, ponytails and flowing locks, as if nothing had changed since the sixties when they first stepped aboard these ships. The Cargo Mate on this very ship was a vestige of those days, long haired, tattooed, and never fully sober. It was widely known that he was always, to some extent, under the influence, but never too much while on duty.

Off duty was an entirely different matter, and his antics were legendary. On my first voyage aboard that fine vessel, we stopped on some god-forsaken little island somewhere, with nothing much to offer for sailors on liberty, so the Captain authorized a cook-out, and "Beer on the Pier". These events were generally pleasant, with crew members from every department and from every level spending some time together eating and drinking, telling their shipmates overly intimate details of their sexual preferences, and garnering themselves nicknames in the process.

This drunken sot of a Chief Mate, whose name was probably Otis, was more about the beer than the pier that night, though likely had been working a private stock of something stronger than beer prior to the festivities. He was more than just wobbly, he was shit-talking, snot-slinging, falling down drunk. He announced, way too loudly, that he had to take a piss. He must have felt, that a senior officer isn't too proud to whip out his Johnson and piss in public in front of the entire crew. He decided that dropping his pants in what was technically the workplace, in the presence of his female co-workers was not insanely stupid, and so off to the edge of the pier he waddled, to pee between the ship and the dock.

The ship was held off the dock with giant fenders, big thick rubber balls, as big as a car, or bigger, and the ship stood a good 10 feet from the edge of the pier. He chose the area right next to the gangway, to ensure that the entire gangway watch and anyone on deck, on any starboard deck really, would have clear and unadulterated view of his manhood as it leaked what little dignity he still had.

It might have made sense, in some twisted drunken way, if he had stood close enough to the gangway to hold on, but no, he stepped right up to the edge of the pier, 15 feet above the water, balanced on the curb at the edge of the pier, tottering dangerously, looking down, focusing intently on maintaining his grip perhaps. His fall was almost slow motion, and it appeared that he actually fell asleep standing there with his pickle in his hand while 50 or so of his co-workers watched. He just sort of slowly fell forward maintaining his dick in hand posture, no cry, no wind-milling arms, no attempt to recover his balance.

Fortunately the big splash seemed to wake him up. He appeared genuinely surprised to be in the water. The gangway watch tossed him a life ring, swung a boom out, and lowered a harness for him. There seemed to be no consequence for the action, he remained cargo officer, keeping his job and privileges, and having had little respect from his coworkers to begin with, relatively speaking, he lost nothing as a result of the incident.

I grew to love that ship, and the island of Guam, and as many of its female inhabitants as would let me. While we did spend quite a bit of time on that wonderful Island, we also travelled, as ships will do. We followed the 7th fleet to the *remote reaches* (69) of the south Pacific, that rare corner of the earth where still there exist uncharted waters. Navigational charts tend to be littered with a dense matrix of numbers, called soundings. They represent the depth of the water. Survey ships are constantly mapping the ocean floors. In the not so distant past, surveying was a normal activity for all ships, and one of the skills all deck officers were required to master.

Down there in the *far southern reaches* (70) of the watery world, the charts were filled with vast daunting areas of pure white blankness, with occasional lines of soundings spanning the emptiness, marking the passage of some ship from decades past, logging the depth as it went. Even more frightening was when one of these

THERE I WAS

lines ended abruptly with the symbol of a ship wreck, deep safe soundings, literally thousands of fathoms, mounting abruptly to a tall underwater ship killing peak. They were out there, hidden beneath the white.

This was the realm that Nimitz, Halsey, Spruance and others once wrested from the godless Japanese aggressors. The Seventh Fleet remembers. The Seventh Fleet pays homage. We were enroute to meet the fleet at a tiny flyspeck of a tropical paradise/sand dune called New Caledonia, and passed through several historic battle sites in the Solomon's and Coral Sea. Navy ships go out of their way to visit these places, and solemnly ring a bell when passing over the remains of sunken sisters.

It was amazing how often that bell rang, how many thousands upon thousands of men must have died in a sinking raging inferno, or been left in the water, in the dark, with burning oil slicks, and sharks, and the Japanese tradition of hunting for and shooting at the survivors in the water. I have seen the Seventh fleet ARG (Amphibious Readiness Group), a squadron of ships filled with Marine landing forces, divert hundreds of miles out of its way, to pass close aboard to Guadalcanal, while thousands of Marines line the rails in dress uniforms, saluting their fallen brethren.

The memories of WW2, were still fresh, the scars not healed, the marks of the war were still to be seen. On Saipan, they embrace and honor the past, and the island is filled with the old Japanese pillboxes and fortifications. The beaches are still littered with the rusting hulks of Mike boats and tanks that stormed ashore so many decades ago. Decorative gardens are planted lovingly on them, and roads are literally diverted around them.

Saipan is about one hundred and 30 miles north of Guam. When the US took back Guam later in the war, Saipan was still occupied, but stranded and isolated. The Navy made a point to send one bomber to Saipan each day to make a token attack and let them know that they were next. The Japanese soldiers had families there, along with civilian workers. They told their civilians and even their military, that the Americans were Barbarians that would roast them alive and eat them. So when the US came, there was no surrendering. Not that the Japanese culture was in any way amenable to surrender. So the Japanese civilians and military fought every inch, being backed up eventually to a tall cliff overlooking the Pacific, where they proceeded to leap off like Lemmings rather than be taken by the enemy.

Eight wonderful months I spent on that ship, studying, visiting and re-living the Pacific Campaign. I sailed into Sasebo harbor in Japan where the US Navy maintains a small base, I steamed past the tall radio towers that once broadcast that fatal message "Tora Tora Tora" on that fateful day, December 7th, 1941. Sasebo had been the Japanese Naval High Command, so it was fitting the US Navy commandeer it and turn it into their Naval Headquarters under the occupation.

THERE I WAS

Guam, Saipan, Sasebo, Okinawa, Pusan Korea, Hong Kong, Singapore, Sydney Australia, Thailand, Chuuk, Borneo, Brunei, Manila. It was a glorious eight months, the first of many such tours, but eight months is a long tour, and I was ready to go home. Like my dad always used to tell me: "Get moving." Military Sealift Command had manning issues, and was infamous for long tours, and difficulty getting relieved.

We were enroute to Yokosuka Japan, in Tokyo bay where a relief was allegedly waiting for me. Of course, the normally week long run was beset with heavy weather, complete with storm diversions. We got called off to make unscheduled service calls to random 7th fleet elements, and the one week trip was now stretching into its third week.

Finally, after delivering the much needed soda pop and junk food that that particular destroyer squadron could not live without, we were again pointed in the direction of Yokosuka. Barely had my pencil laid the new course on the chart when the Distress call came in. A US Merchant, under charter by Military Sealift Command, but with a fully commercial, civilian union crew was adrift in the middle of the pacific somewhere between Midway and Japan, just a few hundred miles away, and lucky us, we were the closest asset. Hooray.

We found our stricken sister, drifting about in this lonely patch of ocean, hundreds of miles from the nearest land, and thousands of miles from home. Commercial crews are small, that ship, like most commercial ships, would have only four deck officers (including the Captain), and six deck seamen. Military Sealift Command ships are brimming with 'Deckies' of all stripes, a half dozen officers, 40 or 50 deck seamen, just the ticket to help this enormous behemoth rig herself for tow.

This ship was owned by the government, and was filled to the brim with military cargo. Being a government owned ship, they actually had a tow rig stowed neatly beneath the forecastle (pronounced Fo'csle) in a gear locker. It was magnificent piece of Marine hardware with wire pendants as thick as a man's arm, an enormous swivel, shackle, tow plate and various other elements of 'jewelry' weighing several tons, that would need to be removed from their tight stow below decks, manipulated out through the narrow hatch, laid on deck assembled correctly (for the first time since leaving the loft where it was manufactured) and deployed.

The poor crew of a half dozen AB's had been at it for a few days, and had only managed to get about a quarter of the gear out. Adding an additional 20 able seamen to that chore would accelerate that task significantly. So I joined the Chief Mate and few dozen other AB's on our launch and off I went to meet this strange ship 2000 miles from the US Shores, and another 2000 again from mother Boston.

Upon arriving, the Chief Mate and I were escorted to the Captain's stateroom, where pleasantries and formalities were exchanged over lunch, and not surprisingly

62

THERE I WAS

several of the officers were from Boston. The great state of Massachusetts is home to one of the major Maritime Academies in addition to having a long proud maritime history, and is well represented in the industry. It was in fact quite surprising, however, to find that this Captain was in fact from my hometown of Needham, and lived less than a mile from the home I grew up in. The world just kept getting smaller.

We spent the day rigging for tow, and finally wrangled the massive bridle in place, ready to join a towline. The Captain of our ship maneuvered close aboard, as only a Military Sealift Command ship handler can, and a rifle with a specially fitted attachment on its barrel launched a 'shot line' at us. We heaved in the shot line, which was connected to a series of thicker and heavier 'messenger' lines until we got one strong enough to wrap on the capstan and haul the heavy towing hawser.

We got the hawser bent on to the bridle and dropped it all off the bow. We climbed back into the boats and headed back to our ship, with our new found friends in tow. Towing speeds are a small fraction of normal transit speeds, so the light at the end of this long tunnel remained out of sight. After a few days, a salvage tug arrived to pick up the tow and bring her to a shipyard somewhere.

We finally made our approach on Yokosuka Japan, just south of Yokohama on Tokyo bay. It is, as you might imagine, an extremely busy port, bustling with merchant traffic, Navy ships, pleasure boaters, and thousands of fishermen. Nothing defines a port more than its fishermen. Every port will have fishing boats, and they are as specific to a region as its food. Japan being an ancient culture with a fish based diet, had elevated fishing to a high art, and being Japan, had managed to artfully embrace the past while moving steadfastly into the future.

Japanese fishing vessels ran the gamut from traditional wooden boats called "Wasen", complete with sails and handmade nets, to massive factory fishing boats that pillaged the oceans for everything from sardines to whales. Fishing boats are always in the way. Technically they have the right of way in most situations, but not always. They aren't supposed to fish in the channels, and they are supposed to yield to deep draft vessels that can only operate within a marked channel, but those rules are not only consistently ignored from one end of the earth to the other, there is a planet wide tradition amongst the Coast Guards of the world, to hold fishermen to a different standard than Merchants. The approach is simple, the Merchant is always wrong.

A fisherman could be drunk, fishing in illegal waters for a protected species, with no lookouts posted, and actively maneuvering to intercept and collide with a Merchant, and the Merchant will be found at fault. In Asia, even more so than the rest of the world, fishermen in small vessels are as thick as flies, and avoiding them is like avoiding rain drops. While it is patently illegal for them to drop gear in the

63

channel, that is apparently a big secret to them, and inevitably you end up steaming through their gear. This not only infuriates the fishermen, but it can foul your propeller.

If the fishermen are nearby, they will rush to their gear, forcing you to maneuver. Given that the only water deep enough for the giant Merchant to maneuver in is within the narrow confines of the channel, there is precious little room to avoid making splinters of some poor fisherman's boat. In the approaches to Tokyo bay, as in other Japanese ports, maneuvering is further complicated by the attack buoys.

Channels are marked by buoys, as are obstructions, anchorages, and other areas needing identification. They are the road signs of the maritime environment. In Japan, it is crime to collide with a buoy, and there is a hefty fine to pay if you do, which is fair. What isn't fair, is that approaching too close a Japanese buoy is considered a collision. When you pass too close to a Tokyo attack buoy, it senses your proximity, and sprays paint on your hull. So your winding, twisting, turning, fisherman avoiding path within the painfully small and narrow area demarcated by the over aggressive buoys, is further limited. I have always suspected that the fishermen are in collusion with the port authority, and intentionally maneuver to drive the barbarian foreigner ships toward the revenue generating navigational aids.

We were prepared with counter measures. Squads of highly skilled deck seaman armed with Bosun chairs, and paint thinner were stationed on deck, ready to drop from the rails in Bosun's chairs, and dangle like Ninja's with scrub brushes and industrial solvents to wash away the damning stains. The authorities would arrive at the pier to demand their tribute, only to find an unstained hull, free from the marks of the evil attack buoys.

We survived the gauntlet of Tokyo Bay, and made it to the anchorage safe and sound. My bags were packed, my travel arranged, and I had a pocket full of cash and a plan. We were already three weeks late arriving to Yokosuka, and I had been scheduled for relief over two months prior. I was ready to go.

Now a little background is in order. At one point during this voyage, a sister Military Sealift Command ship was short of a Mate, and was unable to get underway. They needed someone fast, and so I volunteered. It was my first trip as Second Mate, and I was happy to help. I was in Guam at the time, and flew to Japan, got an arrival visa at the airport and met the ship at Sasebo. The ship was, at this point, already long delayed in departing and had been waiting for me with baited breath. They wasted no time in getting underway. So rushed they were, in fact, that they neglected to get the port agent to have my passport correctly stamped, and so unbeknownst to me, I had left Japan without a proper exit Visa.

THERE I WAS

So there I was... after a brisk boat ride from the anchorage to the immigration office, where I was to get my Seaman's' Arrival visa, authorizing me to step foot in Japan and take a bus to the airport. It is normal for Japanese officials to grunt and moan over your documents. Long drawn out Hmmmmmmmmms, and aaaaahhhhs are common. They will always display their authority over you, and their relentless dedication to the rules and norms in pursuit of administrative perfection. I was expecting the requisite 10 minutes of careful examination of my passport, complete with the vocal punctuation to emphasize that it wasn't just so, but as a dedicated and competent Zen Immigration official, he was aware that perfection is a road and not a destination.

But soon the grunts changed their tone, becoming shorter and sterner. I watched as he called over a supervisor to confer. You can always tell how important a port official is in most countries other than the US, by how ornate their hat is. The person called over to confer, had a nicer hat and was therefore more important in that office. They grunted and moaned together in a well-choreographed duet, occasionally peppered with actual conversation. Another ten minutes. The supervisor then took the passport to his office, where he grunted solo for a good ten minutes more before picking up the phone.

A long phone conversation was followed by yet a third supervisor being called, a comically large hat perched on his tiny head. Now the two of them poured over my passport ooh'ing and aah'ing with noises that sounded to me like the sounds a very angry constipated person might make. The original, bland hatted functionary joined in, and it was now a three part harmony.

It had been several hours at this point, with me sitting on those hard, undersized chairs designed not for a 200 pound American, but for people raised on a less cheeseburger intense diet. Finally after a full three hours or more, it was explained to me, that I had arrived in Japan with an arrival Visa from an airport near Sasebo, and no departure visa, and that meant that I had left Japan illegally. They told me that the Captain of my ship needed to write a letter to explain why this was so, and I needed to present that letter to them once I had it.

So I gathered all my heavy bags, having lugged them already across the ship, down the accommodation ladder, into a boat, out of a boat, into a cab, into this office. Now I lugged them again out of the office, into a cab, onto a boat, back up the accommodation ladder and into the Captain's office. Or more accurately, just outside the Captains office, the Captain was of course himself very busy with port officials, trying to explain where the paint stain had gone. Finally he emerged, still bearing the scars of the administrative battle he had just waged with his very own ornately hatted official. Everyone on the Japanese waterfront wears a hat... with a chinstrap.

THERE I WAS

I had taken the liberty of writing the letter on official Navy letterhead, reducing his effort to just a signature, which he happily provided. So I strapped my 60 pound seabag to my back, my carry on, and my laptop and again lugged them across the ship, down the ladder, onto a boat, out of a boat, into a cab, into the immigration office, where after another three hours of grunting, chanting, and no less than a half dozen consultations, I was gifted with the rubber stamp that I had so desperately been seeking.

Now another cab, to the Navy transportation office where I was to receive plane tickets. I was scheduled for a hellish long journey from Tokyo's Narita airport, to Hawaii with a five hour layover, thence to LA, and on to Boston. 36 hours all told starting in six hours. Already I was 10 hours into it. In keeping with the tone of the day, I had missed the Navy shuttle that made the three hour run to the airport thrice daily and I was forced to take a cab to the train station and ride the dreaded Japanese train to the airport.

Like every other square inch of urban Japan, there was a ballpark crowd packed into the terminal. The average height in Japan in those days was about 5'5" give or take an inch or two. I noticed over the years that they appeared to grow taller, perhaps as their diets changed, or perhaps I imagined it, but there in that train station, like so many of my other experiences in Asia, I stood head and shoulders above a massive crowd of humanity, looking out across a vast sea of wobbling black haired heads, with an occasional orange headed rebel proclaiming his or her individuality. Other westerners were distinctly visible, standing out with their heads and shoulders above the crowd, nodding at one another to acknowledge the odd shared experience.

I found my way to the ticketing machines, and got in line. Japan is a very complex, fast moving, society. They tolerate westerners, and are remarkably polite and hospitable, but so many aspects of their society are unique and profoundly foreign to outsiders that it is like travelling to a different planet.

The ticket machine was of course annotated in Japanese, and fortunately I had had the foresight to ask a local worker at the transportation office to write the name of the Narita stop in the appropriate ideogram. Not that I needed to, every Japanese person within 30 feet of me stood poised and ready to assist the poor foreigner, but they all seemed suitably impressed that I managed to get myself a ticket without significantly delaying the long line.

I was packed into the car like a sardine, pressed up tight to a mass of people who were probably disgusted to be so close to a meat eater. I stood there for the two hour ride, followed the crowd to the air terminal, and managed somehow to find the correct gate. With one bag now checked, I felt liberated, and having several hours to kill I strolled about the airport visiting the brightly colored shops and booths.

THERE I WAS

Japanese snack food is the most interesting mix of culinary oddities imaginable, packaged like western snack food, in bright plastic bags, but instead of potato chips, they were filled with tiny deep fried crabs, or whale jerky, or fish heads, or squid tentacles. It was damn entertaining trying to figure out what was in those crazy bags. Ultraman, Godzilla and Johnny Sako were still alive and well in the toy stores, as well as Pokémon and Hello Kitty. The Japanese word for Pokémon, translates to *Pocket Monster* (71), which would have been damn amusing if I wasn't learning this from the bad English of a store clerk, but in the context of an awkward transaction, it was downright hilarious.

"You like... pocket monster?"

"Beg your pardon?"

"Pocket Monster?" She was ever so pretty, and ever so polite, and it took me a moment to connect that the pocket monster she was referring to was one of the toys arrayed on the shelf in front of me. I smiled at her, and told her that I loved my pocket monster, but had no need for any more, the one I had was all I would ever need. She smiled back, and bowed. I bowed back, and she bowed again. I learned long ago that bowing back and forth could go on forever if you let it, so I elected not to get into a bowing match with this sweet young lady who had unknowingly talked dirty to me.

Eventually, I made it aboard the plane for my first ever JAL flight. I waited with baited breath as the stewardess droned on for a full five minutes, wondering what this seemingly endless and involved monologue was about. The Japanese soliloquy was followed by an abrupt, deeply accented

"Please fasten your seatbelts"... really? Another speech, this one even longer, now I was timing it.

"Smoking is prohibited on this flight," how complex is this language that needs six and half minutes to say no smoking? What are they really saying? It took a full 12 minutes for her to explain the seatbelt in her native tongue, and just three sentences in English. I began to suspect that they were talking about me.

A mere nine hours later we landed in Honolulu. I am cursed with the inability to sleep on an airplane, which I am sure is fortunate for those around me, but by now I had been awake a very long time, and was likely on the verge of a deep vein thrombosis. Airport chairs being specifically designed for discomfort, my only option was to lie on the floor and hope I didn't get trampled.

Upon rising, just seconds after the final boarding call was announced, with the additional rumple and residue of airport floor smeared all over me, I stumbled onto the overcrowded plane to find my seat occupied by an angry and belligerent Japanese businessman. There was much ado, and guttural barking, but in the end, the very plain and obvious number on my boarding pass precisely matching the number on

THERE I WAS

the seat won the day. The bellicose traveler was understandably dismayed to be relegated to the one remaining seat next to an enormous Samoan, who already seemed to be occupying both seats.

Causing a delay on a hot tarmac at the gate before the AC came on and picking fight with the seat squatter didn't exactly endear me to the mostly Japanese passengers that surrounded me, but such was life. I had worked the past 60 days straight without a day off, and had been traveling for two days at this point, and I was not exactly in a friend making state of mind. The final six hours of the flight droned on, each minute dragging into an eternity.

I had not booked a connecting flight in LA, resolving to get a room, a bottle of blessed whiskey, and do some relaxing. This was one of my favorite traditions, spending a few days 'decompressing' in Venice Beach after a long Pacific voyage, but at this stage the beach was still hours and hours away. Apparently, the secret society of allied immigration officers had gotten the word. The problem in Japan had followed me home, the focused deliberation and atonal sound effects replaced with carefully practiced indifference.

I was led to a small side room where I was abandoned for hours. Over a decade of traveling the globe, flying out to meet ships with one way tickets to the Middle East, with my thick beard, and suspicious beady eyes, made me the perfect candidate for harassment. The fact that I was on government orders seemed to matter not at all. My passport, with its extra pages, and rainbow of stamps and stickers, was deemed offensive by the border guards and I was made to suffer for it. The only up–side had been the fact the room was not the dreaded medical exam room empty but for the exam table (complete with stirrups), five gallon tub of KY Jelly and arm length rubber gloves. Still, that room couldn't be far away.

After 2 or three hours, just when I was starting to believe that they had forgotten about me, and just moments before I was about to start screaming and breaking things, I was joined by another petty functionary. Perhaps he was a senior supervisor, I couldn't tell without a hat, but he did have the power to hand me back my passport without a word, and gesture to the door. Free at last.

Of course by now, my baggage had gone unclaimed on the carousel, leaving me to hunt it down. The people in the baggage department are never happy to see you. To them, you are just the next pissed off traveler who is about to yell at them, and while I did keep my promise to myself to neither yell nor become violent with them, they remained surly, unfriendly and only barely helpful.

I emerged from the dark bowels of the lost baggage department, lugging my heavy bags, and stepped into the glorious southern California sunshine, and it was like stepping out of jail. Suddenly, everything was right with the world. Only one more leg to this journey. I blearily, blissfully stumbled into a cab and ordered the taxi to the nearest liquor store on the way to my hotel.

Returning from a long voyage at sea to the normal world can be extremely stressful. Everything is different, from the damnably solid earth that refuses to rock and roll, forcing you to not be catching your balance every second of every day, to the heights of the ceilings. The scale and proportion of things are all disparate, how people interact, the smells, the sounds, everything is profoundly different. Stepping into a house is like stepping into a phone booth, confining and stifling with the walls appearing far too close together. My heavy booted feet, thundering and shaking the trinkets on the shelves and seemingly rendering the wooden structure insubstantial after months of walking on unyielding steel. People everywhere who aren't violent dregs of society, standing too close, and chattering too much.

Working for months on end, with no days off, often in dangerous conditions, or little sleep, or fantastic port calls with *epic adventures* (72), can be physically and mentally draining, and can generate a lot of pent up tension. It can leave one fairly bunched up. When you couple that with the culture shock of re-entering a different world, in a different hemisphere, under a different sky, it can make for a challenging transition.

I had found that travelling straight home after a marathon like the one I was now ending, was more like just starting another Marathon as opposed to the well-earned finish line I was coveting. No matter what you tell your friends and family, they are happy to see you, and will not allow you to sleep for three days to recover. They won't understand that you NEED to get drunk and stay that way long enough for your ass to unclench. So I had learned the value of meandering home instead of B-lining. My meanderings grew longer and more involved as the years passed, but always my first port of entry into the US was a long layover on a beach, or near a pool, and copious amounts of blessed whiskey.

After many long years of planet wide wanderings, with no real ties to anyplace, returning to the land of my birth started to feel more like visiting, than coming home. I had no physical address, and was a perfectly rootless itinerant citizen of planet earth. That just added to the stress of going 'home', which felt less and less like home every time I visited. This had been my first trip back to sea after a brief hiatus. I had forgotten this feeling of detachment, and was thankful that a warm hotel bed and a fifth of Jack Daniels was in my immediate future to help defer having to think about that. The perfect recipe for much needed oblivion.

It only took a week of serious loafing on Venice beach, and gallon or so various fine blessed whiskeys to uncoil enough to consider myself 'relaxed'. The long trip home, didn't really lead home, it led to a lounge chair on Venice beach. I would eventually snap out of the stupor and meander again, I always managed to meander

69

again. This time back to Boston, but there on that beach, watching the impossibly gorgeous Californian girls wiggle past, I realized that my journeys were only just meanderings. That there was no longer a defined finish line, only rest stops, and visits to old haunts.

The end of this journey, like all the others, was really a beginning. A daunting beginning of a long journey to destinations unknown, and with no end in sight.

Part 2 – Old friends and sea stories

"They talk of the dignity of work. The dignity is in leisure."
Herman Melville

There I Was

The adventures live on in the Story

> *"There is no such joy in the tavern as upon the road thereto."* - Cormac McCarthy

The bar was open to the water, and a cool ocean breeze kept the tropical heat at bay. It was a large primitive *pavilion* (73) type structure, big enough to accommodate a crowd. Its thatched grass roof seemed out of place above the beautiful bamboo floor. String lights and lanterns were strategically located to keep the ambiance just right. Jimmy Buffet's "Songs You Know by Heart", and Bob Marley's Greatest Hits were perpetually playing in the background. What few walls it had were adorned with life rings (74) and other maritime tokens from the ships of the patrons who frequented the place.

Soda bottles filled with colored water and small lights were festooned across beams and walls. They appeared decorative but were actually homemade fly traps filled with dyed sugar water, a clever modification would allow the flies in, lured by the light and sugar water, but made it difficult to escape, leaving them to drown in the syrup of their own base urges. They were a perfect metaphor for this bar.

There were plenty of fans to keep the place breezy, and the smells of fried foods and Philipino delicacies roasting in the kitchen filled the air. The building opened up to the beach, which was adorned with Tiki torches and candles on the small tables between the lounge chairs. There was a long dock that led out to a floating houseboat bar filled with working girls and the men who loved them. A long string of 'Nipa' huts ran up the coast where the beach met the jungle, each about 100 feet apart. Some were in clusters, some all alone.

This bar was an old haunt of mine and as I walked in the Bartender, a gorgeous little Filipina named Lucy, welcomed me with a huge smile and a shout:

"One Blessed Whiskey, coming up!" She yelled.

"One for you too Lucy, you know I hate to drink alone."

"Thank you, thank you. You never have to drink alone here, you know that. I'll get Santo, he will be happy to see you"

"I am glad that I caught him here, good luck." Lucy frowned as she put the two glasses on the bar and started pouring the Jack Daniels.

THERE I WAS

"You no hear? Santo lost his foot, can't ship out no more, he always here... make everybody miserable... you want San Miguel, make Boilermaker?"

"No Boilermaker, you are just trying to make me drunk, I am a married man now Lucy. That is bad news about Santo, when did this happen?"

"Last year, some accident on ship, he didn't go to doctor, it got rotten and he had to have it removed halfway to his knee, and I am married too, you flatter yourself."

"Well if I don't, who will?" She laughed "So when did lovely Lucy from Luzon get married, and how many men leapt from bridges when they heard you were off the market?"

"Ha, thousands of them, the death toll was worse than a typhoon." She finished pouring and raised her glass.

"To Marriage." I offered

"I'll drink to that." We downed the brown nectar together, finishing in sync and putting the glasses down together.

"This one on me." She poured a second round and then waved over a bar back and spoke to him in rapid Tagalog; he responded more slowly, in a different dialect, and then walked away quickly.

"Santo will be right here, he will be glad to see you, no one here wants to hear his sea stories."

"That is just wrong, who in their right mind doesn't want to hear sea stories, it is like my dad was always asking me 'what the fuck is wrong with you?'". She got serious for a moment,

"Lots of lonely wives here, husbands at sea for years, or fishermen widows. Lots of the staff here, this the best they can hope for, this village, cleaning toilets or raking the beach. No hope to see faraway places, they don't want to know about the world that they can't see. They just want to find a home that won't blow away every year when the Typhoons come." I nodded my head. Santo didn't have much in common with his own people anymore. I knew that feeling well. I had been there, hell that same problem had led me to this very bar just a few years prior, and I had damn near decided to never go home and settle right here on this beach with this bartender. She raised her glass

"To old friends, and new beginnings"

"AMEN!" I replied, knocking back the shot

"Amen? No praying in my bar, you drive away my godless customers."

"SANTO!" I leapt up and embraced my old friend. Santo and I had met over 25 years before, when we served in the US Navy together.

"Careful, I got a cheap wooden foot, not so easy to stand up when you squeeze me like a big drunken bear"

"Drink?" I offered. He bowed slightly

73

THERE I WAS

"Many thanks!" Lucy poured us a round and I held up my glass.

"To wives and lovers"

"May they never meet!" came the traditional response. Many drinks followed. We retired out to the beach to watch the stars fill the sky and the ships roll across the horizon. The sound of the waves hitting the beach, mixed with the laughter and music from the bar, along with smell of Mother Ocean, the flickering light of the Tiki Torches, and the taste of the blessed whiskey blended into the perfect setting for sea stories.

Lucy brought a bucket of ice, and bottle of Jack Daniels, and would visit us from time to time to see if we needed anything. Santo loved to tell stories, and he loved to hear them.

THE FOUNTAIN

Adventures in Naval Plumbing

> *"The art of the sailor is to leave nothing to chance." – Annie Van De Wiele*

This particular class of Navy ship, had special fittings on the drain pipes to allow for the use of a fire hose to unclog drains. That is to say, a plumber, who on a Navy ship in those days was known as a Hull Technician or HT, could screw a hose to a toilet drain, align the various valves to ensure that the enormous pressures delivered by the fire pumps were aimed directly at the clog and towards the overboard discharge, and charge the drain pipes to fire hose pressures... what could possibly go wrong.

This particular young HT, on that fine Navy day, was making the necessary preparations. His name was Marvin, and he was a big, lanky, happy, southern boy who was perpetually smiling and joking around. I noticed the fire hose connected to a toilet and was understandably curious. He greeted me with an enormous grin and seemed overjoyed to explain the concept to me. He outlined, in his thick easy drawl, the important and careful business of lining up the valves correctly to ensure that the clog was blasted safely into the ocean and not toward some terrible unintended consequence.

Marvin the HT, had been recently promoted to Petty Officer, and was sporting a fresh new single 'Chevron' on his arm. So recent in fact, that he had not even yet been paid at the higher rate, and was only allowed to wear the insignia in a special "frocked" status, while the volumes of naval promotion paperwork churned through the system.

He was admittedly nervous, and took great care tracing the complicated maze of pipes to locate and align all the valves correctly. Plumbing systems on ships are often a complex web of pipe, valves and fittings branching off in bizarre twists and turns as they snake through the ship to form their complicated network.

I was curious, living on a ship is like living inside a giant machine, and one is constantly surrounded by complex mechanical systems. Manipulating a system to blast a clog through an overboard discharge with a fire hose seemed to me to be both interesting and potentially entertaining.

The fateful moment arrived, Marvin made his final checks and slowly opened the hydrant valve, his hand hesitating slightly above the wheel before grabbing it and carefully twisting it to the left. We watched the hose twitch and thicken as the

THERE I WAS

pressure mounted. The fire pumps on this ship developed 125 pounds per square inch of pressure, while delivering 95 Gallons per minute of sea water at fantastic velocities. Marvin brought the valve fully open and started his walk along the affected area to ensure all was going well. The primal scream from the next deck up was our first indication that something had gone horribly wrong.

"MAAAARRRRRRVIIIINNNN!" thundered the enraged voice from above. Marvin's eyes widened and he went deathly pale as he recognized the voice. He scrambled back towards the hydrant to secure the water, but the damage was done. A valve, a single valve, hidden in a hard to access storage space, had been neglected and left open. This valve connected the clogged drain line to a toilet in the officers' quarters. I looked at Marvin and said:

"It is like my dad always used to tell me: 'You are up shits creek now' though he never meant it quite so literally."

This particular ship, had 17 officers, three of whom were members of the Engine department; The Chief Engineer, the Damage Control Assistant, who was Marvin's division officer, and the Main Propulsion Assistant. Naval Officers come in various different flavors, from the regal graduates of the Naval Academy at Annapolis, to the ROTC and OCS officers trained in civilian academic institutions, all the way to the proud Mustangs. A Mustang is an officer who has risen up from the enlisted ranks to obtain a commission or warrant and gain that vaunted and privileged seat in the officer's mess (wardroom).

There are several paths from the enlisted ranks to the wardroom, and one path is that of Warrant Officer. The Navy's warrant officer program provided an opportunity for senior enlisted people to continue to advance, and garner promotions through the later years of their career. They serve in specialized roles within their field, particularly the highly technical roles such as engineering. They are typically old timers approaching their retirement, and placed into leadership roles. Grizzled old salts, tough and leathery, who climbed to the very top of their ladder and then leapt to the next ladder.

The Main Propulsion Assistant himself was one of these very warrant officers, stern and ornery, referred to affectionately by his sailors as "Iron jaw" (75), though never to his face. Iron jaw, at the precise moment that the pressure from the fire hose dislodged the clog, was attending to his physical needs on that fateful toilet connected to the neglected valve. As he sat there reading his newspaper, a fountain of sewage erupted up from that toilet, between his legs, and up the back of his shirt with the full force of a naval fire hose propelling it.

He came running down the passage, still half naked, covered from head to toe in raw sewage, fire shooting from his eyes, and screaming his battle cry "Maaaarrrrrvvvvviiiinnn!!!!!"

THERE I WAS

Earlier that morning, Iron jaw and Marvin would have been mustered together while the daily work assignments were handed out. Marvin standing in ranks with the other mechanics, Iron jaw stern-faced, clenching his teeth, facing the crew in front near the Chief Engineer, and the tiny childlike Damage Control Assistant just days from his Annapolis graduation, anxiously awaiting the day his hormones would burst to life, and finally bestow his destined 'big boy voice'.

Marvin endured the full fury of Iron jaws' wrath, there in that hallway, near that cursed hydrant. Marvin, who was extremely tall, seemed to shrink before the glowering fury of Iron jaw, bug eyed with rage, and with shit splattered so profoundly up the back of his neck that it had built up beneath his ears like grotesque earrings. One couldn't help but imagine the force of that sewage, lifting him from the seat and spraying out in every direction like a sprinkler head.

Marvin spent the next several weeks scouring the ceilings above that doomed toilet, painstakingly removing the star shaped stain that results when sewage is propelled with the force of a jet engine at a flat surface. Days after day, restoring that bathroom to a state of pristine naval shininess under the harsh menacing gaze of Iron jaws yellowed soulless eyes.

He was written up for dereliction of duty, ironically, and lost his newly won stripe, along with his big dopey smile, and spent the rest of his days on that ship, swab in hand, atoning for his sins, and pondering his fate.

The Lucky Seven Seaman's Club

Eastern Cultural extremes

"Truth is in things, and not in words." Herman Melville

We motored into the Port of Keelung, Taiwan, thirteen decks of rolling cargo on a tramp car carrier, and seventeen sea weary seafarers. The ship was chartered to run from Japan to Europe with a cargo of Nissans, but would take whatever cargo it could get on the meandering trip back to Japan. So we loaded Volvos and Saabs in Sweden, BMWs and Volkswagens in Germany, Minis and farm equipment in Ireland, and headed off to Asia.

We had run through the placid sub-tropical Pacific, on a trip long enough that the Dolphins that accompanied us became our friends, with names and imagined back stories. Dolphins love ships, and will converge from every point of the compass to frolic in our bow wake. They love to lead the ship by just a few inches, and small groups will race ahead of the ship, in the standing bow wave 'surfing' just below the surface. Two or three of them will dance about in a complicated seemingly joyful ballet, flitting right and left before peeling off rapidly to one side or the other and erupting gleefully from the water as if they believe that they can fly.

It is quite a show, and one of the pure joys only experienced on a ship at sea. But as entertaining as the wildlife was, we were more than ready for a different type of 'Wild life' entertainment.

It was my first trip to the Far East, and as well travelled as I was already, no one is ever quite prepared for Asia. Everything that humanity has to offer is there, and has been there since history began. From the finest art, architecture, and most finely civilized practices, to the most base and despicable banality imaginable, packed together in the close confines of the most densely packed cities on earth.

It was our second port in the Far East, after Singapore. Singapore is a magnificent city, and has come to be one of my favorite places on earth, but Singapore is at its core... civilized. Singapore is a paragon of law and order, and is nearly a police state, but in an inherently civilized way. It is extraordinarily clean and well-ordered with the historical patina of the British rule of order, polished and rehabbed with a modern and purely Asian slant on the pursuit of perfection.

Keelung, on the other hand, is a bustling port city in the heart of the South China Sea, traditionally Chinese but outside the Communist Regime. Dense, modern, Asian, urban, with towering high-rises, high speed rail, and filled with bright lights and

THERE I WAS

neon; all nestled atop and alongside the rattan and bamboo vestiges of ancient traditions that have endured in place for thousands of years. Ball park crowds on every street. The magnificent contrast of sharply dressed businessmen in Silk Suits and $1000 shoes buying deep fried chicken feet off a wooden goat cart from a pajama clad vendor in a *coolie hat* (76). People, animals, cars, buildings, the future, the past, the amazing immense present all slammed together and stuffed into a package far too small to contain it all.

The port itself was insanely crowded and busy. Ships nested three deep at the dock, more ships coming and going constantly. Fork trucks, flatbeds, and yard tractors zipping back and forth along the waterfront among the multitude of scurrying rats and seabirds. Giant nonchalant Norwegians striding about alongside small fierce looking locals, enroute together no doubt, toward some act of piracy. Activity and clamor prevailed against a backdrop of pure contrast and exquisite complexity.

One crew member had been to Keelung before. He had mentioned briefly that he had visited a small dive bar where he met an interesting 'waitress' who had no tongue. I am sure it was not coincidence but rather an act of profoundly simple yet enviously effective marketing that we found that very same club. A local man on a bicycle pedaled up to the gangway shortly after we pulled in, with a handful of free drink coupons from a local establishment called "The Lucky Seven Seaman's Club". The coupons were printed conveniently with a simple map that directed one from the gate of the cargo terminal to the club, noting some key places of interest along the way. He assured me that this fine establishment did indeed serve Blessed Whiskey. No further decisions required, our way and our opening round were mapped out for us.

A small dangerous van was arranged to ferry us from the WWII era cargo docks to the metropolitan jungle beyond. The smiling polite driver engaged us with proud tales of his beloved city and homeland, joking with us in broken English. He taught us how to order a beer, and say 'don't shoot', and even wrote down the name of the port and dock number in the local symbology, so that we might find our way home. He dropped us off in the heart of the downtown area, just a dozen or so blocks from our destination. We thanked him profusely, tipped him handsomely, and took his card promising to call him for the return trip.

He left us there on a busy street corner, beneath the towering high-rises, as the setting sun painted the sky orange. Cars whipped by at highway speeds, just inches away, as if the curb provided some legitimate barrier between throngs of humanity and full on expressway traffic. The bright signs began to stand out in the failing light, blocking out the sky, and chasing away the darkness. We stood on a main thoroughfare, flanked by modern glass buildings and wide sidewalks teeming with hordes of business workers headed home, and the early nightlife just arriving. Cross streets were smaller, narrow and dark, and lined with an endless stationary parade of food carts. Thousands of food vendors, shoulder to shoulder for miles on end, selling every form of exquisitely prepared, marginally edible substance available to humanity.

Roasted animal body parts on a stick, steamed rice, baskets of giant fried bird feet, fish heads, fried rice, octopi, eels, dead animals hanging upside down, noodles, rice, insects, stir fry, deep fry, rice, and of course rice. We strolled down the endless culinary carnival, sampling the exotic fare, drinking in the sights and sounds and pungent aromas. The air was an odiferous vaporous fog of new and interesting smells that ranged from delicious to disgusting. The savory smell of some animal roasting or frying, coupled with the putrid, pungent lingering stench of the horrific remains of those same animal's recent slaughter in close proximity. The aromatic circle of culinary life.

The streets became narrower, darker and lonelier as we moved along. The vibrant cacophony of the crowd giving way to echoing footsteps down long alleys. Numerous small signs provided the dimly lighted ambiance to this urban underbelly, and one could almost sense that crime was happening in every shadow. A big red number seven against a brightly lighted yellow background marked our destination. The "Lucky Seven Seaman's Club".

Without prior knowledge, one never knows what one will find at a "seaman's club". The proud title having been bestowed on every type of establishment from Church Mission, to whorehouse. You can look forward to some type of delight, be it a home cooked meal, fine liquor reasonably priced, hotel amenities, or feminine companionship, also reasonably priced.

Through the entrance, past the curtain of hanging strings of beads into the long narrow room, with a bar counter to our right and booths to our left. The line of booths was broken by an archway leading to another room. A curtain of beads separated the rooms. As we walked past the archway, a dozen or so girls dressed in short sexy cocktail dresses, could be seen sitting on couches peering back at us and smiling coquettishly as we walked by. It was that type of Seaman's club; I was quite certain there was no chapel in this building.

The host greeted us with a giant toothy smile and seated us all in a large booth towards the back. He assured us that a waitress would be along, and indeed she did arrive shortly thereafter, small pad and pencil in hand. She wrote us a note asking us what we would like to drink, taking our orders silently but for an occasional "mmmm" or "hmmmhmm". We asked her name and she wrote it down for us. We, of course, asked her why she was writing instead of speaking and she wrote that she had no tongue. We concluded that it must be the very same tongue-less waitress that our shipmate had encountered in his previous visit.

The drinks arrived quickly, delivered by four beautiful young 'waitresses' and the host who asked if we would like some company while we drank. The host introduced them by name, and seated them at the table with us. The young ladies sat quietly, demurely, each with a small pad and pencil in hand, and here is where the story takes a disturbing turn. We asked each of these young ladies their names and each of them took pencil in hand and began writing. We all sat quietly, looking quizzically at one another, the oddness of the situation dawning on each of us slowly. When finally one of us asked the question we are all thinking.

"Why do you all write instead of speak?" One of them began writing, and some of the others engaged one another with some odd gestures and strange mumbling that sounding nothing like Chinese, or any other language any of this well-travelled crew had ever heard. "mmbbfffmmmfffmmm..bbbb..ff"

The note of explanation was presented... none of us have tongues....I said it aloud, aghast "None of you have tongues?" Vigorous nodding, a chorus of "mmmmbbbfffmmmbb...aaaa...bbbhhmmm".

For me, suddenly the bar became sinister. As sinister a place as ever I had been, and I had been to some of the nastiest waterfronts on earth, I had been to war, hell I had even been to New Jersey. What possible explanation for this would not be horrible? Did they arrive here and have their tongues removed? Or was tongue removal some local custom or punishment and this one of the places where tongue-less people were consigned. Were they slaves? Unfortunates? Was it some malady contracted from eating the deep fried scorpions from the unsanitary food carts?

Did I even want to know? Had I just crossed some boundary into a dark corner of the underworld? Was this some Keelung version of the hotel California? Would I ever be able to leave? Would I ever be able to reconcile the fact that in this world there existed a whorehouse filled with tongue-less whores? What had these poor girls done to deserve this fate? Had they chosen it? Had it been forced upon them, or was it all less sensational that I was making out to be? Was this more normal here in Asia where food carts would slaughter, butcher and prepare a live animal of your choosing for your culinary pleasure, right there on the street? Were tongue-less whorehouses as common in Asia as Crack houses were in NYC?

Some of my shipmates seemed less disturbed than I, in fact... intrigued was a more accurate description. Perhaps the thought of a silent woman was a dream come true. Perhaps the vast East/West differences already apparent in our Voyage, jaded them to the disturbing nature of it all. Perhaps the deep-fried chicken feet and

THERE I WAS

Octopus I had sampled earlier had rendered me over-sensitive. Either way, I felt an irresistible urge to get the fuck out of there as fast as I could.

In the back of my mind I heard my father's familiar refrain: "Get out!"

Already I had seen too much. Already I knew that my nightmares would be haunted with the sound of "mmmmmffffbbbb...mmm...bb...bb...hmmm" for the rest of my life.

No one cared to join me, so I was forced to venture into that dark alley alone. What was quaintly criminal before, was now downright malevolent. The evening had darkened, and the shadows seemed to be watching me. Off in the distance I heard a loud slap, and then a cry "Straits of Malacca!" whack "Straits of Malacca" whack. I stood there a moment in the alley, beneath the Lucky Seven sign, and a profound calm washed over me. If this alley was filled with the world's most sordid collection of muggers, thieves, murderers or bankers, I was prepared to meet them and die fighting them.

I had imagined, and even come close to, experiencing that death, and it was something I understood. It was a death worthy of a Merchant Marine, and to die fighting was an honorable end. A far better epitaph than "Blind and Crazy from the Black Syphilis of the Keelung Tongue-less Whore", or to die anonymously in some tongue-less salt mine or chained to a sewing machine in some tongue-less sweatshop. Lured into a world of tongue-less slavery through the portal of the tongue-less whorehouse. It occurred to me then that even with tongues and without chains most whores must be slaves to some extent, and it both saddened and angered me.

The anger steeled my resolve. I strode back down the alley as if I owned it, prepared to meet my fate, putting distance between me and that strange sordid den of iniquity. I made my way towards the light, and steered clear of the dark alleys, and away from whorehouses, tongue less or otherwise forever, and somehow found my way back to ship. The shipmates who stayed, survived and returned with their tongues intact, yet they never spoke of the place again, and I never asked, what happens in tongue-less whorehouses, stays in tongue less whorehouses.

Ode to a Grecian Hair Cut

It really is a small world after all

"A sailor's joys are as simple as a child's." - Bernard Moitessier

She was a Pure Car and Truck Carrier that ran back and forth from Asia to Europe. The holds were filled to the brim with Nissans enroute for dozens of European ports from the Mediterranean all the way to the Baltic. Car carriers have huge ramps that are lowered from the ship to the dock, and the cargo is driven on and off. It is a specialized version of the, roll-on/roll-off type of cargo ship, affectionately known as RO/RO's.

We had loaded Nissans in Yokohama, and had run all the way from Japan, through the straits of Malacca and Indian Ocean, up the *Red Sea* (77), and we had just emerged from the Suez Canal into the Med. It had been a long run, two to three weeks at least, and before that we had made the same run from Europe to Japan.

I had spent an entire day in Yokohama trying to find a place to get a haircut, and also to buy a pair of shoes, but had not succeeded in *my mission* (78). I went into dozens of shoe stores, and those few that got past their cultural prejudice against foreigners enough to acknowledge my presence in the store, never had a shoe at or above a size nine and a half. I did find a barber shop or two, but again, generally they just completely ignored me. I was getting pretty shaggy at this point, and the words of my father kept echoing in the back of my mind: "Get a fucking haircut you hippie punk."

Often times there will be some person on the ship who cuts hair, but I never did feel comfortable having some cook or deck seaman act as my part time barber. I could always tell who on board was getting a 'home' haircut, and I never saw what I felt looked like a professional haircut. So I would either allow my hair to grow out and don the traditional Mariner's 'pigtail', or just shave myself bald if the ship was dedicated to a tropical trade route.

I knew that our next port of call would be to Volos Greece. Car carriers unload quickly, especially partial unloads, so port visits were brief. We would only get to spend a few hours in Greece, just enough time for a haircut and maybe a nice meal of Souvlaki and stuffed grape leaves, and of course a fine local vintage.

Back home, I had been getting my hair cut by the same gentleman since age ten. My barber was a kindly old Greek man whose name was, for the sake of this story, Dmitri. I looked forward to going home and telling him of my Grecian hair cutting adventure, as I am particularly fond of Greek haircuts. I am sure Dmitri would expound on how all things are a little better when they are Greek. Dmitri loved to wax poetic about Greece and all things Greek. Being a connoisseur, Mediterranean and a fellow storyteller, he would occasionally share some homemade Greek delights with me, Baklava, homemade wine, or olive oil from a family estate back in the motherland. Walking into his Barbershop was like coming home, comforting in that it was always the same. It was always a small cast of a few regulars, mostly retirees, sitting about reading the paper and discussing the Red Sox, or the Bruins. Short round Dmitri, ironically bald, cutting hair and telling stories in his soothing soft voice, with his dignified Greek accent. I was sure that he would love to hear of my visit to his *beloved homeland* (79).

Volos is perhaps the most perfectly *sheltered harbor* (80) on earth. A *magnificent bay* (81) protected by an arm of tall hills that protrude into the Aegean Sea and hook around to shelter a *grand harbor* (82), leaving only *a* small opening for the ships to pass through, it was like something from a Tolkien novel. I would have six hours ashore, and my first order of business was to find a barber shop and get myself groomed back into a human-like state. It didn't take long to find one close to the waterfront that likely specialized in catering to the shaggy Mariners that wandered in from afar.

After a fine haircut with yet another friendly Greek barber and small waiting room of old timers whose seafaring days were behind them, but still enjoyed telling sea stories on the waterfront, then *a wonderful dinner* (83) of authentic Greek food and wine I headed back to the ship. After bouncing off every port between Volos and Gdansk through at least a dozen different countries, watching the longshoremen become paler and paler, I finally boarded the Lufthansa flight home. By then I was ready for another haircut and was looking forward to sharing stories of my old friend's homeland.

When I told Dmitri that I been to Volos, I was surprised to find out that he had not only been born and raised in Volos, but had learned to cut hair there. He asked me where exactly I had gotten my hair cut. I told him, and in what is perhaps the most amazing incidence of 'it's a small world' in my long experience of 'it's a small world', I had gotten my haircut at the very shop where Dmitri had learned the trade.

I was skeptical of course, Barber shop stories being very similar to sea stories in the liberties taken with the truth, but Dmitri indeed had an old faded black and white photo of the storefront with a younger version himself standing in front, though with a full head of neatly trimmed hair. The Sea God's work in strange ways, using human hair to weave the intricate fabric of nautical tapestry across oceans and continents, to connect two small barber shops from two proud maritime cities.

Panama Canal

How Air Conditioning Ruined the Merchant Marine

"What's in a life without Camaraderie? For setting sail on a ship with a band of merry brothers by your side is much more gratifying than drifting aimlessly on a boat lost alone at sea." - Siam A. Cheeda

We were heaving anchor near the eastern approaches to the Panama Canal just before sunrise. I was the ship's Bosun, and the Chief Mate and I were alone on the bow, in the dim tropical twilight, preparing for the day's transit. The steady, metronomic, industrial scale clanking of the mighty anchor chain as it passed along *the wildcat* (84) gear and down into the chain locker below us echoed across the perfectly still glassy waters of the anchorage. Occasionally, the thundering deck-shaking cacophony of the massive pile of chain settling beneath us, interrupted the steady mechanical beat of the windlass heaving on the anchor.

The Chief Mate was operating the winch as I directed a fire hose at the anchor chain while it travelled up the hawse pipe, to wash the mud and bottom muck off the chain. I raised my fist up to the Mate to signal him to stop, and shut down the hose for a moment. The chain had fouled on some rope. We had picked up some 1" diameter nylon rope off the bottom. I started pulling the rope off the chain, picked up the hose nozzle again, and pointed one finger in the air over my head and moved around in a circle to signal the Mate to 'heave away' again. We went off and on this way for next half hour or so as we methodically retrieved the anchor and rope, all while hosing down the chain and anchor.

Soon the tone of the clanking changed slightly, as the tension on the chain increased, and the lead of the chain went to near vertical as it came out of the hawse. I shouted back to the Mate,

"Anchors Aweigh!" He relayed the info to the Bridge via walkie-talkie. The Captain acknowledged, and the Mate on watch made the log entry that we were now underway, and that all the rules had changed. I felt that surge of joy knowing that we were now underway, and a new voyage was beginning. The Pacific was beckoning. We continued heaving until the anchor was housed and clean. The Mate went about tending to the anchor gear, making the anchor ready to drop on short notice in case it was needed during the transit. I started untangling and coiling the

THERE I WAS

several hundred feet of rope that was piled up on the bow in a giant *rat's nest* (85). The Chief Mate, or "The Mate", whose name was Bill, finished his task and came over to me.

"Find yourself a nice Christmas present, didjya Bosun?"

"It looks pretty new, it's in good shape, but I don't really have much use or room for it. I'll just coil it up here until I figure out what to do with it." The Mate nodded,

"When you finish with that, meet me back by the Pilot ladder on the Port Side."

"Aye Mate" I spent the next 20 minutes laying the rope into a neat working coil about six feet across and four feet tall. We steamed slowly through the anchorage and up the river towards the first set of locks. The river was wide, but the size of the ship made it seem narrow. The still water and jungle overgrown banks in the early morning light, with a wisps of fog clinging to the water seemed like something out of Apocalypse now, and I could almost hear Martin Sheen's voice narrating the voyage and describing the insane Colonel that awaited us upriver.

I drained and stowed the fire hose, and double checked the anchor gear to see how the Mate had left it, so that I would be prepared to drop it quickly in a panic if something went wrong. By the time I got back to the Pilot ladder the pilot boat was already approaching. We would be taking on a Pilot and half dozen or so line handlers. The Panama Canal is one of the few places on earth where the Pilot has more authority than the Captain. The Captain cannot veto or counter the directions of the Pilot, and the Pilot takes the responsibility from the Captain in the event of a mishap.

The Pilot boat made its careful approach, maneuvering perfectly alongside the ship, to the rope ladder draped down the side of the hull. As the Pilot came up through the break in the rails, stepping onto the ship, he saw the Mate and broke into a huge grin.

"Billy Boy!"

"Benito!" They launched into a hearty embrace, back patting and laughing. The Canal Authority begins the Pilots' training by sending them each to one of the various US Maritime Academies. Bill and Benito were old classmates from Maine Maritime Academy. Bill handed Benito a fresh new Red Sox hat, which he immediately donned. Benito was similarly prepared with a hat bearing star shaped logo and 'ACP' monogram of the Panama Canal Authority. They wandered off towards the Bridge laughing, leaving me to board the line handlers.

I gathered up the line handlers, and brought them to the bow. The Canal Authority required that only ACP personnel be used for rigging and line handling while in the locks and canal. They would spend the entire day on the bow under the tropical sun, mostly sleeping, until the moment when they all burst to life in a frenzy of activity as we passed through the locks at either end of the canal. The Mate

THERE I WAS

and I would sit up there with them, ready to drop the anchor in event of an emergency, and to assist the line handlers as necessary. It would be a long, mostly uneventful day.

The first set of locks, the 'Gatun' locks, came up quickly. The locks had been built by the US Army Corps of Engineers at the turn of the 20th Century during Teddy Roosevelt's administration. The Gatun facility was composed of three pairs of locks, each one a chamber large enough for a ship to steam into, with massive steel doors that swung open to allow the ship to steam in or out. The locks stepped down from Gatun Lake, raising or lowering the ships to or from sea level. The lake water would drain into the stepped locks, filling it and raising the ship in the lock below, or lowering the ship in the draining lock to the next level, where the gates would swing open again, allowing the ship to proceed to the next level.

It was truly amazing under any circumstance, to climb a hill nine stories tall, in a 100,000 ton, 900 foot long ship, but given that the canal had been built nearly 100 years before, it was mind boggling. The gates had that sturdy riveted look of industrial revolution era steel work. There were no pumps to move the billions of gallons of water that flowed through the locks each day, just gravity, and the rumor was that the doors were so well balanced on their hinges that the motor that opened and closed them was tiny, and had replaced a single horse.

There were rail tracks along either side of the locks, upon which travelled the small locomotive "mules" that tugged the ships through the locks. The 'mules' were constantly tooting whistle signals to the line handlers, who scurried around the deck, tying off the lines, or heaving messengers to get the lines from ship to shore and vice versa. Transiting the locks is an experience you never forget. I stood by to operate the winch for the line handlers if they needed it, as Bill silently watched and communicated with the Bridge via handheld radio. As we passed through the final lock into Gatun Lake, the line handlers all settled in. They would not be needed again for another six hours or so at the Pedro Miguel locks on the Pacific side.

I looked over at the tall coil of line, that I had recovered with the anchor that morning, and wondered what to do with it. I walked over to the line handler in charge, and asked him if he and his crew had any use for the line. His eyes widened as he nodded vigorously, and announced the windfall to his compadres in rapid Spanish. The entire crew converged on the pile of line like a pack of wolves on a fresh kill, knives out, hacking at the line, fragments and tufts of nylon flying like confetti as they divvied up the rope.

The thick line, like most rope, was composed of smaller threads. The threads on this rope were of Para cord sized twisted nylon twine, and soon they began disassembling the rope and re-working it, as only a gang of seaman could, it into nets, bags, belts, handles and straps for their bags. It was impressive to watch. Soon

87

THERE I WAS

the entire coil was gone, transformed into a few neat piles of finished goods, and a few fragments of stray fiber too small to be utilized into something useful. Bill and I watched and commented on the impressive 'marlinspike' seamanship being displayed before us.

The crew cleaned up what little mess was left and then came up to Bill and I en-masse to present us each with a large magnificently crafted hammock, woven from the threads of the line in a fishnet that tapered down to a beautifully tied sling knot at either end. We thanked them profusely, everyone seeming to have benefited well from the transaction. We all then settled down for the long run through the lake. The line handlers tucked themselves into every available, tiny patch of shade on the bow, slinging hammocks, or rolling out bedrolls from their kits. One of them even managed to produce a guitar and started picking a lilting Panamanian ballad, adding a perfectly appropriate musical score to the scene.

I elected to utilize my new hammock to embrace the local custom of 'afternoon siesta'. I found a spot in the shade and slung the hammock up neatly, and climbed in. It was remarkably comfortable.

"You gotta try this out Bill, it is amazing"

"You don't have to tell me, I spent many a night sleeping on deck in a hammock before Air Conditioning ruined the Merchant Marine"

"Air conditioning ruined the Merchant Marine?"

"It did, look around, does it get any better than this? Everyone hanging out together, enjoying each other's company, making music, they'll be singing and stories before long. This is what every night was like in the tropics before AC. People came out and hung out on deck, socializing and experiencing life at sea, instead of hiding in their rooms watching TV."

Bill was a crusty old salt and was speaking from experience. He had started in the Navy during WWII, and then enrolled in Maine Maritime Academy to obtain his license following the war. There were six academies overall, Massachusetts, Maine, SUNY Fort Skyler, California, Texas A&M, and the Federal Merchant Marine Academy at Kings Point in NYC. They were all good schools, and each had their reputation, but I always admired Maine for living up to their reputation. People who wanted to work in the Maritime industry went to Maine. They weren't just passing through on their way to a legal career, or at a power plant somewhere, they went to sea, and spent their lives working on ships. Bill was the perfect exemplar of that.

He sat there, staring ahead down the channel watching for traffic. His bald head tanned deep brown from a life on deck in the sun. What few wisps of hair that remained were bleached stark white by the sun. His big bullet of a head sat squarely on his shoulders without the benefit of a neck. His face was creased and lined with deep crow's feet at the corners of his eyes from long years of squinting at the horizon. He loved to share the wealth of his experience, and listening to him discuss how AC had fundamentally changed society on ships, was like listening to history incarnate describe the past.

I pulled my hat down over my eyes as I settled into my hammock.

"Bill... tell me a story." I said in my best mockery of a child's voice. Bill grinned.

"Oh you want a story eh, I got lots of stories." Bill was a gifted storyteller, and this was the perfect time and place for a story. The line handlers seemed to notice that the afternoon's entertainment was beginning, and perked up.

"This story is about a 'Phantom'. Boredom can be a powerful inspiration. As you know, Mariners are no strangers to boredom, but it can go awry, and this is a story of how far from the reservation that boredom can drive a man." Bill paused for effect, before beginning his story.

"His *final masterpiece* (86) was a *grand tribute* (87) to the Captain. We had been steaming in the North Atlantic with the Allied fleet in foul weather for weeks on end, and his legend had grown with each passing day."

"He started small and unobtrusively, and was more of a distracting curiosity at first, but each successive performance increased in its boldness and audacity. Before long, everyone had an opinion, and he was the primary source of entertainment and conversation on the ship." Bill spoke slowly, savoring the words, and matching the pace of the story to align with the pace of a ship lazily crossing Gatun Lake on a tropical afternoon.

"Long sea voyages are filled with drab routine and boredom, and once captured, the attention of a ship's crew can become electrified and rapt in the blink of an eye." We all nodded, each one of us had experienced the effects of boredom on a long sea voyage.

"He had captured our attention, this man... this Phantom, he had our full and undivided attention. We constantly wondered where, when and how he would strike next." Bill paused again, and raised his binoculars to his eyes, scanning the channel ahead for traffic.

"His performances increased in both frequency and difficulty until his swan song there in the Captain's office. That was his final act and we never heard from him again. Maintaining his anonymity was his greatest talent and was the driving force of his fame. Each successive act defied all reason and logic. It was truly amazing that someone could perform thusly in such public places, on such a crowded vessel and remain anonymous." Bill picked up the pace slightly:

"Navy ships are small places filled to the brim with people. There are places that never sleep on Navy ships, places that are occupied with throngs of people around the clock, and yet he managed to execute his art publicly in these places, leaving

89

THERE I WAS

behind his magnificent sculptured handiwork, while escaping detection every time." Bill paused to communicate with the Bridge, leaving us hanging for a moment

"Bridge – Bow, we have Eastbound traffic fine on the port bow, just coming round the Frijole Turn. Tell Benito to try to avoid hitting them, if he needs some instruction in ship handling, I can come up there"

"I am sure he will do just fine" Came the Captain's terse reply. Bill grinned ever so slightly.

"Now where was I? Ah yes, the Phantoms swan song…" He leaned back smiling, his raspy voice softening as he told the story

"His *piece de resistance* (88) impressed even Mr. Stevens the Captain, as stoic a stone-faced commander as ever commanded a Navy Vessel. He called a few of his officers to his stateroom to view the handiwork gifted to him just moments before. He had been working at his desk and stepped into the head for a quick sprinkle, gone not more than a minute or two, and returned to find that monument of hubris and disrespect waiting for him on his desk. It sat there neatly coiled and perfectly presented, still steaming slightly."

"The Captain was the latest, and final, victim of the Phantom Shitter. When he struck at movie night, mid-feature, we were impressed. When he left his mark on the messdecks in broad daylight, we were amazed, but the Captain's gift, as turds were hereafter referred to, was downright awe-inspiring. In deference to both the Artist, and the recipient of his talent, we named the piece "The Steaming Stevie". There was a murmur of approval from the audience. Nothing like a good sea story to pass the time. If only we had some blessed bilge wine to share it would have been perfect.

Bill had been through the canal hundreds of times, and knew every inch of it. We passed through the town of Gamboa, and headed into the "Galliard Cut", this was the part of the canal that stopped the French dead in their tracks leaving them to abandon the project. The Galliard cut was a notch in the mountain deep and wide enough to drive a ship through.

When the French had started digging the canal in the late 1800's, their approach to the high mortality of workers due to disease and unsafe working conditions was to try and add workers faster than they died. Classic colonial European arrogance. This, of course, made new workers harder and harder to come by. This when coupled with the acceleration of disease mortality, led to the project to grind to a halt.

Enter Teddy Roosevelt. Teddy took over, and assigned the project to the US Army Corps of Engineers who immediately incorporated sanitation to the workers camps, stemming the Cholera outbreak. American technological know-how was added to the mix with the addition of state of the art steam powered excavating equipment, and the installation of rail systems to remove the spoils, and the outcome was this wonder of modern engineering that we were all navigating at that moment. The walls of the cut rose almost vertically a dozen stories or so above us. Just sheer cliff carved out of the stone hills by Ohio and New York Steam shovels, and the sweat of the Panamanian and immigrant workers.

By the time we got to the Pedro Miguel locks, the sun was getting low. Between the sun, the stories, and the soothing guitar music, we were all baked into a state of dull tropical submission. The passage through the Pedro Miguel locks was enough to wake us all back up. Once through the locks, the line handlers gathered all their gear, and climbed back down the ladder to the awaiting pilot boat, waving goodbye as we steamed off beneath the Bridge of the Americas, into the setting sun.

Djibouti Africa

Continental weight differences

"The march of conquest through wild provinces, may be the march of Mind; but not the march of Love." Herman Melville

We were headed to Djibouti Africa, just south of Ethiopia in the Gulf of Aden. It's pronounced *Ja-Booty* (89), which is obviously fun to say, and on a ship full of dumb-ass Navy sailors, led to an inordinate amount of Booty jokes. Djibouti is as third world as it gets, and we got an immediate taste for just how different this place was compared to the rest of our experience only moments after pulling in to the tiny primitive port.

We had just finished tying up, and were gathering at the gangway in preparation for our last port visit prior to the alcohol free Persian Gulf. A tall slender local man, dark as night and thin as a rail, was walking down the pier wearing a long linen robe. He stopped abruptly, hiked up his skirt, and squatted then and there, dropping a deuce as tight as a rabbits' right there on the dock, then stood and walked off like nothing had happened. Welcome to Djibouti.

There was a meandering dirt road that connected the Port to the town. It was *a long rutted road across a dusty brown landscape* (90) littered with *scrub* (91) to either side. It was along this road that we learned that Djiboutian goats apparently don't like Americans. They attacked us on sight, which stopped being amusing just as soon as their iron hard heads started making contact. Knowing that these goats might represent the entire wealth of some poor local farmer, we chose not to take a stand and fight, but elected rather to evacuate the area with extreme prejudice.

This visit took place in the early 80's during the peak of the Ethiopian famine. There was then, as there likely still is, a French foreign legion outpost there, and a small downtown area. There were a few dozen of us, randomly walking together towards town. We would soon break up into our own individual little cliques but as we all were heading the same way at the same time, we travelled together. There is safety in numbers, and we had already determined that there were killer goats here.

There was among us an African American body builder named Arthur. Now, anytime you gather up a few dozen fleet sailors, especially during a deployment, there will be some serious weightlifters in the crowd, and indeed there were on this outing, but just the one African American. As we strode into town, we were again assaulted, but this time by a crowd of giggling children. We had been warned, and we were armed with tons of hard candy and small change.

THERE I WAS

They begged and laughed and offered us tours and taxi's and invited us to join them in their games. Then they saw Arthur, and their joy turned to complete amazement. The rest of us ceased to exist in the world, as they crowded around him, grabbing his biceps, and pawing at him. Perhaps they have never seen such a physique on a black man, they were far less impressed with the white body builders who also accompanied us. We took the opportunity to escape, leaving Arthur and his compatriots, for the time being, well cared for by an adoring crowd of happy children.

Whether the entire city was a dirty, open sewered barrio, or our sailor's instinct just automatically led us to those parts of town I will never know, but there we were, wandering about the dark alleys and streets of the Port of Delorah, Djibouti, Africa in search of adventure. There were bars aplenty, but they were noticeably lacking in refrigeration, so we had to choose between warm beer, and rotgut hard liquor that tasted as if it had been distilled in a dirty bathtub, a whiskey far less blessed.

Most of the Africans we encountered were much smaller than us, lean wiry and lacking meat. We overfed Americans were thicker and heavier, and being young military, we were muscular and healthy looking. The local working girls found this exciting, and as we walked into the bars, the larger members of our group would look up to see a laughing African girl run across the bar and launch herself into our arms, perfectly confident that we would catch them. It happened in every bar we entered, in some kind of strange African Hooker tradition.

The girls were genuinely disappointed in sales that night, given the emergence of that new dreaded disease AIDS, and how prevalent it was in Africa that time. That and the feeling of danger from the sulking locals and dangerous looking French Legionnaires made a person reluctant to take ones pants' off, or wander off into the dark backroom alone with a stranger.

The Legionnaires were out in force. They were mostly hard-core Polish and Eastern European mercenaries who had joined the legion not to forget, but to evade prosecution. Scar-faced, scowling, hardened killers by all accounts. There was one in particular, whose name was probably Grgzgrchvk, and he was racist to boot. He made the mistake of making harsh racial comments to a local in the presence of giant Arthur, who aside from being enormous, was always on the edge of a steroid induced rage.

Arthur and Grgzgrchvk went at it, and Arthur's tremendous size and strength, and the steroids, seemed to be the match for the badass professional killer Grgzgrchvk. This appeared to surprise the living hell out of not only Grggrchvk, but the small handful of other consonant laden soldiery that accompanied him. The four of them decided to join in the fray. I don't know if it was over-confidence, soldiers

THERE I WAS

honor, stupidity, willingness to die, or just the joy of combat but the four of them decided that they were a match for the eight of us.

The amazing part is, how very close they were to being a match for the eight of us. It turns out that you can nearly wear yourself out knocking down Polish Mercenaries and they will just keep getting up. They were tireless, ferocious and fearless and each and every one of us was good and bloody by the time it was over. We left the bar under our own power and moved to the next bar for one final drink before heading back to the ship.

The bars all seemed much the same, one room, crowded and dark, with dirt floors and oil lamps or a handful of flickering light bulbs. A few locals, who went from laughing and happy to silent and scowling as we entered, maybe a few steely eyed legionnaires sitting in a corner, facing the door, giving us the hairy eyeball, and of course a tiny hooker or two who would inevitably, squeal with delight, race across the room and leap with wild abandon at me or Arthur.

The bathrooms, were usually at the very front of the building, and were nothing more than a hole in the floor that drained into the open sewer in the street. The disgusting bathrooms had been a topic of conversation all night, and fortunately, between drinking only straight hard liquor, and all the sweating, I had managed to avoid having to use the 'facilities' so far, but one can only avoid the bathroom so long when one is drinking like a sailor.

The room was small, and floor was funnel shaped, sloping from every corner into the hole in the middle. There was only a candle, made from some rancid animal fat, and even the foul stench of that burning offal could not overcome the horrific, redolent reek that emanated from that disgusting pit. I stood there contemplating whether or not to vomit, when a slushing splashing sound from the hole made it clear that I was not alone in there, there was some living creature sloshing about in that fetid abyss.

That was reason enough for me to leave my dick in my pants and exit with all the alacrity I could muster. It was like my dad always used to tell me: "Get out." The need, of course, remained. My steadily decreasing inhibition, coupled with the impairment of judgment that inevitably comes with drinking whiskey and getting punched repeatedly in the head, led me to the conclusion that the street was an open sewer anyway, I could therefore cut out the middle toilet and just pee right there in the street.

It was just fortune's sense of humor that led the one cop in the entire town to walk down that particular street at that moment. The cops were different than the other locals. Not lean, not wiry, not malnourished, but thick and healthy, with well-fed bodies, sharp clean khakis and the third world requisite automatic weapon. He

94

approached my friends as I stood off to the side attending to business and then barked at me when he realized I was defiling his beloved sewer.

There was the language barrier to contend with, in addition to our drunkenness and the stupidity of my shipmate who was one of those people who assumed that if someone didn't understand English, you simply needed to talk louder. My well intentioned idiot friend shouting and gesticulating like a moron, and the small crowd of very large, recently blooded Americans, began to make the Cop nervous, and his hand wandered closer and closer to the trigger on this Uzi.

I suddenly realized that he was speaking French. I had taken French for years in high school, and even had a French Canadian uncle, and I could curse fluently in that language. I had enough French to communicate that I was deeply sorry for soiling the street, and that we would not cause any more trouble, and offered him my hand in friendship, with just enough of a $20 bill showing to ensure everyone knew what was happening, and that they too should shake the hand of this fine civil servant. Soon the matter was cleared up to everyone's satisfaction and we were on our way back to the ship.

Bribing your way out of a jam in the third world is not an uncommon event, I thought nothing of it, and given that I had gone toe to toe with a professional mercenary and had had no less than a dozen hookers launch themselves and fly through the air at me like Circus acrobats, I wasn't even sure the cop would make it into my sea-story, but it made to everyone else's sea story.

The next day, it was the talk of the ship. Everyone was amazed and impressed, and asked me repeatedly where I had learned to speak African.

Part 3 Moments of Truth

"You can never cross the ocean unless you have the courage to lose sight of the shore" – Christopher Columbus

THERE I WAS

Small Boat, Big Ocean

The things that go wrong

> *"To young men contemplating a voyage I would say go." – Joshua Slocum*

Santo Laughed out loud. "Where did you learn to speak African, HA". He poured another drink

"I can tell you there are no Philipino's there in the French Foreign Legion, fuck no." he said as he sipped his whiskey. The booze had thickened his already strong accent, so it came out as "... Pilipinos dere in dee Prench Porin Lidgon, Puck no."

"I am going to miss that accent Santo, not a lot of Pinoys in Ithaca NY"

"What you talking about?"

"I am retiring, I stepped off my last ship this afternoon, and crossed the Bridge over Shit River for the last time"

"What the fuck Cliff, are you crazy?" (Wat the puck Clip, are you crayssee)

"I have been called that before, but this might be the sanest thing I have ever done"

"Bullshit." (Boolchit)"Why leave, you think you will <u>like</u> being ashore every day, trust me, you won't. I would kill to go back"

"I have a child now Santo, she needs her father, and I need to make sure that I am not constantly risking making her an orphan every day when I go to work."

"You Captain now, how dangerous is that? You get paper cuts maybe?"

"Tell that to Richie Phillips."

"Aaah, how often that happen?"

"Anything can happen anytime, Santo, I learned that a long time ago, but it was just as true this morning as it was 25 years ago.

"Anything? Anytime? That's true everywhere" (Anyting? Anytime? Dats true ebrywhere."

"More so at sea, my friend, for example... It was winter in the North Atlantic," Santo smiled. Nothing like a good story to make a point. Santo loved stories about our first ship together 25 years before, in the Navy. "We were steaming with the NATO flotilla, MyFirstNavyShip, right after you left. We had been doing destroyer squadron tactics for days on end. The weather had been brutally rough, but it had calmed down just enough, maybe 10-15 foot seas, that they decided to do some 'training'. Boat operations, you know, just tall enough to be dangerous, but not tall enough that someone would get court martialed if one of us died. Perfect training opportunity." Santo was nodding, as a Navy Boatswains Mate he had been involved

THERE I WAS

in more than just a few open ocean boat Ops before. He knew all about naval 'training opportunities'.

Just then Lucy showed up with an issue that Santo had to deal with right away. He led me back to the bar where a small group of cadets from some local maritime academy had just settled down for some heavy drinking.

"You wait here at the bar, I be back soon, these boys are going out to sea for their first training cruise next week, tell them sea stories, tell them everywhere you been, give them something to live up to. I won't be long."

THERE I WAS

Land of the Ice King

The End of the World

> *"A ship in port is safe, but that's not what ships are built for." – Grace Hopper*

She was my first Merchant. Just days after pulling the bent fork from the bloody cheek of young Jun, we left Port Hueneme (pronounced Wa-nee-mee, for reasons unknown), bound for Christchurch New Zealand and thence to McMurdo Station, Antarctica. The Motor Vessel MyFirstMerchant was built to support the Antarctic Mission. She had a reinforced bow, an oversized propeller for pushing through pack ice, and a Captain who was rumored to be made of ice. She was unique in that she had a *specially modified cargo hold* (92) that could be converted into a large scale berthing to evacuate the entirety of the Antarctic mission personnel in the event of an emergency. The number four cargo hold was modified to carry people by adding bathrooms in the wings. A vertical wall was added at the outer edges of the hold where the hull flared out, and scores of toilets, sinks and shower stalls were added to accommodate the hundreds of people who could be inhabiting the mission at any given time. A complex erector set that magically transformed into a network of intricately connected beds was also permanently stowed in the wings awaiting the day when hundreds of scared cold people would be forced to unstow them, and hopefully be clever enough to get them assembled.

This hold was referred to as "The Slave Quarters" which is the actual term used in Naval Architecture for a cargo hold that accommodates people. The PC movement was but in its infancy in those days, and had apparently not yet found its way to the South Seas.

The space had never been used for human cargo thankfully, and the bathrooms existed solely as a means for the Captain to punish people he didn't like. Many a poor Mariner that crossed sabers with Captain NameWitheld found themselves spending their entire tour scrubbing rust encrusted hoppers and sinks in the dank depths of a *dark smelly hold* (93).

The MV MyFirstMerchant had been in Polar service, under Captain NameWithheld for the better part of a decade. Capt. NameWithheld's specialty earned him the nickname "Iceman". Piloting through Arctic ice is a dangerously treacherous affair. Ice that is perfectly uniform in appearance, can be composed of equal parts slushy young ice, softer than baby-shit, and jagged mature, hull-rending ice, harder than steel.

On any trip to the Antarctic, you must pass through the South Seas. The South Seas are the only body of water on the earth that span the entire scope of the earths'

THERE I WAS

longitude, encircling the south Polar Regions entirely. The absence of land across this span allows the mighty Austral winds to fetch uninterrupted across vast distances in regions where the powerful storm generating Coriolis effects are at their strongest. The winds littorally (pun intended) whip around that entire slice of the globe, stirring up fierce storms and heavy seas.

Storm passage is never pleasant. Even a cape transit where the seas are generally head-on or following, can be terrifying and uncomfortable, but when the seas cut across your beam, hitting you broadside, it is frightening enough to bring religion to even the hardest bitten Mariner. We emerged from the storms into the calmer Austral Polar Regions. The water thickened into a surreally quiet slushy soup. The roaring white frothy bow wake was replaced with a sculpted standing bow wave that surged silently though the oatmeal thick water. Then comes the ice. Sea ice takes many forms, from giant icebergs, to hard pack-ice, to 'pancake' ice like giant white lily pads stretching from one horizon to the other.

The sound of the ship cutting through the water is so constantly and persistently in the background that one scarcely notices it; until it is gone. It is eerily replaced with the tortured groaning and cracking of pack ice, punctuated with the thunderous explosions of smaller bergy bits calving off of the towering, city sized tabular bergs. Sometimes it is quiet enough to hear the murmured rumblings of "Growler" bergs, in which the seas have carved and etched giant *acoustical chambers* (94) at the waterline that generate, amplify and launch strange growling sounds at passing ships. The voices of the sea gods are loud as you approach the land of the Ice King.

Day by day the ice thickens, since the only approach to Land is through the ice. The ice pack is so thick and difficult that are only 2-3 weeks at the peak of the Austral summer in early February when it is thin and soft enough to challenge. The Captain weaves his way through the ice, somehow surmising from the featureless white expanse which ice would slosh down the hull harmlessly and which would not yield but instead penetrate. Occasionally the ship would hit a harder bit, which would bump, grind or screech its way down the side of the ship sending shivers through the steel and up our spines into our very souls. If there is a hell, it sounds like a ship pounding through pack ice, (and likely has rap music playing the background as well).

Patches of open water appeared between the fields of ice, like lakes or ponds amid a jagged frozen landscape. Killer whales frequent these expanses, broaching, playing, hunting, or just hurling their massive bulk at speeds that defy the imagination. Herds of seals started to appear as well, swimming in schools, or lounging about on the ice. Honking at us angrily for disturbing their repose. We approached McMurdo Sound through one of these large patches of open water.

THERE I WAS

There were, of course, bits and pieces of ice floating in the water along the pier. I eyeballed these suspiciously knowing that they could make the mooring difficult and wondered if I would be called to lower a boat into the water and do some harbor maintenance. No tugs out here, far south of nowhere, to push away the obstructions. The Captain didn't seem to give them a second thought, and brought the ship in softly at a gentle angle as one would expect, but he didn't shallow out gradually coming up parallel to the dock as I expected. In an amazing feat of ship handling, he brought the bow in at that angle, nearly touching, maybe even lightly kissing the dock at the far seaward point. He then crab walked the ship while holding that precise angle the entire length of the dock, gently shoveling the ice aside like a snow plow. He stopped right on time, kicked the stern in smartly and we were alongside with no ice fulcrums to poke holes in our hull or make tying up or maneuvering difficult.

McMurdo is a Wilderness station sitting on a rocky outcrop in McMurdo Sound, adjacent to the Ross Ice Shelf. The small cluster of buildings sit in the shadow of Mt. Erebus, overlooking the sound. The US Navy operates the station. Scientists and the personnel who support them are the main inhabitants. All things Antarctic are governed by an international treaty that limits any effort on that barren ice covered rock to scientific research. No commercial nor military activity is allowed. The military operate the bases, essentially because no one else who is capable of supporting a mission at the end of the earth would be willing to do so without the promise of a profit windfall.

The Treaty was developed and signed back in the late fifties and the nations that were signatory to it each staked their claims to the various sites. Prior to the Treaty the only mark of human kind were the remains of the early expeditions at the beginning of the 20th century, a few remote whaling stations and some hideously polluted, examples of how not to operate a remote research station. The US had McMurdo, and the South Pole station. New Zealand had Scott base nearby with its airfield and an actual pub. New Zealand, being so close was entwined in the history of the place. The Russians, in a scientific victory, had scored the station at the magnetic South Pole, which is not located precisely at the geographic South Pole. The magnetic South Pole is a research gold mine, whereas the geographic pole is a meaningless feather in the cap.

McMurdo was the site of the base camp of one of the early expeditions, the unfortunate Scott expedition. In the early part of the 20th century, in a frenzy of Polar exploration, nations raced to be the first explorer to plant a national flag at the South Pole. Scott commanded several such missions, setting up a base at McMurdo that stands to this very day, unchanged in the frozen perpetual winter of the extreme southern Latitudes. Scott, while intrepid and experienced, through a series

THERE I WAS

of seemingly small miscalculations and errors failed to mount a successful expedition. Among other mistakes, he chose ponies as his preferred beast of burden, and learned the hard way why you never see Eskimo "pony sleds" plying the frozen regions of this world that are actually peopled.

The ponies were not well suited to the extreme conditions at the end of the earth and were shot along the way to provide food for the nearly starved expedition. The weary explorers arrived at the South Pole only to find Amundsen's Norwegian flag already flying at the world's southern extreme. No doubt copious amounts of dog poo reminding them of their equine folly.

They died on the return journey within sight of Mt Erebus beneath which lay their camp. That camp remains there to this day, outside McMurdo Station, almost precisely as they left it; preserved in natures icebox for posterity. The temperatures in the southern extremes never rise above freezing. The unchanged remains of a Weddell seal, slaughtered 100 years ago, sit frozen outside the hut entrance. Strips of meat and blubber hang in the larder alongside boxes of ship biscuit and other provisions. A pot of stew still sits on the cold fire ring, eternally awaiting the return of the doomed party.

The hut is visible as you approach the "Ice Pier" at McMurdo. Given that the temperatures are perpetually below freezing, and that ice and water are everywhere, and don't need to be shipped in, the decision was made to build the pier out of ice. It had been done in the past with success, and I am sure has been done since with success, but that year there were problems.

The ship was under charter to the US Navy and the National Science Foundation. Our cargo was absolutely everything that that small cluster of semi-permanent structures and the people who inhabited them would require for a full year of survival, operations and science. Everything from Band-Aids to soup spoons to diesel fuel.

This ship was a general purpose breakbulk freighter, capable of loading containerized cargo, in addition to every other form of cargo. There is a type of container called a flat rack, which is open on the sides and at the top. On the earliest versions of these racks, the end pieces were not permanently integrated into the container and were removable. They could be lifted off and laid flat on the container deck so as to take up less room when shipped empty. The problem was containers are like Lego blocks, connected with special fittings to keep the load tight and integrated. These collapsible flat racks had to be stacked loosely like lunchmeat or a towering cargo container Napoleon, lashed with straps and chains in a teetering monument to impending doom.

While collapsible flat racks were technically legal, few people used them anymore. We had several dozen of these racks filled with construction materials in holds. The cargo in question was shipped on the collapsible flat racks, would be unloaded in McMurdo, and the cargo removed. The racks would then be broken down, reloaded, then stacked precariously in the number four hold (the slave quarters) and lashed by naval reservists with little or no stevedoring experience. What could possibly go wrong?

We started moving cargo immediately after that magnificent docking, and this ship, with four cargo holds and six cranes started working all four holds at once. Under the best of circumstances with modern port facilities and professional stevedores, the entire ship would take a few days to unload and several more to backload, but this was the edge of the world. The cargo was not met at the dock by a steady stream of tractors and flatbeds rolling in an endless train to the staging yard or warehouse. The lashings were not being removed by people who earned their living handling cargo equipment. The cranes were not being operated by professional stevedores who were paid per lift.

Two weeks were allotted to get unloaded, back load the return trip cargo (Antarctica exports all its waste back to the US, including human waste in refrigerated containers) and get the hell out of there before the ice gets too thick to pound through. Provided absolutely nothing went wrong, to any extent, at any point. Things went smoothly for a few days. We worked 10-14 hours each day and were so energized by the perpetual daylight that there was plenty of time to see the Antarctic sites. We visited Scotts hut, climbed Mount Erebus, and went penguin and seal watching.

Penguins are endlessly amusing, and must be the source of the expression 'odd bird'. On the day a select few of us were permitted to visit the actual South Pole, we made the drive to the air strip. Naval Cargo planes would land here to deliver people and gear, before bouncing along to the South Pole base. We noticed as all the penguins in and around the runway watched the approaching plane, their little empty heads would all turn in unison following the path of the plane. We watched the heads of the penguins standing at the end of the runway, as the plane flew over on its descent to land. Their heads continued following the plane, looking up higher and higher until the plane flew over and behind them, and hundreds of ridiculous little penguins fell over backwards like dominoes.

That day we went farther south. We went so far south that every other direction was north. I stood there at the bottom of the earth, and the Sea Gods made it clear to me which direction my future lie, and where it would take me. All directions pointed to the same place, and no matter which way I turned it would lead me in the same direction, north. The destination was the entire world. I followed up my visit to 90°South Latitude with a voyage through the entire span of earth's longitude in less than six steps. Three hemispheres in one day. Our esteemed Chief Engineer had brought his fiddle and gave us a 'world tour' dancing and playing an Irish Jig around the entire the earth.

But soon the fun was over. On the fourth day there came a storm. Antarctic storms are perhaps the fiercest on earth. Even in 'summer', white-out blizzard conditions have been so extreme that people have been lost in the narrow streets between buildings on base. This storm brought raging wind, seas and ice directly at the ship and ice pier, and the ice pier cracked. Imagine, ice cracking, who would have thought. So our primary unloading surface had a *gaping crack* (95) smack dab in the middle. The Army Corps. Of Engineers had built it, and fixing it was their responsibility. They began to sew it back together by driving piles into the ice along either side of the crack and using wire cable to stitch across the crack. Meanwhile, the two largest cargo holds, had nowhere to land their cargo on the damaged pier. So that cargo had to be lifted from the stranded holds to the other two serviceable holds and offloaded there. This substantially slowed the already snail like pace.

The second storm two days later saw one of the broken halves of the ice pier nearly disintegrated, stranding yet another hold. We were days behind now, and the brief 2 week window was rapidly closing. Summers shine dimly and briefly in the land of the Ice King, and winters' approach is rapid and severe. The storms continued to come, hurling huge blocks of ice onto remaining remnants of the shattered ice pier, and packing more and more ice against the side of the ship.

There was talk of 'wintering over'. The Captain explained this remarkably unfortunate scenario to me as the ship being stuck and forced to remain in place until the same time next year when the ice thins enough to escape. Six months of darkness and temperatures as low as 50-100 below zero sounded like a grim sentence to me.

In response to the dire circumstance we approached our cargo operations with renewed vigor and finally logged the last lift. A storm was brewing and the ice along the seaward side was already dangerously thick. We were underway in minutes, putting the engines at full throttle, reverse and then forward, reverse and then forward, jack-hammering our way through the ridge of ice that strived to pin us to the crumbled remains of the Ice Pier.

Finally underway again, we set about securing for sea and prepared for the ice transit as we beat into the teeth of an impending storm. Passing through pack ice during a storm is like being inside a tin can that has been thrown into a cement mixer; lots of motion and grinding and terrible sounds that motivate a man to set his affairs in order and evaluate his life. The storms subsided as we emerged past the ice into the towering South Seas. The skies were clear and the sun still spent most of the day with us, setting late in the evening just before the midnight watch and rising again a few hours later.

THERE I WAS

The skies were peppered with giant Skua gulls, Gannets and mystical Albatross whose wings never flap a beat. They spend nearly their entire lives at sea, returning to shore only to breed... much like merchant seamen. Albatross are attracted to ships, and will find the currents of rising air generated by the ships passing and park themselves in these currents for as long as the current remains stable. As a ship riding a constant course through a steady regional wind pattern, we began to collect an air escort of Albatross. We had an entire squadron of these majestic birds, parked precisely in their rigid formation around the ship. They hung immobile in the air, capturing lift from the wind and currents, steadfastly gliding alongside.

One such bird, I assumed his name was Al, found a location to suspend himself just aft of the superstructure in an area we called the back porch. He was close aboard and at eye level, three to four feet away from the rail. He spent several days hanging there keeping us company. I greeted him each morning and evening as I left and returned from work. As I passed through the door his head would turn towards me and stare a moment, the rest of his form remaining motionless as the world carved past below. Sometimes he would hold that gaze for several long minutes, maintaining eye contact until nodding slightly in silent acknowledgement before returning his gaze to the endless ocean before us. It has been said that Albatross are the souls of dead Mariners, having met and socialized with Al, I find it easy to believe. I could almost hear the "What the fuck are you looking at?" as he stared me down each day.

The South Pacific was storming when we arrived there. We were beating headlong into 50 foot seas or worse, taking them just enough on the starboard bow to add a long miserable roll to the heavy pitching. The bow would rise up on the wave to its peak and hover briefly for a moment, before falling away and crashing into the trough below then rising up the next wave. From the Bridge, over 40 feet above the waterline, we found ourselves staring up at a wall of water, looming above us like a death sentence.

Often times the next wave would crash over the bow, burying the front of the ship under water, and the agonized strain of her buoyancy heaving up through the thousands of tons of water on deck could be felt in your feet pulsing through the steel. The sensation of the bow falling and then rising is like a weight suddenly added to your back. Or like the floor rising up and pushing against your feet, raising you to a pinnacle where it suddenly diminishes and stops just slightly sooner than you. You are left, for the briefest of moments, floating weightless as the deck falls away without you. Your toes desperately reaching for the deck, trying to grasp an elusive foothold. The gravity does catch up, and you rejoin the deck, hopefully in the same vicinity with similar orientation as when you left it.

THERE I WAS

If there is strong roll with this pitching action, then re-establishing physical contact with the ship is often an exciting experiment in physics. Your orientation remains constant while you hover in free fall, but the ship is still under the profound influence of the powerful hand of Poseidon and it travels on, rotating variously about its three axes. When you finally reconnect, gravity points perhaps not quite in the same line as when you left, and the ship has rearranged itself in space while you have not. All in the span of a few eternally long seconds.

Sleeping and eating in this environment is pure misery. Cooking becomes impossible and cold meals are eaten carefully while one hand and both feet cling desperately to the mess deck tables. Anything not physically bolted to the ship either goes shooting across the room, or gets lifted into that hovering free fall only to land badly somewhere nearby. Often a particularly harsh roll will send everyone and everything flying. The view becomes surreal as your shipmates cling with both hands to the table, their bodies parallel to the floor, as the ship orients itself in sheer defiance of gravity. Objects and the weak of grip are hurled to one side of the room, and only the most dexterous of those left clinging can sufficiently rearrange themselves in time for the return trip on the opposite roll.

Sleeping becomes more of a treasured memory than a nightly event. The more experienced Mariners develop strategies to deal with rough seas. I would stuff blankets and pillows under one side of the mattress, and sleep in the crotch of the built up mound and the wall. I had experimented with hammocks, and found them quite comfortable in all but the heaviest seas, but if the seas get too heavy or the lash point fails, they are transformed instantly from hammock to slingshot with profoundly unpleasant results. No matter what your method, sleep is problematic in high seas, and always there exists the possibility of waking up in mid-air, in inky black darkness, wondering from which direction the floor will come at you.

Rough seas can last for days, especially when crossing the longest stretch of open sea on the planet as we were. Days on end with no sleep, surviving on Saltines and an occasional sandwich can make one pine and yearn earnestly for a nice prison sentence in a federal penitentiary. The dreary hell-like monotony of this particular voyage was broken when the harbinger of our worst fears raised its ugly head.

Cargo moves both to and from the Antarctic, and we had a full, if not heavy, load. Containers, mostly empty, were stacked on the hatch covers, and heavier, cumbersome and irregularly shaped cargoes were stowed in the holds. Containers are designed to stack and have connection points at every corner so that various fittings can be attached to lash and bind them together. Our containers were stacked four high and eight across, and were connected to the deck at the bottom and to each other where they met at the top of one, and the bottom of the next one in the stack.

THERE I WAS

Each vertical stack of containers was independent of the others. Lashing only at the bottom left the stacks wobbly and loose at the top, so special fittings called 'bridges' were put at the top to integrate the stacks together giving them more vertical stability. The severe rolling of the South Seas and south pacific transit, coupled with the lack of skill of the amateur Stevedores, had caused these bridge fittings to loosen and stacks were leaning with each roll. From the wheelhouse looking down on deck, the narrow gap between the stacks could be seen widening at the top as the ship rolled one way then the other.

Whenever lashed cargo moves in even the slightest way, it is a nightmare scenario. If the lashings fail then massively heavy objects start dancing about on your decks or within your holds with the potential to destroy the ship in a catastrophic instant. Or they can slowly beat it to death like a 40 ton hammer swinging back and forth with each roll of the ship, liberating other hammers as it swings.

Now, we fortunate few, who were finding it difficult *not* to go hurling through space in the dry confines of the interior with both hands and lots of places to hold on, would get to wander out on a deck fully awash with an angry, angry ocean that continuously hurled small mountains of water at us. We would have to climb an old unsecured extension ladder over 40 feet up to a flat, slick surface with no hand holds, and no rails, which was itself an unstable structure on a heaving deck. We could then manipulate a five foot long iron wrench and tighten up dozens and dozens of fittings as if our lives depended on it, which of course they did.

The pleasure was increased by the harsh reality, that due to the fact that I was new to the Merchant Marine, and had only Navy experience, I was accustomed to being provided rain gear, and had not brought any of my own. So I had the distinct pleasure of spending the longest night of my life in the cold wet darkness, while the fist of Neptune's fury pounded all around me. All for the sake of restoring stability and order to those unruly stacks of cargo containers that had wobbled so slightly, yet so dangerously, as to compel us to tempt this fate.

I finished the task with breath still in my lungs and nearly all of my fingers still fully functional. I survived the precarious dismount down the rickety ladder and made my way through the raging torrent on deck with the few brave (or foolish) shipmates who had had the fortitude (or bad judgment) to venture out there with me. The Captain was the last to walk in from the storm and almost as if the Sea Gods had been waiting for that moment when we all inhaled to breathe a sigh of relief, came the thunderous crash from the number four hold.

Our one solace out there in that watery hell on deck, as we faced death dozens of times each minute, was that "at least it isn't those flat racks down in the number four hold." That thunderous kaboom was followed by the fully expected and much

THERE I WAS

dreaded, clanking, crashing, and screeching of hundreds of tons of loose steel shifting about. Captain NameWithheld stoically about-faced and silently led us out the door to the number four access hatch.

The Captain didn't need to tell us how to proceed, we groped our way about that raging watery gauntlet gathering lanterns, chains, tools, and rope, and all met on the starboard side near the access to the hold. The ship had just started rolling to starboard and without speaking we all stuck our heads over the side and looked anxiously at the hull to see if any of the loose cargo would come rocketing out... not yet anyway.

We were fortunate in that the number four hold had been modified for human cargo, and there was easy access and space to stage equipment within the hold. We were far more fortunate than we realized at the time, any other hold on the ship and there would likely already have been a gaping hole in the hull at or below the waterline. We entered the hold and found much what we expected.

There had been four stacks of flat racks on the bottom level of the hold and one of them had blown its lashings on the outboard side. This allowed the racks to slide almost freely, constrained only slightly by the few lashings that still held. Each time the ship rolled dozens of racks and end pieces, some as long as 40 feet, and each weighing several tons, would slide 5-10 feet slamming into the teetering stack next to it, or into the wall outboard of it. There against that wall was the telltale sign of good fortune of how rusty toilets saved our lives. That wall was getting severely battered and had already been penetrated and gashed in several places. That wall did not belong there. A wall like that did not exist in any other cargo holds on that ship, nor on any other ship of that class, or any class for that matter. For the number of ships built in the last century that were capable of transporting human cargo in a cargo hold was likely just one... Ours.

So instead of those demon racks battering the weak inner surface of the hull below the waterline, they battered the structural necessities of the physical architecture developed in the trade of human bondage. Those walls that had been specified by the Navy as a longshot contingency, had so far prevented catastrophe, but it was still up to us to wrangle several hundred tons of wild steel.

So the longest night of my life, was closely followed by the longest day of my life. The decision was made to divert the ship towards the closest port, to bring us nearer to rescue assets, and to find a smoother course. The Captain and the Navigator collaborated and decided upon a course. Changing course is normally the most routine of events, but in our current condition it was the most dangerous moment we would face on this already significantly dangerous trip. The turn would have to be made 130° to port. This would entail turning broadside to the seas into the trough before steadying up with the seas broad on the port quarter. The odds were about

THERE I WAS

even that the ship would lean enough during that turn to impart sufficient momentum to the loose cargo to launch it through the starboard side hull, introducing the ocean to the number four hold and starting the clock on the ships then inevitable trip to the bottom.

The lifeboats were made ready, and we all stood there on deck, near the port lifeboats, peering over the side with trepidation waiting for the telltale sound, fury and spectacle of cargo bashing its way free of the hold into the sea. The longest night and the longest day of my life was punctuated in between, by the longest three minutes of my life as we made that fateful turn. Surviving that, the fun part started.

There were only about a half dozen of us that braved that dark hold. The Captain was wise enough not order anyone in there who was unwilling to go. Four of the nine members of the deck department and two engineers. The Engineers brought their formidable metal working skills to the party, and would cut wire rope and chain rapidly with a torch, versus the deck department's slower mechanical cutters. They brought steel and welding gear and would add lash points where needed or fabricate metal bracing to shore up the lashings.

The deck crew went to work trying to lasso the loose cargo and get it strapped down. We had the Engineers cut us long lengths of cable and we would fasten one end, and make suicide runs throwing ropes and tying 'messengers' to the loose cable end trying to get it over the shifting pile, and then get that end turned onto a fitting where we could fasten or tension it. More of them broke than survived, and we lost another stack of racks in the process. Each time the ship rolled the cargo would slide and strain what lashings remained, or ones we had just secured. When they failed the wire would snap violently, whipping about like an enormous weed whacker. Often some component of the rig would pop and shoot like a six pound bullet across the hold ricocheting around like a pinball. The fact that everyone survived that maelstrom of flying metal with no worse than a few flesh wounds, broken bones and bruises is the single most miraculous event I have ever witnessed. It was touch and go for most of the day, but it was a numbers game and as long as we kept installing more lashings than we lost... we were winning. Soon the load shifted less and less, and our lashings got tighter and tighter and before long the rogue flat racks moved no more. They were held securely by an enormous web of chain and wire lashings, crisscrossing from every angle like a giant cargo Gulliver bound up by Mariner Lilliputians.

After that last lashing was placed, we all just gathered along the starboard side and looked at the immense damage done to the wall that had saved our ship. Each of us imagined how this night might have played out if this damage had been to the hull and not the buffer wall that existed in no other ship but our own. We stood there a long time contemplating it and all at once seemed to realize that the seas had calmed, and snapped out of our reverie together. The cooks had done their part and a magnificent hot meal of Prime Rib awaited us in the mess decks. As I trudged towards my stateroom after dinner, I could almost hear the words of my father's nightly refrain "Get your ass to bed!"

Tales From the Arabian Gulf

The origins of hate

> *To the last, I grapple with thee; From Hell's heart, I stab at thee; for hate's sake, I spit my last breath at thee."* Herman Melville, <u>Moby Dick</u>

GAINING PERSPECTIVE

The bright sun assaulted my eyes as I stepped out from the cool dark restaurant onto the searing hot Tarmac. The stark temperature and humidity difference between the wonderfully air conditioned inside and the hot humid hell outside caused moisture to condense on my clothes and skin, fogging up my sunglasses. I could see the heat rising in waves off of the seemingly vast tarmac that lie between me and my ship. I knew the ship was less than a mile away, but it was invisible through the dust and haze.

The port of Fujairah sits like a sentry at the Eastern side of the Straits of Hormuz outside the Persian Gulf. Fujairah is one of the Seven United Arab Emirates and doesn't enjoy rich oil resources like its neighbors. Its economy is driven mainly by the trade in the region. It is a major 'bunkering' (fueling) port, as it is the last gas stop before the straits of Hormuz and the Gulf.

A heavily armed Arab guard saw me loitering and eyeballed me suspiciously. It isn't easy mustering enough phlegm to correctly pronounce "Don't shoot" and "Which way to the big boat" in Arabic. The Arabic language is very guttural, with the words starting deep in the throat before finally being finally being hocked out through the mouth with angry vigor. My pronunciation was likely terrible, it takes a lifetime of drinking warm goat's milk to get the pronunciations correct. Adding a solid dose of anger helps considerably. He pointed in the direction of my ship and indicated that I should move along.

I had stepped ashore in the sandy confines of greater Araby, here in the port of Fujairah, during a 12 hour visit for fuel and supplies. The port was a fenced in compound that existed in isolation, unconnected to any city, town, village or other signs of life. There was an oil terminal, dry cargo operations, and a livestock facility. For the sailor on liberty, there was only a small lonely duty free shop, a tiny Indian restaurant, and lots of hateful stares from the wizened Bedouins who worked the port. It was no less than 115 degrees in the shade, and everything was brown.

The port sits at the base of a ring of craggy rock hills that rise dramatically and vertically from the searing hot sand of the desert. The air is thick with a fine brown dust that covers everything, filling your eyes, and your lungs, and rendering your spit and snot the color and texture of mud. The dust had a strong sour smell, which even when mingled with the powerful stench of Bunker oil, was nothing compared to the eye-watering reek that emanated from the enormous camel and sheep paddocks. The stench was so thick, that it seemed almost visible, a tangible gut twisting miasma of viscous olfactory offense.

I sojourned out into the merciless, oppressive sun, the foul stenches of the desert comingled with the hot dust coating my mouth and nose, filling my lungs, making them feel like sandpaper. There, on that blisteringly hot tarmac, as my eyes shed brown muddy tears, I had an epiphany. I came to a profound and deep understanding of this place, this culture, and radicalism in general. I realized that if I had choice between living here, in this hell on earth, or strapping a bomb to myself and running into a crowd of people I didn't like, I would give it some very serious thought.

THE SONG OF THE ARABIAN GULF

The sky glowed with an eerie dull orange light, reminiscent of the Hollywood version of hell. It was midnight and overcast, but bright enough to see by, like being near a campfire. The reflections of the massive oil rigs in the flat calm waters made them seem like giant monsters looming over us.

Dozens of them littered the horizon, from one end to the other. Each with a towering stack rising hundreds of feet above the water, erupting with a mighty orange flame as the rigs burned the Natural Gas off of the wellhead. They stood like torch-bearing sentinels lighting the way across the Persian Gulf.

The waterway was carpeted with vessels of all sizes. Oil rig support boats, coastal trade, behemoth oil tankers, and of course, hundreds of the small wooden Dhows that were the maritime workhorses of the region. Dhows could be seen from Asia to Arabia, and were common throughout the Indian Ocean, but they were most common here in the Persian Gulf.

The Persian Gulf an ancient place, even among ancient places. The earliest known trade routes on earth, both overland and over water were between Persia and the Indus valley, and many aspects of life here seemed to have advanced very little since then. Certainly the Dhows had remained a fixture in the local maritime environment since the days of Sinbad.

We travelled slowly through the maze of traffic and oil platforms, guided by the eerie rig candles shooting fire into the sky. Like navigating in a pinball machine, we changed course constantly, carving a curving slashing zig zag through the calm waters. The radio chatter was a surreal mix of professional Arab port authorities and ships officers, local fishermen, Texas hillbilly rig operators, and the ever present song of the Arabian Gulf. For as long as there has been VHF radios, local Arab Dhow operators have had a spiteful tradition of baiting Philipino Dhow crews on the radio.

It is done in a very specific way. Randomly, out of the blue, almost intentionally to fill the rare silences, in English, usually with a thick Arab accent, a high pitched falsetto voice broadcasts in a very sing-song manner:

"Phillipinoooo Muuuunkey....Fuuuuck you". Variations include abrupt guttural angry: "Fuck you Monkey!" or

"Fuck you Phillipino", but always in addition to the soft, sinister, song of the Arabian Sea.

"Phillipinoooo Muuunkey... Fuuuck you" is constantly punctuating the radio traffic. Interspersed in the busy chatter of a harbor approach, or between Texas drawled tug boaters towing a rig, or suddenly amid the pure silence on a quiet 2AM watch. The novelty of it wears off on your first day, after the first few hundred times you hear it, and it fades into the already surreal background like just another clown in a three ring circus.

TARGETS OF OPPORTUNITY

The silence was shattered by the thunder of running boots on steel decks as the mine response team scrambled to their stations. From the straits of Hormuz, all through the Persian Gulf both the Iranians and Iraqis set mines in the gulf. The land war had not gone well for either side, so they had each decided to wage less bloody war on each other's shipping. We knew of the threat, and posted lookouts along the weatherdecks. Anything seen floating in the water was assumed to be a mine, prompting us to man our Battle Stations, and the .50 Caliber guns.A livestock carrier on a regular run carried sheep from the southern gulf to Kuwait a few times a week. She was nicknamed the "Arabian Love Boat" by Fifth Fleet veterans and had been a fixture in the gulf for as long as anyone could remember. When livestock perish during a voyage, from heat, illness, poor conditions or STD's, the crew simply discharge the carcasses overboard, leaving a constant trail of bloated dead sheep all along the Saudi Coast from Bahrain to Kuwait. The ever present floating bodies were perfectly suited as training aids for mine response drills. So when operating in that area, which was also an area known to be heavily mined, several times a day the call would go out on the PA:

"WOOLY MINE ON THE STARBOARD BOW, BEARING 040 RELATIVE AT 600 YARDS, AWAY THE MINE RESPONSE TEAMS, WEAPONS FREE". The announcement was always followed by the stomping of booted feet racing down the passageways and across the decks to guns. The clanking preparations of a .50 caliber machine gun being crewed, locked, and loaded, were followed by the staccato 'rat-a-tat-tat' of the shooting guns mixed with syncopated accompaniment of the spent shells clattering onto the deck and rolling about as the ship maneuvered frantically to avoid the dreaded mutton. The outcome was always the same, the bloated gas filled carcass was reduced to sheep burger, leaving a greasy chum slick, a more sanitary Persian Gulf, and a better trained crew.

BRAZEN CULTURAL DIFFERENCES

Throngs of Arab businessmen in their perfectly white cotton robes and black and red headdresses crowded in alongside westerners in the bustling lounge of the Gulf Hotel in Manama Bahrain. The posh hotel, with its 10 restaurants was an oasis of Western decadence just a stone's throw from the magnificent Grand Mosque. The tall cool atrium was an extravagant monument to oil rich opulence. Giant potted date palms towered over the fountain in the lobby, giving the illusion of being outdoors, minus the oppressive heat and dust.

When the loud conversation and clinking glasses suddenly stopped, the only sound was the tiny roar of the fountain, like the faint voices of the sea gods in the distance.

Bahrain is a small island nation state in the Persian Gulf that houses the headquarters for the US Fifth fleet. As Arab states go, they land somewhere on the tolerance spectrum between the medieval conservatism of Saudi Arabia, and the modern open-mindedness of Dubai.

Civilian clothing that constitutes normal attire anywhere else on earth, was considered scandalous, and could get a girl arrested. Showing some leg, or cleavage or even just her hair, was the cultural equivalent of being naked in public. Attitudes slowly changed over the years, and nowadays, women in full western regalia, complete with cleavage and tight pants can walk down the street in many Islamic nations without the risk of being stoned to death, but not at this point in history.

In that bar, on that day, the small group of young Navy sailor girls in their tight shorts, tiny tank tops, and all that exposed skin challenged the extreme limit of Arab tolerance. This particular group were a bit rough around the edges, and had pushed the envelope for 'liberty attire' to its very edge, dressing in clothes that at best raised eyebrows, and at worst would raise an alarm.

The entire bar went silent as the brazen women entered, talking loudly. One particularly bold young lady, with a painted-on tee shirt emblazoned with a confederate flag and daisy dukes, caught an Arab man staring at her. She boldly stared back and finally said

"In America, women can dress any way they want." Without missing a beat, the man calmly responded

THERE I WAS

"And yet you *choose* to dress like a prostitute." The entire bar roared with laughter and the tension evaporated. The embarrassed girls stormed out to find a less judgmental watering hole, and dull murmur of conversation resumed.

VESSEL ATTACK BONUS

The unforgiving desert sun beat down relentlessly, illuminating the stark white hull of the Naval Oceanographic survey ship as we wound our way up the Euphrates River, making us an easy target. Dour Navy sailors, in desert camo and flak jackets manned their posts, scanning the dusty brown horizon for signs of trouble. They were tasked with protecting this Naval Vessel, with its civilian crew, and civil service scientists.

The fighting was still heavy in Umm Qasr, and the Navy wanted to send ships to support the push to Basra. The most recent bathymetric data available were some old British surveys from the 1940's; so they sent us up the river, so to speak, to map the bottom. Each morning as the sun painted the desert sky purple, we would follow the winding river through the endless sandbox to the survey area.

Every crack of gunfire off in the distance triggered an agitated reaction from the security team. A dozen binoculars would rise to a dozen helmeted heads in a mass Pavlovian response. The action was getting nearer. Our small survey launches were surveying closer inshore while we covered the deeper waters mid-stream. I stood on the bridgewing with my Navigator and the Chief of the Navy security team. Surveying within the tight confines of the river require a lot of maneuvering, so the Bridge was crowded and busy.

Off in the distance, behind some god-awful sand dune in that furnace of a desert, a lone bedraggled Bedouin must have been bored and decided to take a pot shot at the giant glowing white steel target on the river. A sharp crack in the distance was followed almost immediately by the loud 'tink' of the bullet hitting steel just a few feet from us on the wing.

The reactions of the civilians, vs. the reactions of the Navy couldn't have been more different. There were a handful of each on the port bridgewing when it happened, and both reacted initially with a stunned silence. The Navy, of course, reacted more quickly, snatching their walkie talkies, or their weapons, locking and loading, and scurrying about like someone had just kicked a hornet's nest.

The crew's reaction may have stunned them even more than the bullet. The Navy coming frantically to life shook the Merchant Marines from our stunned state, and all at once, every one of us, cheered at the top of our lungs.

Merchant Marines in a time of war, and in general, get paid extra when the danger level rises. Ships crews get an 'ammo bonus' when a certain percentage of the cargo is ammunition, and an even bigger bonus if that ship enters a war zone. Then there is the vaunted "vessel attack" bonus, a hefty payout, like an extra paycheck or two that crews get if their unarmed, non-combatant vessel comes under fire.

The young Navy boys knew nothing of the 'vessel attack' bonus. They had no inkling that that one bullet would put over a month's pay into each of our pockets, they just stopped dead in their tracks and stared in wide eyed disbelief. Why would anyone cheer when coming under hostile fire? It was quite a happy moment for most of us, and our lighthearted high-fiving and 'yippi-ki-yaying' agitated them to no end.

This was serious business to them, and we were not treating it with the stern taciturn resolve that they felt it merited. I ordered the steward to prepare a special meal in celebration that night, and once we were safely out of the river and into the gulf a nice American cookout restored the balance and set their minds at ease.

CROSSING THE POND

You never forget your first

> *"You can't cross the sea merely by standing and staring at the water."*
> *Rabindranath Tagore*

The impenetrable darkness of the night was shredded by the erratic beams of searchlights everywhere, sweeping the water, and shooting off in crazy directions as the ships rolled in the heavy seas. People on deck everywhere, shouting into walkie talkies, binoculars trained on the water searching for that poor bastard that fell in.

Two weeks earlier, six allied ships rendezvoused off the coast of Halifax Nova Scotia, high in the North Atlantic in heavy seas. One each: US, Canadian, British, Dutch, German, and Portuguese gathered to form the NATO squadron. We would spend the next six months together conducting squadron maneuvers, but our first order of business was a night of revelry in our first *port of call* (96), Halifax Nova Scotia.

We stayed only one night in Halifax prior to a long ocean crossing and a schedule filled to the last second with drills and training exercises. So there we were, leaving Halifax harbor on a rough stormy day, just as hungover as a crew can be. Halifax sits at the Far Eastern end of Nova Scotia, and when one leaves the shelter of her harbor, one lands quite abruptly into the full fury of the North Atlantic. So the rocking and rolling began; not a gentle, calming rocking and rolling that makes one feel alive and salty, but a furious jerking, 'hold on for your life', rolling that makes one regret enlisting. The kind of rolling that drives even those without horrific hangovers to vomit in protest.

Now we were tactical. Hungover and seasick or not, the squadron was formed, and therefore must drill. In those days, the Russians would park spy ships up and down the North American coast. They dressed them up as "Trawlers", but it was no secret what they were really up to. They followed along with us, making a point to be irritating assholes every chance they got.

Pollution laws were looser back then, and the normal practice was to poke a few holes in the trash bags and throw them overboard. The Russians would of course pick the bags out of the water to gather what intelligence they could. Our Captain did not appreciate having his waste examined, so he decided to do something about it. The crew was assembled into the helo hanger one day, and he called for volunteers. There were trash bags at the ready, and a tall narrow tent that was normally used as

THERE I WAS

a temporary *guard shack* (97), and at least 100 of us shit in those bags, and then covered the shit with 'love notes' we wrote to Ivan. The love notes were cleverly disguised as telex radio messages, and we even stamped them "Secret", to pique their interest. Top secret sports scores, and AP news reports annotated with colorful and salty anecdotes. We each, literally, gave a shit for our country that day.

Our Soviet counterparts did not see the humor in our offering and in response they decided to shine spotlights at us to blind our lookouts. Our good Captain had no patience for godless Bolsheviks, and he decided to remind them of the difference between a warship and a spy ship. So he did a little 'illuminating' of his own.

Navy ships have extremely powerful targeting RADARs, capable of beaming over a megawatt of microwave radiation directly at a target. Not the gentle low power sweeping search RADARs of a peaceful merchant, but hard core military targeting RADARs that focus an intense narrow beam of microwave radiation precisely at a target, lighting it up in the 'eyes' of the missile.

We lit up the Russians at full gain. A normal ship might never know. They might notice some static in the electronics, buzzing in the speakers, a blown receiver or two, maybe someone in a direct line of sight might feel a little warm, but spy ships exist to monitor transmissions, even RADAR transmissions, so they knew. They likely had some pretty fancy electronics, and that much energy beaming at them was certainly wreaking havoc with them. Eventually they just called us on the VHF and asked us to stop. They backed off considerably after that.

The Russians stayed with us for the entire crossing, and we messed with them every chance we could. The squadron would surround them, or head straight at them, or race off in different directions, whatever we could do to irritate them.

One night a bad storm blew in, kicking up 20–30 foot seas. We heard a call over the radio that a Russian Sailor had gone overboard. The squadron reacted immediately. Nothing is more impressive than watching a full destroyer squadron that has been drilling relentlessly for weeks on end respond to an emergency. Within five minutes there were five helicopters in the air, precisely coordinated with five ships in a perfect formation sweeping a search grid. Each minute that passed lessened his chance of survival. We continued the fruitless search for hours, but we never found him. The ocean won that day.

The Russians eventually called off the search. The voice coming from the radio in emotional broken English told us that they would never forgot how their NATO adversaries put aside their differences and put their helicopters in the air and their people on deck in those dangerous seas to help out their Soviet rivals.

That event, while a potent reminder of our salty brotherhood, put a solid damper on the *cat* (98) and mouse games. The Russians kept their distance after that, and we

THERE I WAS

didn't have the heart to mess with them anymore. Our drill routine was more somber until we steamed together enroute to Northern Europe.

We travelled to Copenhagen Denmark, which, like every other deep water port on earth, has at least one fine British Pub located conveniently close to the docks. Copenhagen, of course, had just such a pub, and a gathering of our squadron mates of all ethnicities was planned. It was a snowy November evening and a small group of us walked down the waterfront together on our way to the evening's festivities.

Now I can't say if it was just my ship, or if this was common throughout the navy, but of the 227 officers and crew of that fine ship, at least half a dozen had played professional baseball in the minor leagues. All of them were good enough to get to the minors, maybe even good enough to stay in the minors, but none had been good enough to achieve the ultimate goal of reaching the *Major leagues* (99).

For many of them that meant the derailment of their lifelong plan and I suspect that precious few of them had a plan B. The Navy, perhaps even more than the other services, is filled with a diaspora of lost souls who had come to some crossroads in life, and chose to leave land and life ashore behind and explore the watery part of the world.

It was all to the benefit of our softball team, and to the detriment of a small handful of enormous Danish Vikings who chanced upon the four of us, myself and three of these minor-league ex-pats wandering about on the Copenhagen waterfront on that snowy evening.

It was ostensibly playful and good natured enough to start, a snowball and a laugh hurled casually. The Vikings perhaps were under the false impression that their tremendous size advantage and life in a land of near perpetual winter gave them some sort of advantage in a snowball fight. They did not understand that in America, young men spend the entirety of every summer of their lives perfecting the fine art of hurling a small heavy ball at extremely high velocities with pinpoint accuracy.

Nothing in their Viking heritage prepared them for the maelstrom of snowy pain that rained down on them from every point of the compass. The culmination of endless summers practicing the throw to home, the fastball, or the fielder's choice, coupled with no small measure of naval gunnery expertise, shocked those blond behemoths to their core. Four small (by Viking Standards) skinny Americans outgunning the princes of a snow kingdom in a game of showmanship.

Never had one of those Vikings launched a throw from centerfield to home plate, bouncing it neatly into the tiny target of the catcher's mitt some 200 feet away. Our centerfielder figured out early on that as strong as those Vikings were, they simply could not throw with any accuracy at that range. He just parked himself comfortably out of their range and lobbed long arching bombshells across the docks at the hapless locals. They were already busy dodging the rapid fire torrent of snowballs that were being relentlessly rifled at them from two former professional infielders who, but for their lack of hitting skills, would have been fielding in the major leagues.

Almost immediately following that first Viking salvo, the condescending Teutonic scorn that had carried them into that melee, transformed from amazement to concern, to panic. Too proud to surrender they continued to fight their losing battle in a proud but foolish display of vain gallantry.

We had them pinned down between the water and a small dock tractor and reduced the pace of our attack from a staccato rapid fire assault to a more leisurely sniping siege. We took the opportunity to build up our stock of ammo and were considering a full advance on *target* (100) with the intent of driving them into the water or forcing surrender when a few of our shipmates happened along seeking a source of blessed whiskey, camaraderie and perhaps feminine companionship.

This afforded us an opportunity to relent, and ask our new Scandinavian friends if they cared to show us the way to our destined watering hole and join us for drinks. This was conveyed from across the field of fire, using sign language. The extended pinky and thumb tilted towards the mouth 'come drink with us' sign being one of the most universally recognized hand signals on waterfronts across the globe. So off we went together, Americans of every color and enormous Vikings alike, in search of our intended British Pub. It was conveniently close to the waterfront, as British Pubs are prone to be.

At that particular time in history, it was nearly impossible for an American sailor to walk into a bar in his full Crackerjack uniform in most any country on the planet, and not have Bruce Springsteen's "Born in the USA" cranked up to full volume. We became accustomed to it, and took it as a compliment, which was usually the spirit in which it was intended.

That night, one particular subject of the British crown, after tipping a few pints of warm lumpy beer, came to the conclusion that he didn't like Bruce Springsteen. He decided to share the sentiment by shouting at the top of his voice:

"Bruce Springsteen is a fookin' Wanker." Now I had no idea what a Wanker was, but I was pretty sure it was bad, so I responded, also at high volume:

"Well so is the fucking Queen." That is when the entire bar went from Jolly and Loud to tense and dead silent. What came next was predictable, except that being British, they were inherently civilized, and perfectly polite. Rather than break out into a free for all riot, it was kept between myself and the hardened badass career military bastard who chose me as his *punching bag* (101) that night. He kept knocking me down, and I kept getting up, over and over again until I could get up no more, but I was not about to give him that satisfaction. It was there and then, on that beer soaked floor, that I learned yet another important maritime life lesson that I carried with me forever. Quoting Monty Python in a British Pub, regardless of the situation, will make you friends. As I lay there, bleeding, and unable to rise, the smug arrogant bastard smirked at me and went to walk away, I shouted at him in my best Monty Python accent,

"Oh I see, running away ay, YOU YELLOW BASTARD COME BACK! I'LL BITE YOUR BLOODY LEGS OFF" Every Brit in the place roared with laughter, and suddenly I was lifted from the floor and placed in a position of honor at the bar, with a collection of thick dark malted beverages arrayed in front of me. Never pass up an opportunity to play the Monty Python card in a British Pub.

Culture Clash

The role of cultural mediator.

"The pessimist complains about the wind; the optimist expects it to change; the realist adjusts the sails." – William Arthur Ward

Achieving the rank of Captain, changes things considerably. Seldom was I required to practice the maritime skills I had been focused on developing for so long. Politics and legal compliance, negotiating and mediating were now my day to day routine.

In rare moments I was called to be the expert Mariner, when the level of expertise required was high. The Captain drives the ship when the channel gets narrow. The only way to dock a ship is to firmly believe that you can, and that belief takes a lifetime to develop. Those moments came mostly in the middle of the night, when an inexperienced watch officer would get in over his head and call me at 2AM.

Stumbling groggily to the Bridge, I would have to assess a complex situation by looking at the cluttered RADAR, and the thick crowd of lights on the horizon, each one another ship wanting to collide with me; sifting through the torrent of stuttering nonsense, as the nearly panicked young watch officer attempts to explain the situation as he or she understood it. By the time the Captain is called, a crisis is at some stage of development and something needs to be done immediately.

That is actually what I lived for, as Captain. By the time I got to that lofty height, complex maneuvers, docking and complicated high traffic situations were old friends. I had mastered these skills and wouldn't have stuck it out long enough to become Captain if I didn't enjoy it.

Military Sealift Command ships are owned by the Navy, but operated fully by civilian contract Mariners. We were working in the Persian Gulf and had business in Dubai. It was my responsibility to get the ship provisioned and fueled, repairs arranged, crew changes effected and all the other mundane inport routine of the ship, all in the context of doing business in an Arab culture. It was also my job to attend to the desires, and meet the objectives of the vessels owner, the US Navy.

No two cultures could be more opposed than the culture of the US Military, and the culture of Middle Eastern business. When a ship arrives in port, it is a bustling chaotic beehive of activity. There are fuel barges waiting to come alongside, and sewage trucks waiting to pump, food deliveries, crew waiting to come aboard, with their counterparts on the ship anxious to get relieved and go home. None of this begins until the Captain or one of his officers engages in the business transactions needed to arrange these *necessaries* (102). The Captain merely represents the owner, and usually he or she is the sole representative of the owner.

When it is a Navy owned ship, the Navy often sends military officers to meet with the Captain, and perhaps join the meeting with the local functionaries to add more fun to the already hectic procedures. Contrary to popular opinion, doing business with Arabs is an extremely civilized affair. You sit down, you offer them tea, and you spend a few moments in polite discourse, asking them how business is, and how their families are.

Each meeting starts, with the parties treating each other as people before getting down to business. Over the years I got to know some of these businessmen and we became friendly. I genuinely enjoyed hearing the stories of their businesses and families, and hearing of the trajectory of their children's lives over the years as they grew up. It is an inherently civilized practice, and a great way to do business. Likely the practice was as old as history, and I would imagine, and we would discuss, how Sinbad himself may have conducted business at this very waterfront, in much this very manner.

When Military officers have business to conduct, especially when they are principles in the transaction, in this case the owners of the ship, and the purchasers of the goods and services, they are all business. They storm into a room and get right down to business, forsaking the niceties and norms. This inevitably leads to disastrous effects. That type of abrupt behavior is considered extremely rude, the cultural equivalent of entering a business meeting and farting with volume and vigor, then hocking up a loogie and spitting it on the floor.

The Arabs, following the norms of their politesse, would not storm out of the room or loudly announce their indignation, they would continue to sip their tea, but a cold icy frost would develop in the relationship. Their eyes would narrow and get steely, and when the meeting was over things would start going wrong. Prices would rise. Shipments would be late. The wrong items would arrive. Everything that could go wrong, would go wrong, and there is no explaining to the Navy that it was all due to an overzealous mid-ranking officer who was just a little too abrupt for Arab sensibilities.

The Navy officers were not intentionally trying to be rude by any means, most of them would sooner fall on a sword than intentionally offend. Military culture has its own set of civilized niceties, but military business is a much different affair than commercial business and it is approached much differently. This was one of those places where the teeth didn't mesh. That is one of the reasons that the Navy hires civilians to run these ships for them. It was up to me to prevent the clash of cultures and the inevitable negative consequences that would ensue.

THERE I WAS

So there I was... in my office with my most senior officers, the morning before pulling into port. Were we discussing the navigational plan for transiting a busy waterway? No, that was routine by now. Were we discussing anti-terrorism measures and security? That was a different meeting for later. No, we sat there around the conference table outlining our strategy to keep the Navy away from my office for a full ten minutes while I engaged the locals in the accepted cultural pre-business activities. The Chief Engineer was there, and my Chief Mate, as well as my other deck officers and the AB's who would be standing the gangway watch.

The Chief Engineer had a lot of work being done, we had to fuel, and there was steel work and mechanical contractors, and it was a complicated ballet to get it all scheduled and done on time. So together we schemed to develop an elaborate plan to run interference on our naval bosses and overlords for the sake of getting their work done, despite them.

The Chief Mate was going to wait on the pier for the Navy contingent to arrive. The deck gang would be putting on a show of rigging safety nets around the gangway to provide an excuse to state that the gangway wasn't ready just yet. All Arab businessmen would be directed immediately to the Captain's office.

If the Navy noticed an Arab using the gangway when they were told it was not ready. The Navy would be told that the vessel was still under quarantine and only port officials were allowed to board. They would also note to the Navy that the Arab officials didn't care about the ships safety rules, and that they too could use the gangway if they insisted, but it was against Military Sealift Command policy to use it until it was rigged safe. Rare is the Navy officer who would violate a safety protocol without a valid reason.

The Navy would then be subjected to rigorous security screening at the gangway; careful inspection of ID's, detailed log entries. They were military officers serving in the Middle East during a war, they would not be bothered by access point security, and would actually be impressed at the precautions we mere civilians were taking for their vessel. From there, the gangway watch would respond to the Chief Mate's question of my whereabouts by telling them all that I was with the Chief Engineer in the Engine Room discussing the repair.

The Chief Engineer would be in the Engine Room, and one of his Assistant Engineers would be in the control room to meet the Chief Mate and the contingent of Navy Officers. The Assistant Engineer would confirm that the Captain and Chief Engineer were in the Engine Room and page the Chief Engineer. The Chief Engineer would take his sweet time responding, and then call the control room from the intercom located near a particularly loud *piece* (103) of *equipment* (104) and make a high volume unintelligible show of responding. Followed by another delay as the Chief Engineer eventually wandered up, only to tell them all that the Captain left for the Bridge. Attempts would be made to engage the officers in conversation to delay them further.

The Chief Mate would then take them to Bridge via the most circuitous route possible, having arranged his deck crew in various tasks and work around the ship that would necessitate detours. The Navigator would be on the Bridge, and inform everyone that he was indeed expecting the Captain any minute now. This would create another open ended delay that hopefully was ended by the Captain calling and asking them to all join him in his cabin with the properly prepared port agents. Should the naval officers become impatient, the plan was to page the Captain, who would milk that delay for all it was worth.

At any time in this charade the Captain could contact the Chief Mate by radio to abort the delaying tactics and bring about the meeting of minds. This rigmarole became routine, and we had several plans with different approaches, in case the same officers arrived on subsequent trips. Code words were established, to inform the players that 'plan B' was being launched. The Chief Mate would have "Mr. Kagen" paged if we needed to shift to plan B.

It was a lot of effort, indeed, to avoid a simple social faux pas, but absolutely necessary. It was a small price to pay, and was one of the few operations we participated in that allowed us to engage our creativity. We had tried talking to the officers that arrived, to explain the formalities, but Navy officers when dealing with Merchant officers, like to do more talking than listening. We were lowly civilians, and many of them did not agree with the idea that we were running Navy ships.

So we composed these elaborate ruses, as part of our duty and obligation to conduct the business of the ship, and the results were always infinitely smoother operations, with an added entertainment value. Like my dad always used to tell me: "Just shut up and get it done"

The 5%

You call this a storm?

> *"The fishermen know that the sea is dangerous and the storm terrible, but they have never found these dangers sufficient reason for remaining ashore."— Vincent Van Gogh, Painter*

Life aboard ship is 95% boredom, 5% sheer terror. Every maritime career is peppered with stories, or moments where some poor swab was faced with death, dismemberment, marriage, or some other heinous catastrophe and is left with a new perspective into his or her own character. Everyone is likely to face such moments in their lives, Mariners just face them more frequently.

In the old Navy, where I was baptized in fire and salt water, your shipmates would have been testing you from the moment you arrived on ship to see how you might behave when the explosions started and the lights went out. They might actually have placed you in some real or constructed danger to take your measure. Things are kinder and gentler now, and crews must wait for real danger to arise to take stock of the greenhorns. No more, "Man-up you Pussy, the safest direction to drag that hose is towards the fire, you might actually survive that, if you head back this way you are sure to die." Those days are past, but these stories remain.

These dangers are often the experiences that forever shape the character of the Mariners who face them. How a man responds to fear is character defining, and at some point in their career Mariners will likely stare death in the face and be forced to account. In the face of such danger, the course of my life changed, and revealed to me that I was meant for a Maritime existence. These moments, this 5% of sheer terror, can easily become the defining moments of your life, or just exciting interludes that punctuate the boredom. Like this moment...

I was riding what is known as a product tanker at the edge of the tropical latitudes. Product tankers, unlike the behemoth black oil tankers filled with thick viscous crude, were smaller and loaded with more reasonable quantities of lighter refined cargoes. Chemicals, light oils, gasoline, even vegetable oils moved in these handy 'pocket' tankers. We were moving Naphtha, a highly volatile, somewhat explosive chemical used in making mothballs and presumably other things as it is hard to imagine that 40,000 tons of mothballs ever existed, much less was needed for future production of more mothballs.

The tropical latitudes extend to about twenty three and half degrees either side of the equator. The sun shines at its most direct in these latitudes, always directly

126

above, 12 hours each day, every day. The relentless sunshine boils the humid air making it rise and cool, releasing its heat and moisture into towering black thunderheads. All that solar energy, moving air, and giant clouds, along with the always kinetic mother ocean combine to express their massive potential energy in a variety of interesting ways.

One of the more interesting ways is a rare type of lightning called "ball lightning". It is, as described, a fiery ephemeral ball of electricity floating in mid-air like an electrically charged phantom. Lightning of any kind is alarming to a tankerman, especially on tankers filled with highly refined 'aromatics', the light oils and products prone to producing explosive vapors. Ball lighting adds a new dimension of terror to the already terrifying prospect of a lightning strike. The rarity of the phenomena adds to the effect, as precious few have even heard of it, much less experienced it. On that day we were attacked by it.

We were heading south through these meteorologically active latitudes and it was a strange and ominous day. Towering thunderheads loomed large and threatening at every point of the compass, in otherwise bright and sunny skies. The air had that sharp odor it takes prior to rain, but with a faint sulfurous smell like the fury of brimstone escaping the heated confines of hell. There was no rain, some of the thunderheads looked ready, and even had tendrils of scud dangling beneath them, but it did not appear to make it all the way to the water, seemingly evaporating before completing its fall to earth. This left these mighty Cumulo-Nimbus clouds looking like giant angry jelly fish, drifting with the currents, awaiting their prey. There was lightning everywhere, beneath the clouds, between the clouds, far away from the clouds, coming from above, from the side, even starting at the water and shooting up.

Thunder rumbled or exploded in the distance, or sometimes directly above like the mocking laughter of an angry god. I was on watch on the Bridge, a young AB, with my Mate, a sharp witted acerbic man whose skill with dangerous liquid cargoes was as exceptional as his lack of social skills with fellow humans. The Captain and Chief Engineer were there on the Bridge as well, serene and commanding, pointedly acting calm and un-disturbed by the numerous gigawatts of electrical Naphtha detonating fireworks erupting all around us.

Suddenly it just appeared in front of us, slightly off the starboard bow, maybe a hundred feet in the air. It hovered a moment, glowing and hissing, and floating erratically. It twitched and jerked as if on the strings of a bad puppeteer, and then it seemed to take notice of us. It transitioned immediately from its random erratic motions to a sudden and drastic motion directly toward the ship. We all stopped breathing, and watched the giant ball of flame advance towards us, and settle on the foremast. It stayed there a moment, a hissing and crackling surreal ball of plasma,

127

and then slowly began to sink towards the forward tank tops. We each hissed in a sharp breath as we watched the enormous fuse settling slowly down the mast towards *our oblivion* (105). 40,000 tons of a gasoline like hydrocarbon awaited just feet below, with the explosive potential of a small nuclear bomb.

Slightly past the halfway point down the mast, it just popped with a sharp crack, and a quick change of color before disintegrating and fading away forever. No trace left but the stench of sulfur and fear lingering behind. The ever unflappable Captain nudged the Chief Engineer with his elbow and deadpanned: "You don't see that every day."

Part 4 – Into the drink

"The sea is the same as it has been since before men ever went on it in boats." - *Ernest Hemingway*

The hand of Poseidon

Wrong Side of the Hull

> *"There are places and moments in which one is so completely alone*
> *that one sees the world entire." Jules Renard"*

Santo was back in no time, the cadets had had enough of old man sea stories and losing money at pool and were happy to move on.

"Welcome back, everything ok?"

"Everything fine." (Ebryting pine) "Some local bigshot want special treatment, he need to see the owner. I give him the best Nipa on the beach, a free drink and send the prettiest girls to wait on him, now he is happy he the most important man on the beach."

"So where was I?"

"You were telling me why you suddenly want to run ashore and hide from big bad ocean, like a little girl."

"Puck you, you pilthy mudderpukker."

"See, you belong here, you sound like native Pinoy."

"I am too handsome to be Pinoy."

"HA! You no smart enough to be Pinoy, now tell me your story."

"Ok, ok, relax, back to the story... I got the word that it was my crew that was manning the boat that day, and I was the sternhook. So I set my affairs in order and mustered up at the boat deck. The squadron was spread out from one horizon to the next, couldn't even see them through the rain and mist. We had to do some personnel transfers, move a few people around from ship to ship, in heavy seas and poor visibility." I signaled to Lucy to bring more whiskey.

"Billy Bob was the Coxswain, fresh from training and had never driven that boat outside the harbor. Art was the Bowhook, and Lt. Pike was the Boat Officer, so they at least tried to balance out the rookie Coxswain and Sternhook with some salt."

Santo responded "Big Art from (prum) Arkansas, whatever (wot-ebber) happen to him?"

"I haven't seen him in more than 20 years, if I had to guess he is still trying to make Chief, or was stabbed in a bar fight."

"He liked to fight (pite)."

I continued, "He could drive the hell out of a boat too. Remember, he didn't like to lower the boat on the brake, he said the flywheel would govern the speed of the fall, and the brake was for emergencies, and lowering the boat carefully and slowly in a controlled fashion was not how it was designed to be lowered. Fucking maniac. So we fell fast, bounced down the side of the ship and hit the water hard, but we did manage to clear the falls with our heads still on our shoulders.”

“Bill had zero experience in open ocean boat ops, none. The ship maneuvered to create a nice sheltered lee, but the second we came out from under the lee, it got nasty. All of a sudden, it was just us and the big ocean, all alone. We were headed for the Dutch ship first. She was out there a few miles away, just barely visible on the horizon, blowing her damn horn to give us direction. We had to drop off an Engineer who was going home early for some emergency. The Dutch Navy is union, so they were always heading into port early, ahead of everyone else. It was against their union rules to run low on Heineken. So they would get to enjoy the luxuries of French Normandy while the rest of the squadron slaved on in naval servitude.”

“The seas were tall enough that we could only see the Dutch ship when we crested a wave. Up the back side of a wave to the crest, where the horizon would greet us and gift us with bearings and a peek at our destination and the other ships in the formation. Then over the top, back into the trough and up the next wave. It was a careful process, and cresting a wave in heavy seas requires some skill, and momentum. Too fast, and the ride gets rough, slamming or pitching dangerously. Too slow, and the seas can overtake you, and you get ‘pooped’, with a wave breaking across your stern.”

“That is exactly what happened to us, Santo. You can imagine how uncomfortable that can be for the Sternhook. The boat crested a breaking wave, and didn’t have enough speed to shoot clear of the whitewater, we got caught in the curl, and Neptune’s cold hand reached out and plucked me off of that boat and into that icy cold brine before I had any idea of what had happened.” I stopped to sip my whiskey, and remember the moment, the roaring white shocking cold punch in the face. It was like it was happening again.

“One moment, we are climbing what seemed to be a too steep, too green wave, and the next moment, I’m thrashing about in a turbulent watery hell. My fine Navy Kapok life vest served me well, and I popped up just in time to see my boat cresting the next wave, steaming away from me. I was the sternhook, I could see every one of them, but they were all looking ahead, I had no idea if they had even noticed I was gone.”

“As I was drifting out there, completely at the mercy of wind and seas, all I could think of was all the different ways there are to die out there, all the close calls that I had survived. I always imagined I would die in a bar fight, or in a fire. I never expected to slowly freeze to death, bobbing in the ocean like a bottle with a note in it. It’s like my dad always used to tell me: ‘Boy... you’re fucked now’”

131

The Panamaniac

For your life

> *Out of sight of land the sailor feels safe. It is the beach that worries him." – Charles Davis*

There are many journeys in life, and they all have a beginning, and they all end. As one journey ends, often another begins. The journey of boyhood ends, if all goes well, as the journey of manhood begins. Some journeys can change your life so profoundly that they forever shape every voyage that follows.

I left that Grand Cayman anchorage with freshly cut teeth, proud to have withstood the rigors of my first solo watch. Our mission was to escort our Battleship to Panama, where she would transit the canal without us, meet another escort on the Pacific side and venture to the exotic Far East. We poor Atlantic escorts would have to settle for a brief visit in the port of Cristobal in Colon, Panama. Cristobal, like most of Central America in those days, was a fairly lawless place. It was an industrial port city on the Atlantic side of the Panama Canal, and was one of the original rail heads that bridged oceans prior to the digging of the Canal.

This would be my first real foreign port. We had stopped in Key West and had some hearty adventures there, and while it was certainly exotic, it was still most definitely the good old US of A. We visited St. Thomas in the US Virgin Islands, and Puerto Rico, which are technically US Territories, nearly foreign, sort of Caribbean lite, but US nonetheless.

So when we docked at the gritty commercial waterfront in Cristobal, we could tell the difference. The US Navy has a practice of 'briefing' its sailors before releasing them onto some poor unsuspecting port. Important information is passed along to the crew, such as local customs, exchange rates, what happens to drunk sailors when they get arrested, what diseases they are likely to contract depending which high risk behavior they engage in, and most importantly: *the areas that are forbidden* (106).

The Navy knows where the bad neighborhoods are, and sets them off limits to the sailors on liberty. In Cristobal, some particular Barrio was specifically identified and placed strictly off limits, anyone caught violating would be punished and restricted to the ship on future port visits.

The forbidden zones are high crime areas, filled with illicit drug use, prostitution and violence; all the things that sailors like best. So it was kind of the Navy to spare the crew the time and effort of searching for these things and conveniently point us in the right direction.

133

THERE I WAS

I was invited to accompany a group of deck seaman for a night on the town. It was a gang of rabble rousing, tattooed, thrill seeking adventurers who were not planning on visiting the local museums or touring the classical Spanish architecture. In fact, our destination was none other than the forbidden Barrio. There were six of us, including one particularly rambunctious swashbuckler that I will call Flynn. Flynn had elevated bar fighting to an art form. It was he that had made my very first port of call in Key West such a memorable experience.

Key West is the last Island in the Florida Keys, just 90 miles north of Cuba. It was for the most part, like most of the keys, a sleepy little tropical Island. It is in fact the original Margurittaville, home to the great maritime troubadour Jimmy Buffett, and previously a favorite haunt of Ernest Hemmingway. Key West has a very large gay population, and in those days, it was one of the few places where gay people could be comfortably and safely openly homosexual.

We were there on Halloween, and there is nothing quite so entertaining and fun as a gay Halloween parade in a tropical paradise. There weren't many bars on that tiny Island, but we tried to visit them all. Flynn and I were out with a small group, and when I ran out of money and started to head back to the ship, Flynn refused to allow it. He said that the rest of the night was on him. Unbeknownst to me, Flynn had also nearly run out of money, but being somewhat enlightened and in no way homophobic, he led us into the gay bars, where you could be certain to get a least one or two drinks bought for you.

He made sure to inform the men buying us drinks that we were straight, but that never mattered. Flynn made sure to leave after the second drink, informing us that after two, you were unfairly leading them on, and were inviting someone to make a pass at you.

After getting good and liquored up, and spreading good cheer throughout the island, Flynn decided it was high time that we started chasing women, and so to the strip club we went. We found what we were looking for at the end of a long alley that opened up into a small courtyard, where the entrances to three bars were located. One of the bars was a local strip club. It was probably named the "*Pirates Cove* (107)".

Whether it was the Halloween festivities, the out of the way location, or the heterosexual nature of the place; it was surprisingly empty. We entered into a wide room filled with empty round tables that stood between us and the stage, with the bar along one side to our right. No customers, just the bartender and a small handful of burly bouncers who seemed surprised to see us. We ordered up a round of drinks, sat down and wondered if the management had remembered to schedule the naked women.

Fortunately, a naked woman did appear. She mounted the stage dramatically, with no music, strutting purposefully out on stage, the bar dropping silent as the

THERE I WAS

sound of her three inch pumps clacked across the stage. She made as if to walk past the pole, but at the last minute shot her arm out grabbing the pole, and spun around dramatically as Cyndi Lauper's "She Bop" thundered on through the massive speakers. We erupted in applause, cheering with that crazy, maniacal abandon that naked women arouse in a band of sailors on liberty. The stripper, who was probably named Candi, in addition to being extraordinarily beautiful, was also in fact an excellent dancer, she had obviously had some actual dance training. She was artistically interpreting Cyndi Lauper's song about female masturbation as only a stripper could, and to say it was a memorable experience, would be a profound understatement.

On top of being a swashbuckler, or perhaps as part of his swashbuckling repertoire, Flynn was quite a ladies man. Candi, with her artful expression of erotic self-love, and her glitter speckled nipples, had invoked the swashbuckler in Flynn and moved him to dance. Not being content to dance alone, on the floor, Flynn decided that there was room on the stage for one more. Under normal circumstances, if a patron were to mount the stage, the dancing stops quite abruptly, but Flynn's gymnastic leap to the stage, subsequent cartwheel landing into a full split seemed to impress her. She decided, to the dismay of the bouncers, that she now had a worthy dance partner.

For a brief moment, there on the pole, the two of them spun about, gyrating at one another in a magnificent physical display of sexual attraction. Perhaps it was the boredom, perhaps it was the quality of the performance, but the music played on, and bouncers just seemed amused. That is, until Flynn's shirt came off, at that point, the game changed. The music stopped, the lights came on, and the angry shouting began. Three enormous bouncers raced across the room at the stage.

In true swashbuckler fashion, Flynn grabbed Candi by the waist, dipped her slightly, and planted a giant wet kiss on her, before leaping off the stage, onto the nearest table. From there, Flynn ran across the tabletops towards the door. It was truly amazing to watch, even the bouncers stopped a moment to admire the feat, but a moment only, and soon they too were racing towards the door. Our drunken haze was lifting, and the realization that Flynn was being pursued by local heathens came upon us and we too made a B-line to the door, just behind the bouncers. We emerged into the alley to see Flynn, with three bouncers hot on his tail, running across the courtyard to the alley.

But swashbucklers don't flee their enemies, and as soon as he reached the entrance to the alley, Flynn stopped abruptly and turned to meet his pursuers. It was a magnificently tactical move, the alley was narrow enough that they could only come at him from the front, one or two at a time, depending on the extent of the individual bouncer's level of steroid abuse. Flynn was prone to wearing a cowboy belt, complete with an enormous buckle the size of a dinner plate, the sole purpose of which was to even the odds in just such a situation. The belt was off with a practiced flourish, and whipping about with the well drilled flair of a set of Bruce Lee Nunchuks.

Right at that moment, just seconds after Flynn turned and faced his attackers, belt buckle a-flyin', several things happened all at once; at the far end of the alley out on the street, the shore patrol arrived (unbeknownst to Flynn), and back at the our end of the alley, a small platoon of bouncers erupted into the courtyard from the other two bars. They paused a moment, looking back and forth between my pack of drunken sailors, and three of their brethren engaging a maniacal hellion wielding a homemade flail like some crazed Viking/Cowboy hybrid. We could see the indecision in their eyes, to assist their friends would put us behind them, we were likely involved, or about to be, but not yet actively enough to warrant any action, and we all stood there in an odd Mexican standoff while Flynn hooted, howled and laughed as he wielded his mighty belt buckle of death.

The shore patrol were not nearly so indecisive. They thundered down the alley, Billy clubs drawn, and seeing a crazed drunk threatening a gaggle of bouncers with a weapon, they used their keen Shore Patrol senses and training to determine that they had stumbled upon a drunken sailor incident.

Shore Patrol exists almost exclusively to deal with drunken sailor incidents, and they know exactly what to do with a drunken sailor... (Ear-lie in the morning). Soon the alley was filled with them. They swept in, subdued Flynn, inserted themselves between the bouncers and Flynn and assured everyone that the matter was handled. The bouncers were reluctant to let Flynn's antics go unpunished, and pressed down the alley towards the van as Shore Patrol were carting Flynn away. The other bar bouncers started moving that way to support their friends, which alarmed the Shore Patrol, and motivated us to enter the alley as well.

The bouncers soon realized that the near even ratio of bouncer to Shore Patrol did not account for my crew of additional drunken sailors and found themselves trapped in alley, surrounded by the US Navy. The Shore Patrol noticed how the addition of drunken sailors had noticeably changed the aggressive demeanor of the bouncers and restrained their own ingrained response towards drunken sailors. As the entire show moved out of the alley into the bright lights of the street, the mounting chaos subsided, and the Shore Patrol managed to convince the bouncers to return to their bars, which were now completely without bouncer protection.

As a reward to us, for turning the tide with the bouncers, they elected not to beat us with Billy Clubs and throw is in the brig, and allowed us to proceed. Flynn was returned to the ship to face the music. Being broke, and having had enough adventure for one night, we also wandered back to the ship. Flynn would be facing

THERE I WAS

what was known in the Navy as "Non-judicial punishment" delivered at "Captain's Mast".

The Capt. had the authority to dole out various punishments, including fines, restriction to the ship, extra duty, etc. Mast was held the next morning, and of course Flynn was restricted to the ship, but the next day, Flynn apparently decided that the punishment was unfair and that there was swashbuckling yet to do. There is no swashbuckling, like shipboard swashbuckling, and so that evening at 5PM, when the crew was lining up at the gangway to go ashore, there was Flynn, not in his drab Navy dungarees ready for extra duty, but in full redneck regalia, complete with his lethal belt buckle.

The watch was well aware that Flynn was restricted to the ship, and had been expecting him to show up in work clothes ready for extra duty. So they were understandably surprised to see him preparing to leave the ship for a night of festivity. The gangway watch consisted of four people. The officer of the Deck, or OOD, the Petty Officer of the Watch, the Messenger of Watch, and the Roving Security patrol.

The messenger and roving security watch were sporting batons, and the POOW was armed with a pistol, more than enough juice to defend a narrow gangway against a belt buckle attack. The tensions rose on the gangway, and became physical as Flynn tried to force his way past the OOD, out came the belt buckle. Now Flynn was wise enough not to bring a belt buckle to a gun fight, and knowing full well the POOW could not leave his post at the gangway, Flynn scrambled up a ladder bolted to a nearby wall, up two stories to the "02 Level" with the watch close behind, and a few spectators for good measure. The watch, which was now reinforced with the Master at Arms, and few other members of the duty section, now had Flynn surrounded at the rail, two stories above the gangway, his belt-buckle keeping them at bay.

The gangway watch has to keep a Watchstander in sight of the gangway at all times. The gangway being outdoors, was appropriately fitted with a large awning, which was attached to two stanchions at one end, and to the superstructure of the ship at the other. It was simply a rectangular frame with a thick blue tarp stretched out within, mounted horizontally and flat in the small area between the superstructure and the gangway. Flynn was above that very awning as the Watch closed in on him, and with one final twirl of the belt buckle above his head, and hearty rebel yell for effect, he vaulted over the rail, and onto the awning below, rolling off of it, directly onto the gangway.

This was no small feat as the both the awning and the gangway were narrow, and missing would have landed him in the water between the ship and the pier. The gangway is not exactly an even surface, and is covered with lateral cross members

137

THERE I WAS

for traction. Flynn landed poorly, and apparently turned an ankle, and his dramatic escape was rendered somewhat less dramatic as his dash to freedom was reduced to a rapid limp to freedom. The Watch, and we spectators, simply stared, slack jawed, as he fled down the pier at full hobble. He returned a few hours later, tail tucked neatly between his legs, pale and sweaty from the pain in his ankle.

Flynn's restriction lasted through the next two port visits, and our adventures on St. Thomas and in Puerto Rico were not nearly so eventful without him, but now in Panama he was free again. So there we were, standing on the pier at the base of the gangway on a decrepit old cargo dock in a third world port city on one of the busiest waterways on earth. We walked along the waterfront, six of us, an equal mix of us young bucks with some crusty old salts. We were led by a tall, lanky, seasoned old Boatswains Mate whose name was Art. He had been in the Navy for over 15 years, and should have been much higher in rank, but his hard drinking, bar brawling ways had earned him more than one demotion.

The docks were a dirty dingy place, rat infested and rusty, smelling of diesel fuel and garbage, but compared to what lay beyond the gate it was paradise. There were taxis and vans for hire waiting at the gate, we climbed in and told the driver to bring us to the Barrio. He literally stopped, and turned around to try and dissuade us, he said that most cabbies won't even enter the Barrio, and we would be making a very dangerous and foolish mistake to go there, but we were in no mood for good advice and to the Barrio we proceeded.

The stark urban poverty of those streets was like nothing I had ever imagined. I had been in poor neighborhoods in Boston, but they were wealthy estates by comparison. The roads we travelled were unpaved, open sewers. The buildings were rickety shacks, made of cobbled shipping pallets and corrugated steel, tiny and crammed full with entire extended families. Half naked children played in the filth, and alongside the road, people filled plastic containers with the filthy sewage and drainage that stagnated in the ditches. It was like walking into a late night CARE commercial only with the disgusting stench and oppressing humid heat to bring it home. The people just stared at us with either blank expressions, or open anger and hate.

The bar had a small sign with a badly painted picture of a duck, and the name "Ojo Dorado". It had a dirt floor and oil lamps for light, and it went instantly quiet as we entered. There were a dozen or so locals in the place, mostly men, each with a short machete hanging from his belt. As we entered, our enormous Arkansan Art, strode up to the bar, and bought a round for the house, softening the mood slightly, not as much as we would have hoped, but certainly enough for the locals to suffer our presence for the moment.

THERE I WAS

Art was a good natured country boy, always sporting a half grin, and ready with a joke.

"That ought to buy us about half an hour." He announced to no one in particular. He warned us casually:

"Watch your back in here boys, these fellers will kill y'all for your boots". He ambled across the bar with his easy cowboy stride, and found us a nice corner table close to the door, continuing his lecture on how to drink in a dangerous bar.

"Keep your back to the wall, and your eye on the locals, and ALWAYS know where the door is." At the time, I didn't realize how important that advice was, or how I would carry it with me forever after.

The cabbie that brought us here, had promised us cold beer and women, and we were not disappointed. The "Cerveza" was indeed "Frio", and soon after we settled into our table in the far corner, several working girls emerged from the back room. Before long, someone arrived with a boom box and some bootleg pirate Cassettes and the room was filled with sounds of Madonna, Michael Jackson, Oingo Boingo, Van Halen, and Prince. Cerveza Frio, Chiquita's and Musica, life was good.

Several beers into the night, I was getting quite friendly with the lovely little Chiquita that was sitting on my lap, and I was nearly buzzed enough to consider her generous offer to adjourn to the back room, when Flynn's swashbuckling ways interfered, changing my perspective on life forever.

I don't know what Flynn did, except that he upset one of the locals enough to motivate him to violence, which is what Flynn did best really. The difference this time, was that we were not in a strip club in Key West, or a roadhouse in Jacksonville FL, we were in a dank little dirt floored bar in the third world surrounded for miles by the starkest poverty on earth. Every one of us had more money in our pockets than these people earned in a year. The majority of the men in this bar would gladly kill us just for sport. But most significantly, every single one of them had a 12–18 inch machete hanging from their belt, that is they did right up until that moment, when they went from their belts, into their hands.

We were sitting at a big round table, Flynn was sitting next to me, and both of us with our chairs turned out a way so as to be facing the room. I was very focused on the gorgeous little seniorita on my lap, and my attention was drawn away suddenly by the sharp solid "thud" of a machete being slammed into the table. One of the locals had taken a dead on overhand shot with said machete, straight at Flynn's forehead. Flynn had the presence of mind to divert the blow to the side, it no doubt not being the first time someone had aimed a hand weapon at his head, though it was likely the first edged weapon to be so aimed.

My head snapped up at the sound, I looked up to see the knife buried in the table, a local standing in front of me, with a bug eyed Flynn still holding his wrist. I

139

THERE I WAS

watched as Flynn's expression went from surprised fear to rage in the blink of an eye, and he let loose with a blood curdling roar as he grabbed his 90 pound assailant and lifted him over his head. That is when all hell broke loose.

Suddenly, everyone in the bar was moving all at once. No less than a dozen locals seemed to be converging on our table in unison.

My sweet little seniorita evaporated like a puff of smoke, and as I turned to scan the bar, I saw a mob of angry machete wielding Panamanians surging across the room at a dead run. By the time I got to my feet, one of them had closed the distance and decided I was his business. He swung that machete like a sword in a long sweeping horizontal arc at my head, with a determined look of murder in his eyes. I leaned back just in time, and felt the tip of it graze my nose.

This was for real. This was no gathering of suburban punks in an alley behind the gym fighting for bragging rights, not some scuffle with bouncers, or a joust with Marines, these little unwashed fuckers were trying their hardest to remove my head from my body. I stumbled back a step, and came up against the table. My attacker, over swung spinning himself around a little and took a moment to recover and turn, which gave me just enough time to grab the stool I had been sitting on.

Now I have seen hundreds of Westerns, and there are precious few westerns that don't have a bar room fight scene, and those scenes, like so many Hollywood bar room fight scenes, almost always involve a chair being broken over someone's head. The result is always the same, the chair shatters, the victim stumbles, maybe gets knocked out cold, if he is a good guy he recovers and fights on. The results are very predictable, but apparently the stools in the old west were of a far inferior quality. Not rock solid jungle hardwood like this stool.

I held the stool out in front of me while he hacked at it, and as I fended him off, I became more confident and more aggressive, and he started to back up. His air of enraged avenger began to melt into a more wide eyed look of concern and fear. Suddenly the unarmed, surprised gringo, was now a seriously pissed off, stool wielding giant twice his size, in peak military physical condition. I felt his fear and it was like fuel on a fire. He took another haymaker swing at me, when I swatted it away with the stool, it sent him off balance and spinning away from me. I took the opportunity to slam the little bastard with my stool. The stool didn't shatter. It didn't even dent or loosen up, hell it didn't even vibrate. It hit his head with a sickening crunching sound that I still hear in my nightmares, and sent him tumbling to the floor in a heap, with a horrific dent in his head. I stopped and stared at the motionless body on the floor for a moment... or an eternity, slack jawed, heart pounding, when Art grabbed my arm, and started screaming:

"Let's get the fuck out of here! Get to the door! Everyone Move!" He barked that out like only a career military Non-commissioned officer could. Loud, commanding,

140

THERE I WAS

business like, no-fear, just a rapid assessment of what needed to be done, and the wherewithal to scream it at the people who needed to do it. We scrambled to the door, Flynn had picked up a machete and had three of them backed into a corner when Art dragged him to the door. We made it to the street and Art kept barking orders. He had us formed into a platoon and running in step through the muddy streets of the barrio back towards the ship in seconds flat. I can only imagine what it looked like to the locals, six massive Americans running through the muddy streets of the barrio in formation singing, one of them still holding a bloody machete. "I don't know but I been told..." being followed by a giant cowboy screaming and 'YEE HAWing' at the top of his voice.

That was the first time I ever fought for my life. That moment the machete whizzed past my face, and the next 90 or so seconds that followed, are carved indelibly on my consciousness. I have fought for my life many times since, and every fight since that night I approach as if my life were at stake, since one never knows, and it would be foolish to assume otherwise. But that day was the last day I was ever surprised by the murderous intent of violent attack. Anyone mad enough to swing at you, could be mad enough to kill you, fighting is serious and lethal business

I never learned what Flynn had done, if anything, to provoke the attack. We didn't talk too much about it afterwards. In hindsight, just being there was provocation enough, throwing around money, flirting with their women, being loud obnoxious gringos in the barrio, hell even just wearing a belt buckle that ridiculous was reason enough I suppose. That was the second lesson, they don't need a reason to come after you.

In the third world in those days, the average yearly income was less than $300. Between us, we had ten times that much cash, not to mention jewelry, nice clothes, watches, and fancy redneck belt buckles. It even looked like a trophy. Imagine the thought of a payday of ten times your yearly income. Imagine how that might motivate you, even if you weren't desperate or hungry, or living in abject poverty. It was like an immense veil was lifted exposing a dark dangerous world that had previously only been a shadowy rumor. That day I was forever changed. That day, in a dark little bar in the Barrio, under flickering oil lamps, I realized that everything I thought I knew about the world was wrong. I approached everything differently from that moment forward.

141

The Rotterdam Shipyard

High above the Drydock

"Anyone can hold the helm when the sea is calm." Publilius Syrus

Gunter was a stern faced, rigid man, whose natural expression was a scowl. He had grey teeth and watery eyes behind round wire rimmed glasses. His florid complexion and bulbous nose were streaked with the rosaceous markings that described a life laden with beer, schnitzel and schnapps. Gunter, myself, and a ship rigger whose name was probably Jan were about to get lifted 100 feet in the air by a crane.

We had finished with the annual run to Thule Greenland at the top of the world and were ready for more arctic adventures, but ships need to rest too, especially ships in Polar service. So off to the shop we went for an oil change and tune up... so to speak.

Ships get serviced at shipyards. Most major services require dry-docking. Dry-docks are possibly the most industrial, and most dangerous environment on earth. This particular ship from the bottom of the keel to the main deck was probably 4-5 stories, and then the ship's superstructure, masts and cranes, rose up above the main deck another 10 stories or more. The ship was over 500 feet long, and about 95 feet wide. This giant machine essentially sits propped up within a huge box, lined on the edges with cranes the size of water towers, tall enough to loom over the entire ship, constantly driving back and forth with heavy loads suspended from their hooks.

The dock, the ship itself, and everything attached to it, is a machine. Everything is steel. Everything is heavy and its substance measured in tons. Always, there is some massive piece of steel, 10 tons or more, dangling from a wire over your head. Or being suspended in place, high above, as some welder or rigger clinging to the ship like a spider attaches it to the superstructure, sending a rain of fiery hot slag cascading down to the deck below like a swarm of molten bees.

Needless to say, not the safest environment, and I came to the conclusion early in my career that the best way to survive a shipyard is to assume that the shipyard itself, and everyone in it, is trying their hardest to kill me. This may seem paranoid, but in a situation as dangerous as that, pure paranoia is perhaps the only mindset that will keep you alert enough to survive the hundreds of potentially lethal hazards that one will encounter every day.

THERE I WAS

This visit to the shipyard involved completely re-rigging the cranes, which meant replacing every inch of wire on all six cranes. There were three pairs of cranes on this ship mounted on tall masts between the cargo holds. Most of the cranes on this ship stowed vertically. That is to say, when not in use, the boom was raised as high as it would go, almost vertically, till it came to rest against the lower yardarm, where the crew would lash it to mast to secure it for sea.

Ship riggers spent all their time aloft. We would climb with them occasionally, but most of the aerial work was left to them. When climbing, we were required to use safety gear, harnesses, belaying lines, fall arresting gear etc. The riggers had no such requirements and could be seen high above the deck daily monkeying through the rigging like spiders, performing feats of acrobatic prowess that would leave the flying Wallendas breathless.

It took a few days to get all the cranes rigged, and once rigged, they needed to pass the inspection of some shipyard engineer, a white hat. Everyone in a shipyard wears a hardhat, and in most shipyards, the white hard-hats are high ranking people, like senior engineers, managers, inspectors etc., generally it meant a person who didn't get dirty. This white hat was the severe grim faced German whose name was probably Gunter, and he was as uptight as the riggers were relaxed.

The plan was that Gunter, Jan and myself would climb inside a crane 'basket' to inspect the crane rig from top to bottom. I was to bring a grease gun, and apply grease to the sheaves while we were up there. This basket was a steel cage about three feet wide by six feet long, just over three feet high, and open at the top. It had four sling points at the corners, and a special harness that would attach to the cargo hook to be lifted by the crane. The drydock crane operator would then lift the basket filled with people, high above the ship and drydock to inspect every inch of crane wire, sheave and boom. Perfectly normal thing to do in a shipyard, common sense notwithstanding.

The abruptness with which the crane operator jerked us aloft was our first indication that something was amiss. We all just sort of looked at one another and then at the crane operators booth, but the glare off the windshield and the distance made it difficult to see his bleary red eyes and unfocused gaze. Gunter was either barking into his radio or coughing up a hairball, he seemed angry, but he was a German engineer so that might very well have been his pleasant voice.

The crane operator started whipping us around with wild abandon, bouncing us off of various parts of the ships superstructure, and Gunter's furious sputtering grew more intense. At one point, as we were being lifted up and over the mast, we could hear the sound of the riggers below laughing at our plight above the din of Gunter's near hysterical screaming. We could almost hear Gunter's cholesterol saturated heart thundering in protest. As we passed over the next mast, the crane operator in a

143

drunken miscalculation coupled with the associated alcohol induced loss of reflex, didn't quite hoist the basket high enough as we slewed across the mast top. The bottom of the basket hit the cross top as it passed the small open platform at the top of the mast, tilting the basket over nearly onto the its side as it traversed.

Jan took the opportunity to bail out, and scrambled out of the basket onto the small platform at the top of the masthead as we passed. Gunter and I were not so lucky as to escape. The basket was getting battered, and was already dented badly. The sling points where the harness connected to the basket were starting to loosen up. I had a good grip on the wire, and felt that if necessary I could scramble up the sling pendant to the cargo hook if the basket started to break up from all the slamming about. My opportunity for escape came just a few moments later, and following Jan's example I abandoned the drunken carnival ride for the safety of a nearby scaffold as we passed close by.

Gunter's face was a bright red and he was frothing at the lips like a rabid drill sergeant as he watched me scramble to safety. At this point, everyone in the shipyard was now watching the show, and finally, someone either took the initiative, or heeded Gunter's impassioned pleas, and the basket suddenly jerked to a stop.

Gunter just dangled there as the basket swayed back and forth like a pendulum, still jabbering away at full volume, and he continued to scream into his radio as the basket was gently lowered to the deck. He stormed out of the basket like a man possessed. It was decided that in addition to a more sober crane operator, a newer, safer version of the basket would be used on the next attempt. One that was taller, chest height, much harder to fall out of, or escape from. I am not sure what irritated Gunter and the other white hats more, the drunken operator banging his human cargo about the superstructure, or Jan and I deciding to abandon the basket and take our chances elsewhere.

GENERAL QUARTERS

Buttercups and burn boxes

> *"It is not the ship so much as the skillful sailing that assures the prosperous voyage." – George William Curtis*

A half dozen or so of us stood in the rapidly rising water as the room slowly flooded. Water was shooting like a fire hose from burst pipes, and seeping in through cracked seams in the hull. More water was leaking in from the flooded space next door through the water–tight door that had been wrenched and warped enough to fail under the strain of all the water pressure building up on the other side.

We scrambled around as best we could, hammering wooden plugs into *holes and cracks* (108), closing valves, patching holes, but the water kept rising. We cobbled a large K-shaped shoring brace with heavy timbers against the leaking door to keep it from failing and spilling the watery contents of the adjoining room into ours. Both the space next to us, and the space above us were flooded. The water continued to rise, it was thigh deep now. That's when we heard the knocking in the space next door. There were people in there.

We tapped the walls to try and ascertain the level of water in that room. We tried screaming through the door, but heard nothing save the frantic tapping. We had to open that door to save our shipmates. We knocked down the heavy timbers that were holding the door closed and the door bulged towards us leaking water as it pressed up tightly against the watertight mechanism that was straining against the pressure. This made it obvious that there was more water on the other side than on ours.

We all held on tightly as we readied to open the door, preparing for the tidal wave that would follow as the water levels equalized. The door was a standard Navy watertight door, a series of mechanical linkages would rotate the metal levers, called 'dogs', out from the door frame onto wedges on the door face, squeezing the door's gasket into the 'knife edge' on the door frame, 'dogging it down' and making it water tight. The linkages all tied back to a lever arm that operated the dogs.

Our team leader stood by the door and pulled the lever arm, removing the dogs from the door, and stepped back as the thick steel door flung open ahead of a small tsunami of water that surged into the room. When it settled down, the water went from thigh deep to chest deep in an instant.

Meanwhile, just a few hundred feet away, in a different room, they were dealing with different set of problems. Another group of sailors were preparing to open another door, but instead of holding back water, this one was holding back fire.

THERE I WAS

There were six people, in full turnout gear, jammed into a tiny area at the access point to the burning room. Two hose teams, each with a Nozzleman and a Hoseman. The #1 hose team had the firefighting nozzle and was tasked with attacking the fire. The #2 hose team had a long four foot wand, called an applicator, which was angled at the end, attached to the nozzle, and created a shroud of fine mist that enveloped and protected the hose teams from the intense heat.

The "Access Man" laden with tools, stood at the door engaged in the careful process of opening the door and bridging the gap between raging inferno and staging area. The On Scene Leader (OSL) stood between the hose teams with a hand on each Nozzle man's shoulder, directing the actions of the entire team.

The door and wall were red hot, and the #1 hose was spraying the full force of the fire hose at the wall to cool it down. The salt water from the hose, flashed into steam instantly, turning the room into a searing hot wet sauna. The access man was hammering the wall to knock off the crusted salt and brine that was left when the water flashed to steam. The OSL shouted to his team

"STANDBY TO ACCESS THE SPACE, WATER OFF #1!" The team stopped cooling the hot bulkhead and shifted their positions, with the access man closest to the door, and the two hose teams with the OSL between them lined up at the door opening. The OSL shouted

"WATER ON #2!" The #2 Nozzleman pushed the bail on his nozzle and a thick fog of water vapor erupted from the applicator head, surrounding the accessman.

"CRACK THE DOOR!" Screamed the OSL. The accessman tried to muscle the lever on the door, but it was jammed from the heat. He pulled a hammer from his bag and began pounding the dogs till they relented. He reached up over his shoulder and grabbed the applicator with one hand, and the door handle with the other, and quickly cracked the door open six inches while simultaneously inserting the applicator head into the space, helping to beat back the intense heat. Black smoke filled the room.

"WATER ON #1!" The #1 Nozzleman opened his bail up to the spray setting

"#1 MOVE UP, ACCESSMAN GIVE US ANOTHER 12 INCHES!" The accessman pulled the door open another foot and flames, smoke and heat blasted from the opening. The #1 Nozzleman began moving the nozzle in a tight vertical figure eight pattern, beating the flames back. The OSL shouted to his team:

"STANBY TO ACCESS THE SPACE... NOW!" The accessman opened the door slowly as the #1 Nozzleman expanded his pattern into a tall vertical oval, playing water on the full area of the door as it widened open. The accessman got the door fully open, latched it securely, and backed away. Now for the critical task of stepping into a raging inferno.

THERE I WAS

"ENTER THE SPACE!" The team entered. The OSL was scribbling a brief symbolic shorthand on special message templates and handing them to a phone talker who lagged behind the action a few paces, and translated the symbols into Navy English and shouted the information into the sound powered head set.

"AT TIME 1422, TEAMS 1 AND 2 ENTERED SPACE 2-225-0-E, 5 MEN ENTERED THE SPACE"

This team had drilled together for months, 3-5 times per week for an hour or two, simulated fire, or flood, or damage. They knew every step, every procedure, and every protocol. They knew every square inch of their ship.

The hose teams had been selected from the sharpest sailors and the best performers. But a drill, is a drill, and it isn't searing hot, and there isn't an impenetrable haze of black smoke. They were surrounded by intense heat and a viscous greasy miasma of the byproducts of combustion, mixing painfully with the hot steam from the vaporized firefighting water. The #2 Nozzleman lost his nerve, dropped the hose and ran.

Back in the flooded space, now chin deep, the team had decided that the only way out was up. They knew that there was flooding above, but they had established communications with people above who said that the water was only waist deep. But in the space beneath the shorter members of the team had to hold on to pipes or angle irons in the overhead to stay above water. My good friend Mac was dangling from a pipe with one arm, the other arm swinging a hammer furiously at a plug in a burst pipe while the water erupting from the pipe sprayed into his scowling determined face. The only way out was up a ladder through a 'scuttle', a small round hatch just barely big enough for a man, if he wasn't too broad shouldered or fat.

The plan was to force open the scuttle against the weight of the water and then climb up against the flow of water like a sewer rat up storm drain. The strongest amongst us, a burly weightlifter named Jack, was directed to the top of the ladder, and then people arranged in line to follow. It was important to go in close succession, to help each other fight their way upstream. Right as Jake made it to the top of the ladder, and went to grab the wheel, all the water inside the ship took its toll, and the ship lolled heavily to port, throwing Jake off the ladder, and causing the water to slosh about, dislodging several sailors into the water.

The ship settled out at about a 10 degree list. The free floating seaman were recovered, and the evacuation resumed. Jake threw his formidable bulk into heaving the hatch scuttle open, and managed to get it flipped up, and a solid stream of water poured down. Jake squeezed his enormous bulk through the opening against the flow, and those behind him followed with the heavy force of the water beating down on the top of their heads.

THERE I WAS

Back up in the oven, the #2 Hoseman, keeping his head, moved forward to recover the nozzle. It was fortunate that it hadn't been the #1 nozzle that was dropped, as that one, without an applicator was delivering the full force of fire hose pressure, and lacking strong hands to guide and control it, would have whipped about like a rocket propelled bullwhip with an eight pound brass weight at the tip.

Down in the flooding space, the last of the sodden sailors emerged from the hole just as the ship shifted again, lolling over another 10 degrees. All the sailors managed to hold on, and keep their feet under them. When the ship finally settled, the flashing yellow light and loud buzzing signaled the end of the drill. The instructors walked into the space and the water began to rapidly drain out. The fires were shut down, and the teams backed out of the space. We had almost forgotten that it was a drill, it had been so lifelike.

The flooding drills had taken place in the three room "Buttercup" trainer. The entire building had been engineered to roll and shift at the whim of the controller. The building next door was one of several 'burn buildings'. The more life-like the training, the more effective it was. There is no way to know who will drop the hose and run until you put them in a burning room, and an actual emergency is not the time to be learning that.

The Navy has several "Damage Control" schools, and they are amazing and necessary parts of the sailor experience. That training starts in Boot camp and continues throughout a fleet sailor's career. That was one of many days spent on the fire grounds, learning how to cope with a runaway hose, or a burning liquid fire, or a "Boiling Liquid Evaporating Vapor Explosion" or BLEVE for short. One never forgets ones first vertical descent down a stair into a raging oil fire. Or how incredibly effective a blanket of firefighting foam is on a fuel or aircraft fire.

There is nothing more valuable than learning what it is like to run out of air in your breathing apparatus, when the consequences aren't a painful choking death. That day, (and the next) we did it all under the watchful eyes of the instructors before returning to our ship wiser, and likely burnt in more than one place. Most of us had the opportunity to use those skills at some point, fighting a real fire or two, and knew before going into those actual inferno's who among us was likely to panic and who likely to rise to the occasion and maybe save the day.

Part 5 – The Tipping Point

"A sea captain when he stands upon the bridge, or looks out from his deck-house, thinks much about God and about the world. Away in the valley yonder among the corn and the poppies men may well forget all things except the warmth of the sun upon the face, and the kind shadow under the hedge; but he who journeys through storm and darkness must needs think and think." - William Butler Yeats, The Celtic Twilight

In The Water

So There I was

> *"Every man must do two things alone; he must do his own believing and his own dying."* Martin Luther

"It was freezing cold, I was puking up salt water, there were waves and spray everywhere, in my face, in my mouth, and I was in that trough all alone. The boat had just crested the last wave, oblivious that I was gone. I was rising up on the next wave, and it was taking forever." I stopped. Santo was quiet. Even if he had never been there, he had imagined it before. It was every Mariner's worst nightmare. I added some ice to my whiskey, and swirled it around a little.

"When I came to the top of the next wave, they were still heading away. There was so much water in my eyes, I couldn't tell if they were scrambling, or what was going on in the boat, only that it was moving away from me. A big orange blur motoring away, taking my hope of survival along with it. I was alone, in the water, in the middle of the Atlantic. It suddenly just seemed perfectly quiet Santo, like all the roaring ocean had just completely quieted down, and I just accepted that I was living my last few minutes on earth."

Santo was quiet, sipping his whiskey and imagining or remembering what is like to be in the water as your boat motored away without you.

"It's funny what you think about Santo, at times like that. The strangest things come back to you. Things that changed your life mixed in with perfectly random and meaningless memories that you hadn't thought of in years. It is like time stands still, and your brain clicks on to fast forward, and just regurgitates every odd memory you have ever had."

OPEN OCEAN RIVERBOAT

Where Brown Water Meets Blue.

"The good seaman weathers the storm he cannot avoid, and avoids the storm he cannot weather." – Proverb

Usually the life of blue water Mariner is markedly different from that of a brown water Mariner. Those brave (or foolish) few who crew the blue water large ocean vessels generally work for months at a time, and in between ships are off for months at a time. The typical tour is four months working, four months ashore. The inland and coastal brown water rotations tend to be briefer, and more varied, two weeks on, two weeks off, or 30 day on, 30 days off, 10 and 10, or one week on, one off. Some even work a semi-normal schedule going home each night, or working a few long shifts each week.

I was primarily a blue water practitioner, but like many I did dabble in smaller craft. When I first got my Third Mates license, finally becoming a licensed officer, finding a job as a Third Mate on the unlimited tonnage ships was difficult. The unlimited tonnage class of license was the highest level in the licensing hierarchy, and many blue water officers felt that working on limited tonnage vessels was beneath them.

I had a mentor advise me to take any licensed job that I could get, so long as it advanced my career, or taught me a skill that would prepare me for the ultimate role of Unlimited Master. It was he that taught me that one could 'ship handle' a boat, and that if one was extremely careful in how one applied engine and rudder, doing so using a precise technique, then the boat would handle like a ship, and I would be developing my ship handling skills. This turned out to be true, and immensely useful in my career.

So I took a job on a 70' yacht, and was introduced to the wonderful world of both small craft, and specifically pleasure boating. My intent was to spend a summer on the yacht and dock and undock a few times every day, and get a few hundred under my belt, but the great food, gorgeous women, high living and ego building effect of being a big license in a small pond turned 'one summer' into more than two years. I did eventually go back to the deep blue, trading the high gloss white aluminum hulls trimmed with chrome and black glass, for my beloved rusty, thick black steel-hulled work horses, bristling with cargo equipment.

Having lived and worked in the yachting community, I knew that yachts were migratory creatures. Many of them 'summering' in New England, and 'wintering'

THERE I WAS

down south in Lauderdale. Yacht licenses are often limited to inland waters, or the owners are not comfortable or willing to embark on a long journey, and so delivery crews are hired to deliver the boat from one place to the next. There are always boats that need delivering somewhere, and a person with both small boat experience, and an unlimited license will have no problem finding a spot on a delivery crew.

Even some of the more experienced, veteran small boat Captains are uncomfortable losing sight of land, people who are capable AND willing to take a 50 foot yacht across an ocean are a rare commodity. Delivery jobs can be as simple as spending a day taking a 20 foot pleasure boat from Boston to Provincetown, to as complicated as delivering a 120 foot mega-yacht from the shipyard in Holland where it was built, to Fort Lauderdale or San Diego. Every fall the yachts migrate down the east coast, and every spring they travel back up, just ahead of the striped bass.

These jobs were brief, interesting, and helped me extend my time ashore between ships. I started out doing an occasional delivery for a friend or colleague on a boat that I was familiar with, but soon my name got out there, becoming known to a few brokers, and delivery services, and the calls became more frequent. I found myself spending more time delivering boats, than not delivering boats, and in a position where I didn't really need to go back to sea. That got me wondering if I should go back to sea that particular winter or try an extended run at delivery. The delivery work was getting more interesting as my scope expanded.

The thing about doing deliveries in a mercenary manner, responding to the call of a yacht broker, or delivery service, was that you never know what to expect. You could arrive to find a sparkling shiny new luxury yacht, with the finest appurtenances, ready for a smooth sail to some fine destination, or you could find a run-down commercial water taxi on its last legs, cobbled together with bad repairs and high hopes preparing to set to sail from Jersey City to Baltimore through bad weather.

Delivery crews, like all maritime crews, were a mix of ocean professionals, fugitives, social outcasts, pariahs, and adventurers. You meet them when you arrive. In the world of smaller craft, crews required less credentialing, especially in the engineering Department. This was a peculiar idiosyncrasy. At the unlimited tonnage levels, the Engineers were graduates of the maritime academies, some of the finest engineering schools on earth, and the Engineers were easily the most qualified and competent engineers on the planet. Below the unlimited class, in boats that were only certified to operate in protected harbors, the boat might not even require a licensed engineer. The 'engineers' that crew them were a mixed bag that were far more akin to mechanics than engineers.

I had decided to explore delivery as a career option, electing not to ship out, and to see if I could make a decent living tramping about the US coastline as opposed to

THERE I WAS

long voyages to distant lands. I was about a month or two into that experiment, and the seeds of regret were not only sprouted, but in full bloom. As a sideline, it was a good bit of 'extra' money, and having a regular job elsewhere meant being able to say 'no'.

I no longer enjoyed the luxury of discretion, and found myself suffering through a series of calamitous delivery adventures. These included taking a delivery boat from the repossession crew, who neglected to tell us that the dangerous criminal that they had repo'd it from was furious and in pursuit, not far behind. To make 'extra money' look like proper Merchant Marine money, you have to deliver a lot of boats, and that can get old quickly.

I had thought that this job was going to be a good one, it was a 500 ton river casino boat we were delivering from Tampa FL to Gloucester, MA. The boat had been born and raised on the Mississippi, and had been making its way to Gloucester when it stopped for repairs in Tampa. Now that the repairs were done, the next crew of rag-tag itinerant malcontents were flown in to get it the next few thousand miles. I had high hopes for this job, as the 500 ton class is where boats start to look and act like ships.

This girl could carry over 400 passengers, and had three decks. The problem was, that it was never intended to carry them for more than a few hours, and was never designed to be more than a few hundred feet from shore. There were no accommodations, no beds, no showers, not even a kitchen. The fuel tanks were tiny, so we had to plan on making multiple fuel stops. Her river boat hull was far flatter than most ocean hulls, to keep the draft shallow, and since the Mississippi wasn't exactly famous for tall seas, the designers didn't worry about that flat hull creating any roll instability.

The delivery crew consisted of the Captain who, while sober when he arrived, had that smell of a person who is never more than a few hours away from his last drink, or his next. Myself as the Mate, an 'Engineer' who was really just a top of the line diesel mechanic, and three unlicensed crewmen. Now, this particular class of vessel, the 500 ton class, is almost exclusively populated by workboats. Even the largest yachts, through various tricks and naval architectural manipulations of the admeasurement processes, are almost always in the 100 Ton class.

500 Ton crews, it turned out, were not professionally a step above the 100 ton crews. 100 Ton crews may have had junior licenses that were far less credentialed, but they worked on the precious shiny playthings of very wealthy people, in a very desirable and pleasant workplace. By nature, yacht crews, like the vessels they worked on, were polished, sleek, fast and smooth. Hillbillies were rare on yachts, and missing teeth were almost unheard of.

153

THERE I WAS

The 500 ton workboat is down towards the bottom of the workboat food chain, and the crews there did not have that fine glossy polish one was accustomed to seeing on yachts. A 500 ton crew assembled in or around the Gulf of Mexico was going to be graced with more than a few hardcore, Deep South, yee-hawing, confederate flag waving rednecks, and that is exactly what showed up.

The Gulf of Mexico, or GOM as it is known in the Maritime trades, sits above rich oil deposits, and is the birthplace of offshore oil drilling. There are oil rigs everywhere, and of course, the gigantic fleets of workboats that service them. The Captain was a muddled old, never fully sober oil rig supply boat Captain, and while he had a 1500 Ton license, and a lots of experience, was in the throes of an age and alcohol driven career backslide. The Engineer was a magnificent diesel mechanic, who likely grew up with a wrench in his hand, and like the rest of the crew he was from some god awful remote bayou town in Alabama, or Mississippi.

Of the five people that showed up, the sum total of teeth did not total one single full set. Being the only "Yankee", I was the freak. Ignoring my better judgement for the promise of a paycheck and an opportunity for a steady job on a casino boat in mother Gloucester, I set to sea in a battered old riverboat that was never intended for ocean voyaging, accompanied by the cast of Deliverance.

I set the crew to inspecting the lashings on the gaming tables, which had been loosely and poorly tied off on the top deck of the casino. The second deck, below, would normally have had the slot machines, but they were considered too delicate for such a voyage and were being shipped up separately. This created a stability issue, the place normally occupied by heavy slot machines was now empty, but the heavy gaming tables were still 'stacked' above on the third deck. Top heavy is not a desirable load profile, but this is one of those areas where the difference between limited tonnage and unlimited tonnage was stark.

Limited tonnage vessels have much more stability built in, especially steel workboats and they tend to operate in calmer waters, and this is especially true at the low end of the tonnage scale, the 500 Ton. Blue water officers, with unlimited tonnage licenses will do stability calculations, mapping out the center of gravity, and center of buoyancy, and how they interact in a complicated rotational dance around the theoretical metacenter, while limited tonnage officers may not even be aware such words even exist. One doesn't have to be a Naval Architect or Unlimited Master to understand that top heavy and flat bottomed is not the best condition to be in, but this Captain on his soberest day just didn't have the background to understand the depth of that problem.

Stability is the responsibility of the Chief Mate, but even though I had an unlimited Third Mate's license, which was senior to a 500 ton Chief Mate's license, I did not yet have an unlimited Chief Mate's license, and I didn't have the in depth understanding of stability that I would later come to acquire. I knew enough to know that we had a problem. This vessel didn't require stability calculations be entered into the log, as it was but a small riverboat designed for service in sheltered waters, so the builders didn't develop the tables required to make such calculations, so I didn't have the tools I needed to do an in depth stability work-up.

I was more than a little concerned leaving the dock under darkening skies on what was likely to be a difficult voyage. We each staked out an area on the floor, with our sleeping bags. The concession stand became our galley, and we had stocked a supply of canned goods and PB&J to get us through the next week or two. There was a small microwave so the canned beans would at least be warm. Or so we thought.

Our second night out, in a harbinger of things to come, the microwave burst into flames, starting a minor conflagration that took a considerable amount of effort and five fire extinguishers to control. Now our meager galley was a blackened mess that smelled of burnt plastic and ammonium phosphate extinguishing agent. We were now faced with cold beans until the next fueling port in South Carolina.

As the seas started to get rough, I had my first run-in with the crew. Work boat deck hands, in an odd paradox, unlike the officers, tend to be more skilled than their brethren from larger vessels. Workboats tow barges, tug ships, put gear in the water, do ocean construction, and engage in deck work that crews from large transport ships rarely see. So I had good crew, and the language barrier was manageable, given that I spoke a good deal of Redneck. The issue was the cultural difference, most of these men had confederate flags tattooed somewhere on their bodies, and had likely even considered locating those tattoo's on their faces, so proud they were of their hillbilly heritage. Taking orders from a Yankee did not sit well with their deep south sensibilities.

Having survived (barely) an incident of shifting cargo on a freighter not long in the past, and knowing how quickly the seas can stand up tall in the open ocean, and with a fair inkling of what the weather could be like as we approached Cape Hatteras, I needed those gaming tables re-lashed to a much higher standard. The crew had had a long day fighting fire, and were not accustomed to so much rocking and rolling, and wanted to call it a night. This job paid on a daily rate, and they had worked a full twelve, and were not going to get overtime for any more work done that day.

Voices were raised, and in the classic old school maritime tradition, blood was shed. I chose the largest and loudest of them to challenge. I was far more accustomed to dealing with the constant motion of rocking and rolling, and had even learned to use it to my advantage in a fight. I had also been studying martial arts since high school which all served to offset his natural redneck ferocity and extensive experience in road-house brawling.

155

THERE I WAS

I think that others in the crew were considering joining in, as they all started moving towards the fray in a group, when I turned a particularly deep roll to my advantage, using the ships momentum to hurl the giant country boy like a bowling ball at his toothless compatriots, scattering them. During that same roll, as the ship began its return trip and started to roll the other way, even deeper than the last, a lashing popped loudly and dramatically, and a gaming table shifted slightly. The sea gods stepped in to make my point for me. Even with skulls as thick as theirs, it didn't take long for them to realize the wisdom in adding more lashings to the tables to keep them from thrashing about. The fight was over.

We spent a long night lashing the cargo, now comrades in arms, having crossed the cultural divide on a bridge of maritime peril. We followed it up with cold beans, PB&J sandwiches and an extremely unauthorized beer or two to wash it all down. We then settled down on the thinly carpeted steel decks and pretended to sleep as we slid back and forth in our slippery sleeping bags in the heavy seas.

I didn't get much chance to rest, having to report to the wheelhouse to relieve the Captain on watch. No auto-pilot on this old girl, but the Captain had tied the wheel in place, in a ridiculous and almost childish attempt at shirking his duties, and was napping when I arrived. We had, of course, drifted far off course and were heading straight out to sea, eastbound into the Atlantic.

If you have ever been to a ball game, and heard a loud echoing shriek from across the arena, you have heard a portable air horn. It is a small horn that sits on a can of compressed air, and it makes an ungodly loud noise. Most ships have a few of them in the boats, or on the Bridge as back up to the ships horn, or just for general signaling purposes.

Well there was just such a horn, rated at an ear damaging 120 decibels, and I felt that it was the perfect way to awaken a man who had been so heinously derelict in his duties. It was the highlight of the entire voyage. His jerk into a waking state was nearly a convulsion, and his question of "WHAT THE FUCK" was answered abruptly with "That is the 'WE ARE HEADED STRAIGHT TO AFRICA WITH A SLEEPING LOOKOUT' Alarm, you fucking idiot!" His blank bleary eyed stare, slowly morphed into fear and shame, and he just turned around abruptly and lumbered out of the wheelhouse without a word, leaving only the sour aroma of stale cigarettes and unwashed alcoholic behind.

I corrected our course, and settled into my watch imagining that with fires, fisticuffs, and drunk driving behind me, the worst must be over, but alas it was not the case. Mariners develop an ear, and even more so, a feel for their ship. They become intensely attuned to the sound and feel of the ships engines and equipment. The Engineer, whose name was probably Cletus, had come up to the Bridge to chat as he also had realized that the leadership of this endeavor had fallen to us.

THERE I WAS

He was a pleasant, easy going, farm boy from Alabama, who was quick to laugh and loved telling jokes. We were sharing sea stories, coffee and peanut butter sandwiches, when he suddenly went quiet and cocked his head, his big grin slowly melting off his face. Then I noticed it too, the steady purr of the engines had roughened and deepened. His brow furrowed, and he started shaking his head.

"That ain't right" He got up slowly, unfolding his long legs and tattooed arms from the chair, his relaxed laid back demeanor suddenly tensing up like a fighter. The engine noises deepened, becoming more erratic.

He bolted out the door as fast as he could, and I grabbed the PA. "NOW MUSTER ALL HANDS ON DECK." One benefit to having a crew of Southerners is that they are very likely to bring a huge amount of mechanical skill to the table. I mustered up the crew, sent two of them down to the Engine Room to help Cletus, and then gave the air horn to the other to arouse the Captain from his stupor.

The now nearly deaf Captain stumbled up to the wheelhouse, irritated, but wise enough to keep his mouth shut. By now the engine sounds were becoming angry, and the smoke from the stack was darkening. I told the Captain to take the wheel, I warned him that if he let go of the wheel, or fell asleep, wandered off course, got within a mile of another vessel, or so much as thought about drinking, that I would beat him senseless and throw him overboard. He grumbled his acquiescence and I instructed the AB to keep his eye on him and stay on deck. As I made my way down to the Engine Room, the engines stopped, and everything became eerily quiet. The hum of the diesel is ever present at sea, and there is nothing as disconcerting as having it suddenly replaced by the sound of the seas hitting the hull.

When I got to the Engine Room, there was the acrid smell of lubricated equipment that had been running too hot. Something had started to burn. Cletus and his helpers were working feverishly jabbering away in a barely intelligible version of deeply accented engineerese. The engine was down hard, and Cletus wasn't sure he could fix it without parts and tools that we just didn't have on board. The seas were still whipped up tall and the wind was blowing a gale. The engines had been down long enough now that we had lost all momentum, and had laid into the trough, as ships will do when they go dead in the water.

Laying in the trough is a miserable experience under the best of circumstances, like a large ocean going ship in a mild sea. We were in a flat bottomed, top heavy riverboat in a mounting sea, and the rolls became severe. Cletus said that there was no hope of fixing the engines, and no use in trying. I ordered everyone out of the Engine Room and up to the galley.

I checked on the Captain, who to his credit was awake and as alert as I had ever seen him. The direness of the situation had penetrated the thick fog of his bourbon

THERE I WAS

induced haze. I updated him, and told him to start sounding Mayday calls on the VHF, and I was going to go inspect the life rafts in case things got any worse.

Now here we have yet another one of those major differences between open ocean and inland vessels. Ocean vessels would inevitably have what is known as SOLAS grade life rafts. SOLAS was a convention developed by the United Nations, and stood for "Safety Of Life At Sea", and it set standards for things like life rafts, signaling equipment, lifeboats, etc. A SOLAS pack would be a covered raft that self-launched off of a sinking ship, and would be provisioned with everything a person would need to survive at sea for two weeks. Food, water, signaling equipment, various survival gear. Boats intended to operate solely within the confines of a busy river, never more than a mile or two from shore, or farther than a few miles from the nearest rescue asset, have considerably less rigorous safety equipment.

So there I was, holding on for dear life in a boat that was rocking so deeply, that the fear of capsizing grew with each and every roll, looking down at what passed for a life raft on a riverboat. It was called an ILA. Inflatable Lifesaving Apparatus, and was nothing more than a giant inflatable life ring with a trampoline canvas stretched across the donut hole. No provisions, no equipment, just a massive open beach toy that was designed for a few hundred people to cling to for an hour or so on a flat calm river. There were plenty of them, fortunately, enough for 400 people, but it was not good situation by any measure.

Life rafts are stowed in drums nested in cradles on deck at breaks in the rails. They have bottles of compressed gas inside that are triggered to open explosively by tugging the 'painter' line, which runs out of the drum and is secured to the deck. The painter line is pulled out to its full 50-100 foot length, and then the drum is kicked over the side, and opened once in the water.

All of our ILA's were out of date. For a vessel in service, they would need to be inspected and certified on an extremely regular basis. The US Coast Guard is the authority having jurisdiction, and they are damn particular about passenger boats, God love them, but the key phrase is "a vessel in service". This boat had been out of service for some time, and had not had an inspection for years. On the up-side, there were half a dozen of them, and I was sure that at least one of them would work.

I mustered up the crew and had them gather the food, the signaling equipment, flashlights, and any gear that might be useful on an oversized pool float in a heavy sea, and put them into grab and go bags. We set up in the "high stakes room" a small card parlor for poker games on the top deck close to where all the rafts were, and near the Bridge.

I had them gather all the life rings, and hundreds of life preservers and have them ready to throw overboard. I had done more than few ocean rescues in my time, and I noticed that the survivors are always clinging to something that floats. This led

THERE I WAS

to my firmly held belief that you can never have enough things floating in the water if your vessel goes down. It doesn't hurt to pepper the water with hundreds of bright orange polka-dots either, if your sole hope of surviving rests on an aircraft crew being able to spot you from a few thousand feet up in bad visibility.

We all sat together for a moment, quietly pondering the very real possibility of ending up in the water. When I stood my watch that morning, I had seen some signs in the water that made the unpleasant thought of abandoning ship even more unpleasant. Like any job where you spend most of your day outdoors, you will see wildlife. The longer you do it, the better you will get at spotting it. A big part of the job entails staring at the water, and as the years go by, the water reveals more of itself to your trained eye. Sharks at sea are nothing like Hollywood sharks. Their fins do breach the surface, but not so slowly and dramatically as Hollywood suggests. They usually rise up to the surface quickly and abruptly only breaching for a brief moment, leaving a tiny wake for an instant, usually turning or hooking one way or another as they chase some prey.

They are everywhere out there, and it was years before I started seeing them, learning to recognize them from watching the Tuna boils. Once you start seeing them, you can't stop seeing them, and you realize that they have been there all along, under that complex surface that only after years of studying, will the small signs they leave become apparent. I had seen more than a few that morning.

Should we be forced to abandon ship, our chances of survival, while ridiculously slim, were as stacked as I could get them. The crew was scared, but too tough, and too proud to let some damn Yankee see them sweat, and they followed my orders stoically and professionally. We had all silently agreed to fight for our lives together or die trying. I went back to the Bridge to update the Captain.

I was thrilled to see that the Captain was talking to someone on the VHF. We were not alone. He informed me that he had had a response to the Mayday about half an hour ago and that a passing merchant was heading towards us, and that the Coast Guard had been notified and we could expect some help within the hour. I went back to the crew to share the good news, and we all went up to the bow to see if there was any tow gear stowed up there. It was likely that the merchant or Coast Guard would take us in tow, and that would be much easier and safer for everyone if we had a towing bridle already rigged.

It is not uncommon for commercial vessels to have a towing bridle already rigged and ready to assemble and install, and this vessel, of course, did not have that gear. What it did have, was a crew that was more than capable of rigging up a towing bridle from what rope, chain, shackles, duct tape, bubble-gum, and other equipment we could scavenge. It didn't take us long, and by the time the merchant arrived, we had a magnificent towing harness rigged and in place and ready to take a strain.

159

THERE I WAS

Taking a vessel in tow in a heavy sea, is as complicated and dangerous an operation as there is. Being dead in the water meant that we were laid down in the trough, which meant the large lumbering merchant would have to approach with the wind and seas on her beam. The vessels have to get close enough to pass line, which even with a line launching gun, is akin to two people bicycling as fast as they can next to each other and then kissing, without slowing down or killing each other. It took more than a few passes to get maneuvered precisely enough so that we could get the lines passed.

A thin rope with a special baseball sized knot called a "Monkey Fist" tied in the end, was literally shot from a gun across our bow. If we managed to survive that, and wrangle the rope, then the merchant would tie a series of heavier lines to a massive tow line, which we would then heave aboard and rig to the bridle. All on a wet steel deck that was rolling to the point of near verticality, in high winds, with seas breaking the bows. Just another day in the delivery business. We managed to accomplish all that with only a few bruises, and the correct number of appendages intact after the event.

The bridle was rigged, and we all cleared the bow as fast as possible while there was still slack in the towline. Towing 500 tons of steel through the water is done with a very long towline, carefully managed to keep the line in a specific shape, called a catenary, which is a long deep arc, with a large portion of the dip of the arc in the water. It is very important that the towline not clear the water, as that means that the strain is too high, and the line is likely to part.

A nylon line is essentially a massive rubber band. It can stretch and additional 40% of its length before parting. When it does part, it acts just like a rubber band, and snaps back violently. When the line is as thick as a man's leg, and its working capacity is measured in thousands of pounds, then the force of the snapback is enough to rip a man in half before it leaves a huge scar in on the paint job. So we all took our leave of the bow as the line came to tension and watched with no small amount of trepidation as the tow line took the strain.

The merchant maneuvered expertly, managing the towline carefully, and the line took the strain slowly and smoothly with no painful consequences. I set a watch on the bow, and we settled down for the trip in. After a dozen or so bland meals of cold beans and PB&J, all the remaining illicit alcohol, and many a sea story, we finally made our arrival at Charleston South Carolina without a mishap. The engine repairs were going to take a while so we were all paid off and sent on our way.

We met one last time at a local eatery for a well-deserved, long anticipated hot meal, enjoying one last night of, camaraderie, sea stories, good southern cooking, and fine blessed whiskey served from tiny South Carolinian bottles.

THERE I WAS

◼

A BRIDGE TOO FAR

The Sweet Science of Revenge

> *"Retribution, swift vengeance, eternal malice were in his whole aspect"* - Herman Melville, <u>Moby Dick</u>

Cities take pride in their bridges. The *Golden Gate* (109) and Brooklyn Bridges are household names, but most waterfront cities will have a bridge or two of distinction. There is always a story, the first bridge of this type of construction, or the longest span of its day, or the sad number of workers who perished in its construction. These bridges span harbors, and rivers and other navigable waterways, and are generally the factor that end up limiting the size of vessels that travel up that river or into that harbor. The view of these bridges, for the Mariner, is from below.

It is the Navigator's job to know the height of the ship above the waterline, the "Air Draft", and ensure that there was clearance for the ship to pass safely below the bridge. Often times, the clearances were extremely tight, and one would have to time the tide perfectly to ensure a narrow 1-2 feet of clearance to prevent the mast, or stack, or antennas from impacting the bridge. Close tolerances like that were understandably harrowing, particularly for the Captain, with whom ultimate responsibility lied. A ship impacting a bridge is a headline garnering event that in the best case scenario (i.e. no lives lost, no major damage to bridge or ship) is still a career ending moment for a Captain.

So Navigators, under the watchful eye of the Captain, will calculate the height of the tide, and calculate the height of ship above the waterline. They'll consult the Piloting publications for data on the bridges, their height above the waterline, the details of their lights, special signals and protocols, currents peculiar to the area etc. There is much room for error, as the height of a tide is a calculated estimate on any day, and how high a ships sits above the waterline can only be measured by looking at draft marks at the waterline on the hull, which are not always visible to the crew on the ship coming from sea, so often, calculations must suffice.

If one is lucky, a tugboat or Pilot boat will read the draft marks as you enter the harbor and give you a precise value, but all too often, the height above the waterline is a sophisticated guess based on the old draft readings taken when the ship left port an entire ocean ago, and the subsequent calculations based on the Naval architects and engineer's interpretation of how the changed level of fuel and water in the oddly shaped tanks relates to weight and buoyancy.

THERE I WAS

The Navigator will check the salinity of the water, as it significantly affects buoyancy, and using those tank levels and the salinity of the water, calculate how much the ship has risen out of the water based on all that data. Hopefully, the salinity beneath the bridge matches the salinity where the sample was taken, and the pages of calculations were done correctly, and the ship arrives at the bridge within that narrow window of time where the tide is the correct height, so that the ship clears the bridge fully without mishap.

It is not uncommon for a ship to attempt a passage with just a few feet of clearance, and this type of passage inevitably involves precise timing. These passages also involve no small amount of consternation on the part of the Captain. This is one of the many reasons that Captains should strive to maintain good relations with not only their Navigators, but with the crew in general.

This story is about a just such a passage. The ship was entering harbor following an ocean transit from Europe and would be travelling several miles upriver to the port facility. It would need to pass under several bridges to get there. The Navigator was a man of exceptional ability, in both navigation and storytelling, and had made the required calculations, checking them meticulously for accuracy. The ship would pass safely beneath each of bridges with room to spare, though not a lot of room to spare.

The Captain was a nervous man, and a screamer. There are various styles of captaining, and captains can evolve from one style to the next. Many captains start as screamers, and learn the folly of it, growing into the far more effective 'calm as cucumber and always reasonable' style. This Captain was an established screamer, and was intent on remaining one. Screamers are not popular. Screamers are prone to offending crew members, and can end up provoking crew members to extreme behavior. This story should serve as a perfect example of why that approach should be avoided at all cost.

This Captain must have offended a deck seaman so profoundly that this wronged individual decided retribution was in order. How does one exact revenge? How does one pay back a real or imagined slight? I have seen revenge at sea take many forms. The boredom of a long sea voyage can spawn great creativity, elevating revenge to a craft. The high ratio of severely anti-social people often leads to revenge being taken too far.

A common and minor act of revenge is taken out via a person's coffee cup. Coffee is the life blood of a ship, and people often have their own cups, which they may foolishly leave unattended at the coffee mess. Revenge seekers are prone to doing various disgusting things to a person's cup. The most common form of this violation is known as "Rim Dicking", whereby certain parts of the revenge seekers anatomy are rubbed across that part of the cup where the victim's lips apply. Nasty bit of work.

I myself once introduced small doses of a powerful detergent to the flavored creamer of a particularly vile and hateful prick who spread misery for the sheer joy of it. I was the civilian Navigator aboard a Military Sealift Command ship, and he was a Navy Chief. He would come to the Bridge as I stood watch, and loudly berate the young Navy Sailors who stood watch with us civilians on the Bridge. He was a cruel and arrogant bully. When he wasn't inflicting his obnoxious vitriol on innocent bystanders, he was kissing the Captain's ass. His one great skill in life was bootlicking, and the Captain favored his brown nosing ways, soon elevating him to the status of Captain's Pet. This prevented me from banning him from my Bridge and forced me to endure him for hours on end. I turned it around on him, verbally abusing him in kind, but he whined to the Captain, and I was pressured to relent.

Forced, I was, to tolerate him on my Bridge as I stood my eight hours of watch each day, I listened to him abuse those over whom he had power. Hours on end of his ugly hateful gossip took their toll, and I decided I must find a way to get him to leave my Bridge. He kept a container of his effete French Vanilla coffee creamer in the desk that the Navy kept in the chart house.

I decided that the more time he spent in the bathroom, the less time he would have to pollute my Bridge with his foul presence. So I invoked the natural diarrhea inducing properties of industrial grade laundry detergent, and sprinkled just a touch to his already chemical rich coffee additive. I enjoyed the ensuing silences knowing that my actions not only improved the quality of my life, but spared the poor young Navy Sailor from hours of unjustified abuse. It was pure delight watching him grow paler as the days went on, and seeing the bags develop under his eyes, and sensing the mood on the Bridge visibly elevate when the Chief would suddenly stop in mid-tirade, clutch his abdomen and run.

Not as clever an approach as the devious bastard who threw a handful of ball bearings in the dropped ceiling above the stateroom of his target. The constant sound of them rolling back and forth in even the slightest of seas, was a relentless, sleep preventing, grating penance. Another very common form of rebuttal, one to which I was also partial, was to induce sea-sickness in those who were susceptible to it.

This practice was literally a hobby among many, and was often practiced not only as act of revenge, but as a cruel sport. In heavy seas, even a strong stomach is no match for a can of sardines. The smell alone can clear a room, but if that doesn't work, just messily digging in will send all but the immune to the rail. Cigars were another easy way to induce a technicolor yawn, and were a powerful tool in my arsenal to keep my world free of annoying assholes.

THERE I WAS

Those of us who had developed the skill of turning other people bright green learned more subtle approaches. Often just gently rocking yourself as you spoke to someone would slowly and hypnotically bring a person's last meal to the light of day. This approach might also include the strategic and clandestine use of unpleasant odors, not the blunt frontal attack of lighting up a stogie in their face, but a more indirect approach of engaging the person immediately after having smoked a cigar. This was far more discreet, and the victims often didn't even know that they had been targeted.

One of the most elaborate and artful acts of revenge I have witnessed took several weeks of planning and involved training seagulls. This particular ship, was a Military Sealift Command Naval Auxiliary ship, and was one of those ships that the military keeps crewed and ready in case of war or photo opportunity, but doesn't really use all that much. These ships sit in port with skeleton crews who often live ashore, and get to go home each night. The ships a have their own permanent 'berths' on the same pier and many of the crew live nearby and drive to work each day. They park in the same spots each day like normal people. Captains, of course, get assigned a prime parking location right on the pier near the gangway, while most everyone else must trod in from a distant remote parking lot.

The Captain of this ship, was away for two weeks, and so the Chief Mate was left in charge, and rather than allow the Chief to use the vacant spot, the Captain spitefully ordered that his spot remain clear in his absence. This was but one of the Captain's many petty behaviors, and the Chief Mate decided to use these two weeks to even the score. Several times each day the Mate would bring a giant bag of popcorn or potato chips to the Captain's parking spot and feed the seagulls. Each day more and more seagulls would show up, and soon that Captains parking spot became a favorite haunt for the local gulls. The Mate explained to me that seagulls, when they take to flight, are prone to shitting, and that a flock of alighting gulls startled into taking to the sky at once will carpet bomb an area with their poo.

There is a Navy tradition of ringing a bell when a Captain leaves or arrives at a ship. Merchants don't generally follow this practice, but Military Sealift Command is where those two worlds overlap, and this pretentious buffoon of a Captain fancied himself worthy of this military ceremony and insisted that the bell ring for him as he came and went. At the end of that fateful first day back from his hiatus the Captain walked down the gangway towards his pride and joy, the shiny Mercedes SL. The Chief Mate himself stood at the gangway by the bell, waiting for just the right moment before loudly ringing the bell into the microphone of the PA. To ensure the effect he desired, the Chief had been feeding the bird's laxative laced popcorn for the past 24 hours. Over a hundred seagulls, startled by the bell and the approaching asshole, launched themselves to the sky, 'de-ballasting' as they did so, and a foul

THERE I WAS

rain of seagull shit fell from the sky painting the Captain and his precious German car in a vindictive fecal polka-dot. Truly masterful.

Other acts were sublimely simple. I once took a digital watch that sounded a single beep once every half hour, and planted it inside a chair in my brother's studio apartment right before I left for sea. That one beep was not enough to track, but persistent enough to annoy, once every half hour for four long months. Revenge took many forms, and was practiced at many levels, from tiny acts of rebellion, to sophisticated elaborate schemes designed to exact painful retaliation. Our revenant deck seaman on that fine day in that long southern River as we approached that low bridge, had put some thought into his revenge.

If you ask yourself, where does one go to seek supreme retribution, the answer is cruelly simple. To exact supreme punishment upon any person, you simply face that person with their own worst fear. A person's worst fear is the perfect weapon. A tiny bit of effort to even suggest the feared event, can reap the full terror sown by the subjects own tortured musings.

Captains deal every day with potential disasters and their painful repercussions. The object of their distress is public, no secret to anyone on the crew, especially those hands involved in preparing for or mitigating the risk. The Deck department knew that there were low bridges on this transit; it was even tasked with lowering a whip antenna or two to reduce the air draft by a few crucial feet.

This is why no one took notice of the deck seaman, climbing up to the 05 level just above the wheelhouse with a heavy bucket in hand. No one would take note of such an event on any day. Deck seamen are prone to wandering about the decks lugging heavy buckets, and lengths of chain, and giant tools all day long, every day. But this was not just any day, this was the day that the ship would be passing beneath a low bridge, and this disgruntled employee had designed a despicably wonderful prank as a parting gift to the Captain.

Every veteran Mariner knows the sound of a steel on steel collision, or impact. That tortured clanging, groaning, clanking, screeching that screams of tremendous momentum gone horribly awry. Those sounds haunt the dreams of captains, and the lower ranks alike, but it is always the captain that answers for it. Captains own that sound regardless of who or what caused it. In the time honored tradition of maritime scapegoatery, captains take the fall, whether they deserve it or not.

To be fair, not striking any object, particularly a stationary object, is the Captain's sacred obligation. Impacting a stationary object is known as an "allision" and in most every instance, is inexcusable. Maritime law and tradition carefully define accountability regardless of responsibility, and the Captain is accountable for the work of the Navigator, the directions of the Pilot, the error of the Helmsman, or the vagaries of wind and sea, even if they be responsible for the accident.

THERE I WAS

Naturally, captains must learn to live with this reality, and master the fear lest it win, and this contest between captains and the slings and arrows of outrageous fortune is a very public struggle. This Captain dealt with the stress and details of it all by screaming, and berating, and behaving in a manner prone to disgruntling crewmembers. How different this day might have been if that poor Captain had spent but the tiniest bit of effort towards re-gruntling affected crew members, but alas, no such efforts were attempted.

The ship approached the bridge, looming larger each moment, till it hovered over the bow and began to traverse the length of the ship. The Captain, Navigator, and all hands down on deck, watched intently as the massive steel beams approached the tall house at the stern of the vessel. The gallant Navigator looked down at the bow, where the Chief Mate and the Bosun stood by the anchor, as was their normal practice during river transits, knowing that they had the best view of the event. They showed no signs of panic watching the bridge from that perspective, no frantic pointing, no panicked shouting, just rapt professional interest.

The moment arrived, and the Captain stood out on the bridge wing looking up as the bridge loomed overhead, blocking out the sun, to see if it cleared. He stood nervously at the rail, his jaw clenched so tightly that the muscles writhed and twitched visibly. It did, of course, clear the house, the Navigator being of such high caliber, but our friend the disgruntled AB, skillfully out of sight of the Captain, began dumping buckets of chain, and nuts and bolts onto the flat plate steel deck above the wheelhouse, to simulate the horrific sounds that our nervous Captain had been actively fearing his entire career and more importantly... at that very moment. We will never know if a complete mental breakdown was the intent, he seemed surprised and remorseful that he had reduced the Captain to a sputtering mess who needed to be removed from the ship, but intended or not, that was the outcome.

The Captain's tortured screams of "NOOOOOOOO" as the shackles and bolts were hurled across the decks by the vindictive deck seaman, echoed loudly beneath bridge, and many people say they can still be heard at times below that towering span, when the wind and tide are just right. The deck seaman was clever enough to deny any intent, and claimed that 'dropping' the gear was simply an accident. His only punishment was the echoes of those screams in his dreams, and the knowledge that he had been personally responsible for unhinging a man.

RWANDA

Important is Relative

> *"There is nothing more enticing, disenchanting, and enslaving than the life at sea." - Joseph Conrad*

I was sitting in a bamboo chair under an umbrella on Pattya Beach Thailand, decompressing. It had been a particularly difficult voyage, one that resulted in the death of a friend, at the hands of another friend, all due to the conniving scheme of a profoundly evil man. Thailand was the perfect place to drown ones sorrows and forget all the things that trouble you.

I had rented a room on the top floor of a high rise resort hotel right on the water. There were only two rooms on that floor, and the other was vacant, so I had this penthouse to myself. Complete with the rooftop pool and balcony. The room included access to the buffet each morning and night, and was only $50 per day. I had hired a 'Tuk-Tuk', which is like a three wheeled motorcycle rickshaw, to be my personal chauffer, for another $10 day, and ended up recruiting a small army of his friends and family, and had an entire staff waiting on me hand and foot, still all for less than $100/day.

I spent my days lounging on the beach, or by my effectively private pool, while beautiful Thai girls with adorable names like Thoi (toy), Pu, Dang, or Porn served me drinks or rubbed my feet. I had my driver, a butler, a cook, a maid, and even personal bathers. It was like living in a porn movie. Still, the events of the previous voyage weighed heavy on my soul, and even repeated visits to the normally uplifting ping-pong ball show wasn't cheering me up. It is a deep funk that is not lifted by the sight of a vagina so talented that it can launch ping pong balls across the room.

Beach time was over, my driver Boom, was sitting next to me, keeping me company. He looked over, sizing me up:

"Blessed Whiskey?" which with his strong accent came out "Bressid Rishkee?"

"Damn straight my friend, and Cuban Cigars too please." Boom found me a magnificent cigar bar that was outfitted like a British Gentleman's club, with rich paneling and big soft leather seats. They had a huge selection of fine Cuban cigars and an expensive collection of brown liquor. Boom doubled his pay that night, this was exactly what the doctor ordered. The place was filled with both Thai businessmen, ex-pats and tourists, and the conversation was interesting and animated.

THERE I WAS

At one point, the barkeep accidently spilled a plate of Pad Thai in my lap to the horror of owner and staff. I was not upset in the slightest, it was an honest mistake, and aside from the delay in my dinner, there had been enough blessed whiskey at that point that I was in an extremely forgiving mood. This was Asia though, and the owner was upset, and wanted to make amends, and I knew my way around Asia well enough to know that it was important for me, as a grateful and dutiful guest in this fine establishment, to do whatever it took to allow him to regain 'face'.

He apologized profusely and then conferred with Boom, and sent him scurrying out the door. He insisted that I follow him upstairs. One of the wall panels was in fact a hidden door, and the moment we stepped through that door, we were transported out of the West right into the Far East. We emerged from a richly apportioned drawing room into a dark narrow stairway that led up to a dorm style apartment flat composed of dozens of tiny rooms with curtains for doors. Across from the rooms there was a wide open shower area, like a locker room.

The bar owner called out, and a waitress came running from one of the rooms. He barked his orders at her, and then told me that she would wash and dry my clothes for me and he would be back soon with a new shirt. I bowed and thanked him for his kind hospitality. He seemed pleased and dashed back down the stairs. The young lady came over without comment, began disrobing me, clucking at the food stains, and dismissing any of my protests. She brushed off my attempts to disrobe myself, by calling for reinforcements, and soon I was surrounded by a bevy of beautiful Thai women in various stages of undress pulling my clothes off and directing me towards the shower.

Two of them took my clothes and began scrubbing them in buckets, and the other three disrobed themselves completely and dragged me over to the shower where they carefully, and meticulously scrubbed every square inch of me. Apparently cleanliness was extremely important to these ladies. I was familiar with the famous Thai 'soapy', which was traditionally a bath not a shower, and was less about the bathing and more about the other group activities that inevitably ensued, but this was all business. Never had I been so clean, and perhaps never again will I be. It was a surreal experience, standing there while three women chatted and scrubbed, lifting my arm or other various parts to scrub beneath, or bending me this way or that to ensure no part of me was left unscrubbed.

I was towel dried, and a robe was provided for me. I sat and watched while four of the most beautiful women I had ever seen, stood naked drying my clothes with hair dryers, giggling and laughing the entire time. What a wonderful, crazy place. Soon Boom came darting up the stairs with a nice silk shirt that was just my size.

Clean, refreshed, rejuvenated, and with my spirits lifted higher than they had been in weeks, I returned to the bar to find my Pad Thai just being laid out. My delicious, spicy meal was followed by a glorious, blessed single malt Laphroig on ice, and a Cuban Partega. I tipped everyone handsomely, thanked the Bar Owner profusely, and Boom and I enjoyed a nice leisurely drive home.

But later, alone in my room, sitting on the balcony beneath the cool, starry, tropical sky, the past came back to haunt me. The last voyage was a tough ship, in a remote trade. It was a tramp freighter, old and small, and didn't pay very well. I enjoy crane rigging, and these old ships had extremely interesting and complex rigs. They were getting rarer and rarer. This ship was an advanced ship-rigging class for me. The fact that it was plying the Far East trades was a bonus. The old 'breakbulk' ships that load and unload themselves spend more time inport than modern container and RO/RO ships, and when the port is Hong Kong, or Singapore, or some lonely little island in the South Pacific, then there were plenty of ways to enjoy the extra time ashore.

There were two crewmen of note on this ship. Bert and Juan, both deck seamen. Bert was a twitchy violent Vietnam vet who, when medicated properly, was perfectly calm and reasonable. He was small and wiry, and under the right circumstances, extremely dangerous. He was one of those marginal people who was just a touch too violent and frightening for the real world, but still able to serve as contributing member of society in the maritime outskirts of civilization.

We looked out for him, helping to keep him out of trouble, many of us had a 'there but for the grace of God' attitude about him. He was a Veteran, and any issues he had, he had developed in the service of his country. The Bosun was an enormous Scandinavian whose name was probably Sven, he had no problem keeping Bert in line.

I had been running around with a Puerto Rican fellow named Tino. He had a thick accent, and was perpetually smiling and joking. He always wore a bandanna on his head and between that and his classic rolling swagger, he looked just like a pirate. We had flown out of the NY Union Hall together, and it had been one long swashbuckling adventure ever since.

He was always telling me "You are my main man, man", but with his thick accent it came out "Joo, are my Mang, Mang, Mang." I called him Mang cubed, and he loved it. "Mang cubed, I'm Algebraic." He drew out the vowels as he said 'algebraic' in that classically Hispanic way. Tino was friends with another young Puerto Rican deck seaman named Juan. Juan had had the distinct misfortune of getting on the bad side of Bert. In fact, Juan had reported Bert for some serious offense on a previous ship, and it had cost Bert a six month suspension. Bert was not happy with Juan, and had 'coincidently' found his way to Juan's current ship.

Bert had made it clear that he would like nothing more than to remove Juan's intestines with a butter knife and watch him squirm while he did it. Juan was justifiably afraid. Tino, myself, and Sven made certain that Juan was never alone on deck with Bert. We would walk him up to the bow to relieve Bert on lookout, we would keep them working on different equipment. They were on separate watches, so it wasn't that difficult.

Captain Mitchell was an evil, devious bastard who thought the whole affair was amusing, and tried his hardest to thwart our efforts at protecting Juan. He wanted nothing more than to put them alone somewhere to see what happened, and that is exactly what he did. We were inport in a ragged little port in Borneo called Kota Kinabalu, taking on a load of lumber. The Captain waited for a time when Sven, Tino and I were all otherwise occupied, and directed the newly reported Chief Mate who was completely unfamiliar with the situation, to send Juan up on the foremast to assist the AB that was working up there. That AB was Bert.

Tino, Sven and I were working on the dock. Our work was horrifically interrupted by the piercing sound of Juan's' screaming as he plunged from the top of the mast to the deck below. That sound ended abruptly with the sickening crack of his skull smashing on steel. That was the sound that was haunting my nightmares on that beautiful balcony, there in magnificent Thailand. That was the sound that even the frenzied scrubbing of three of the most dedicated personal bathers in Thailand couldn't wash from my memory. That sound, and the image of Bert's smirking face, peeking down over the rail from up on the mast.

We all raced up to the bow to see if we could help Juan, but we found what we expected. The sound of his impact left no doubt. Juan's lifeless corpse lay in a slowly expanding puddle of blood, his head grotesquely stove in from the impact. Bert was nowhere to be found. There were no witnesses, except maybe the Captain. When we found out from the Chief Mate that the Captain had directed him to send Juan up there, Tino went off the deep end, screaming and nearly assaulting the Chief Mate. The police were already on board at this point, and dragged him away. They cared little for his story that the Captain had plotted Juan's death. The Borneo police seemed perfectly satisfied that it was an accident and that the matter needed no further inquiry.

Sven and I went to see the Captain. Normally, when a ship is on a foreign voyage, the crew is bound to the ship until the Captain releases them. The ship can't sail without a full crew, or at least without certain key posts filled, and captains rarely release people from their commitment if there is no relief present. Sven and I had decided that we were leaving today and we were going up there to convince the Captain to make it legal.

He was reluctant at first, but we made it clear without clearly stating so, that his life was in grave danger. He was responsible for the murder of our shipmate and he knew that we knew. Threats to your life should always be taken seriously, more so

THERE I WAS

when they come from an enormous Viking and an enraged Bostonian. We offered him a way out, release us from articles, pay us off in cash, and give us our walking papers.

We stayed in Borneo for as long as it took to bribe the appropriate officials to release Tino. Tino was thankful that we stuck with him, but he didn't talk much. He had plans that he was keeping to himself, and I suspected that Captain Mitchell hadn't seen the last of Tino. Sven headed back to the States to find another ship, and I found my way to Thailand to recover from it.

I didn't stay too long in Thailand, my heart just wasn't in it. Boom and most of his extended family were sad to see me go, and I was sad to leave them, but if I stayed too much longer, I might never have left. So about a month after walking off that ship, I headed back to the states to the Union Hall to catch another ship. Technically, under the union rules, I should have 'repatriated' immediately, and returned dutifully to the States and the Union Hall. I had been in the union long enough to know that simply tucking a hundred dollar bill into the paperwork as you slid it under the transaction window at the hall was all it would take to get the official to overlook almost any lapse in procedure.

I had decided on a different ocean this time. I needed a different sky, and I wanted the weather to match my state of mind, dark grey, cold and solemn. My old friend the North Atlantic. I found a black oil tanker running back and forth from the US East Coast to Europe and Africa. Tankers had become very no-nonsense places since the Exxon Valdez, and people like Bert or Captain Evil were not tolerated. Those types of social misfits were consigned to old battered breakbulk ships in the remote trades. This tanker loaded crude in Africa, ran it to the US, brought refined product to Europe, and then ran in ballast back to Africa to start it all over again. It was a good run, with a fairly set schedule. There were periods of intense work, unloading cargo, washing tanks, loading again, and then a nice calm ocean crossing where you only worked 12 hours each day.

It was my practice, in the days before Internet and Satellite TV and Radio on ships, to bring a short wave radio, and try to tune in to the BBC to get news of the world while at sea. In those days, leaving the dock meant almost completely disconnecting from civilization, your only connectivity to the world ashore was via telex, or $10/minute ship to shore telephone.

On some ships the Radio Officers were sober and kind enough to print out the AP or UPI telex news and post them for the crew, but that was hit or miss. I preferred not to be at the mercy of another for my daily dose of news. I loved the BBC, with their ever so proper, staunchly professional, perfectly enunciated delivery of the important events of the world, carefully presented as objectively as possible, and without the blatant sensationalism of the lesser news services.

THERE I WAS

I would get permission from the Captain to mount the mast and run a makeshift wire antenna from on high, down to the Bridge. The BBC World News came on at the top of each hour Greenwich Mean Time. I would connect each day on my watch during the dinner hour at night, and during the coffee break in the morning. On most ships it would morph into a social event for likeminded people, and would attract a small group of regulars who would arrive at the Bridge twice daily to drink coffee, and listen to the news.

The news that dominated the BBC on that trip, was the news of the genocide in Rwanda. Every day we got the body count, and stories of the horrific slaughters of ethnic Tutsi's at the hands of the Hutu government. We heard the outrage at the epic impotence of the UN. The UN came into existence with a mandate to prevent genocide, it is one of the very reasons that they exist. Yet on the sidelines they stood, taking the opportunity to debate the definition of word 'genocide', while hundreds of thousands of men, women and children were butchered with machetes for no other reason than their ethnic heritage.

We had an African crewman on board this vessel. He was from Tanzania, which borders Rwanda. He was Bantu, but Tanzania is very diverse and he was familiar with ethnic tension. Rwanda was close to home for him. He came to the Bridge each day, and listened intently to the goings on in Rwanda. He offered us insight to the local geography and tribal politics. There was little else on the news each day; for months on end we listened to the BBC's extensive coverage of this disaster.

Early on in the journey, the ship adjusted its route and made several trips bringing crude from Africa to Northern Europe, and runs to the US became fewer and fewer. By the time the trip was finished I hadn't seen the United States in over eight weeks. When I finally wandered back to the US, it was summer and I decided to do some fishing. I found my way to a small cabin in the middle of nowhere, Gods Country, Northern New England, as close to the native brook trout as I could get.

When I finally emerged from the woods, leaving the *glorious landscape* (110), and a small stack of empty whiskey bottles behind, I wandered back down to Boston to visit family and friends. I was anxious to hear word of news in Rwanda.

Had the UN gotten off its over-privileged corrupt ass to make a move to help? Had the US or another Western Democracy interceded to protest the slaughter? It was hard to say, because news of Rwanda was nowhere to be found. Not with the life changing, all important, dramatic OJ Simpson debacle dominating the headlines. Page after page of OJ news, while the genocide raging in Central Africa garnered two inches of column in a tiny font on page 37 of the Boston Globe.

The murder of 700,000 thousand innocents in a strange foreign land, with no oil, no wealth, no value to the US, was not worth reporting, not when one pretty little white girl and her pretty little boyfriend were murdered by a black man here in the

173

THERE I WAS

US. Not to diminish the murder of two innocent people, that was certainly tragic in its own right, but I was dumbfounded that the American media cared little if at all about industrial scale murder.

The OJ story was front and center at every outlet, from the NY Times, to the tabloids. Every TV outlet from '60 minutes' to 'Geraldo' wanted to show that clip of the white Bronco, or had a nice sound clip of the rhyming lawyers. The only thing missing was calliope music. Meanwhile, the genocide raged on. I was forced to climb to the roof of a tall building with my shortwave to escape news of the OJ trial. Even NPR, who at least didn't ignore the Rwandan tragedy, still spent more time reporting the OJ story.

I was thoroughly disillusioned. People just didn't care. The American media, without exception, was ignoring news in favor of sensation. Now not only was Boston feeling less and less like home, but the US started to feel foreign to me. I cared not at all for OJ Simpson. The media was more concerned in stirring up racial discord at home than examining the horrific aftermath of ethnic discord run amok. The people read what they were told to read, watched whatever was put in front of them, and cared very little one way or the other.

There is an old saying in the Merchant Marine: "You can never go home". I was beginning to understand it. I was not the same person anymore, I was now the kind of person who thought that hordes of machete wielding zealots butchering women and children was more important than a sensational murder trial involving a sports star. My tribe disagreed and I endured the odd looks and awkward silences of my friends and family, when I commented on it. It was becoming difficult to find a place here in the States where I still fit in.

Though I didn't know it at the time, I was now approaching that crossroad that so many Merchant Mariners face, where the path diverges away from your past, and your homeland, towards a life of uninterrupted wandering, or perhaps an ex-pat existence in some strange land. I had friends living all over the world, Thailand, Philippines, Dubai, Europe, Singapore, even Egypt. The world was a big place. I didn't yet see this choice coming, but I felt it, the stress of my disillusion and the ever growing feeling that I didn't belong anywhere.

One path would lead farther from home, the other would be another futile attempt at conforming. The wanderings could expand, or they would end, at least temporarily.

Part 6 – Surviving the Story

"A man is born alone and dies alone; and he experiences the good and bad consequences of his karma alone; and he goes alone to hell or the Supreme abode." Chanakya

Redemption

The darkness lifts

"There is but a plank between a sailor and eternity." – Thomas Gibbons

"I had been in the water for a few minutes now, but it was more than an eternity. The water was so cold that I couldn't feel my hands or feet any-more, and every muscle in my body felt stiff and sore. It took forever to come out of that trough to the next crest, it felt like years and years Santo. On the one hand, I was the most alone a person could be, completely and utterly by myself in the middle of the North Atlantic, but on the other hand, everyone I had ever loved was right there with me. I was certain they were all there to escort me to the next place."

"It was damn fortunate for me that Art, Bowhook extraordinaire, in his critical evaluation of the green Coxswain, was in fact worried that we might get pooped, or swamped, or that the rough ride might send someone flying, and was paying close attention. He noticed immediately that one of his greenhorns was missing, and when the seas lifted me again on that next rising wave, after that god awful eternity, I saw the most amazing sight I have ever seen, or will see... the boat was turning back.

Art had taken the wheel, and when the crew spotted me they started pointing and blowing a whistle signal. That whistle, that sound, was the happiest sound I had ever heard Santo. To this day, I can't go to a ballgame without getting weepy. I knew that they had seen me. I tried to wave, but my arms felt so heavy and the seas were so rough..." The memory was so strong I needed to stop, drink whiskey, and listen to Bob Marley sing about Redemption. Off in the distance, in one of the Nipa huts, I thought I heard a loud slap and a then "Straits of Malacca!"

How Not to Get Promoted
When cold blood warms

There are some things you learn best in calm, and some in storm." - Willa Cather

Sometimes, you just don't want to be there. That had never happened to me before, and while I had been in bad situations, on miserable ships with miserable crews, I had always enjoyed *the adventure* (111). I had never come to the end of my shore time and thought "I don't want to go back". This was a first for me. I had spent the previous 3-4 years self-studying for my Unlimited Third Mate's License, which was my ticket to an officer's berth. The vast majority of people with that license obtain it along with their degree from a Maritime academy.

The normal route is four years of college, getting the requisite sea time on the training ships, or as Cadets on merchant ships, and academically preparing for the rigorous 10 or so licensing exams that the Coast Guard requires you pass before issuing the vaunted license. The normal route is not a route I was prone to travelling, and I had crafted my career into an autodidactic training regime that would lead me to that outcome via the more difficult path of the self-educated. Like Melville, "A... ship was my Yale College, my Harvard."

I learned Navigation in the Navy. When my course of study moved to 'cargo handling' I sought and found a berth on a general cargo 'breakbulk' ship, learning everything I could by doing, or apprenticing myself to some crusty veteran. When it came time to broach the topic of dangerous liquids, I dragged my seabag up the gangway of an oil tanker, and learned the ins and outs of the black oil trade by immersing myself in it (the trade, not the black oil).

My education was not confined to the mastery of my trade, I learned of African culture by seeking ships in the African trade routes. I crafted a course in Anthropology/Colonial History, and Sociology studying Apartheid while running bananas from Rio to Capetown. I took the opportunity to study architecture while working a tramp freighter in northern Europe. There is lots of time to read at sea, plenty of opportunity to study, a perfect environment to mix academic pursuits with hands on experience. You can't learn to rig a crane or drive a ship by reading about it, but nothing will so broaden an experience as studying it deeply before immersing yourself in it.

So my learning adventure paid off, in part anyway, with my License to a Merchant Marine Officer, "Third Mate of Ocean Steam or Motor Vessels Any Gross

THERE I WAS

Tonnage". After seven years of Maritime experience, I finally achieved my Unlimited Third Mates" license. This license entitled me also to Master Vessels of up to 100 Gross Tons, and Serve as Chief Mate on vessels of up to 1600 Gross Tons. Given the magnitude of the accomplishment I presumed, wrongly it turns out, that getting the license would be the hard part. I was aware that finding work as a third Mate was difficult, but I had no idea of just how difficult it would be.

Finding a job in the Merchant Marine is never an easy task at the 'entry level', and Third Mate is as entry level as it gets. There are union ships, non-union ships, government ships, commercial ships, brown water limited tonnage work, blue water unlimited tonnage jobs, US flag ships, foreign flag ships, it is a complicated environment. Once you had some experience, and the higher level credentials, things became much easier, but every spring the half dozen major Maritime Academies would graduate hundreds of Third Mates, all with the added benefit of their alumni old boy networks and collegiate job placement services, and there were precious few Third Mate jobs. Fewer every year as the US Flag fleet shrank, crews became smaller, and ships became bigger and more efficient. Certain shipping companies favored particular Maritime Academies, the officer's unions in those days were very closed, almost like exclusive clubs, only opening their books occasionally.

I had climbed to the top of the unlicensed structure as an 'Unlimited Able Seaman' or AB, and was a senior book in a union for unlicensed crew. There is a perpetual and worldwide shortage of AB's, so finding an AB job would never take me more than a few days if I wanted one, even if I didn't have the head of the line privileges that union seniority brought. To find a job via the union, you registered with a union. If you were fortunate enough to be a member of the union, you could register as a member, and would have some status, or if you weren't a member, you could register as an 'applicant' and take whatever jobs the members didn't.

When a job came up, the shipping company would call it into the union, and it would be listed on the 'job board'. The jobs on the board would sit there until the next job call, which were held at specific times during the day, and when the job was called, people who were already registered for work could compete for the job. The job was first offered to senior book members "A Books" or "Group 1" or whatever means that particular union had of differentiating the levels of seniority.

There were usually three levels, ABC or Group 1, 2, or 3, and then applicant. So the job would be offered to 'A-books' and if no 'A-books' applied then to 'B-books', 'C-books' and then lowly applicants. If more than one person at a particular seniority level applied for the job, then the person whose registration card was older got the job. The registration card was valid for a certain amount of time, usually a year. So a person whose card was 364 days old would beat a person whose card was only 363 days old.

178

THERE I WAS

People would get off of a ship, and register their card before taking their vacation, and let their cards ripen for a few months before finding their next ship. My strategy was to register with the two major officers unions and my own unlicensed union, and attend every job call every day, until I found a Mates job, and if my registration card expired prior to finding an officers job, then I would re-register, and ship out unlicensed for four months and come home with a pair of four month old registration cards, and enough money to fund another job hunt. I also sent resumes out to every non-union shipping company on planet earth.

I had spent a year with this approach, and everyone I spoke to thought it was the best approach, but for the second time I had failed to land a third Mate's job and found myself back at my own unlicensed Union Hall looking for an AB job in the dead of winter. I knew that prior to the holidays was a good time to look for a job, and I had registered with that in mind, and had a 'killer card', that was 10-11 months old in November/December, ready for a holiday relief. Great plan, or it would have been had it worked.

So there I was, my officer union cards nearly expired, every day my options shrinking down to just my unlicensed card, no job, nearly broke, and a recent bout of bad fortune with my home and family life. My beloved grandmother had passed away just days before, and I had recently split with my girlfriend, which was ultimately a good thing, it being a horrible relationship, but it did not leave my head in a good place at that moment. So for the first time in my commercial shipping career, I didn't really want to go back to sea.

The typical job was a 120 day tour, which generally came with two months 'vacation' at the end. The vacation was an additional two months' pay, so you worked 120 straight days, and got paid for 180. So your typical Merchant Marine worked four month on, two months off. Many took a full four months off between ships. But not all ships worked that way. Some ships had different schedules, or arrangements with the union. There was one ship that ran black oil up and down the west coast from Long Beach to the Bay Area to Valdez and back, and the schedule was 30 days on, with 30 vacation days. Day for day vacation was the Holy Grail. This was a very sought after ship.

I had registered on the West Coast for two reasons, first because San Francisco was a "Hot" port, with lots of third Mate jobs shipped out recently, and plan B was to catch this tanker should I not find a third Mates job.

Several years before, in a dark episode of labor relations in the maritime industry, most of the tanker companies had decided that they had had enough of the Union Mates and Deck Officers. They were happy enough it seemed, with the Union Engineers (a different union), but they all conspired together to oust the union Deck Officers all at once. One day tankers across the country gave the deck officer unions

179

THERE I WAS

the boot, and replaced them with non-union 'scabs'. This caused an enormous amount of bad blood in the industry, as none of the other unions displayed any of the expected solidarity that was the norm, and the Engineers and Unlicensed unions, fearing the same fate, continued to work on these vessels.

My scheme was to re-register with the officer unions in San Francisco, work this easy one month on, one month off, schedule and shop for a Mate's job during my month off. During my 30 days on the ship, I would be working for a company that hired non-union Mates, and I would see if an unlicensed berth was a foot in the door for non-union opportunities.

I should mention, that my blanket approach to job-hunting was a blatant violation of most union rules, and that the strong union flag waving zealots of organized labor would have been horrified at my mercenary tactics, but at that time, I had no strong allegiances, only a strong desire for a paycheck and honest work in my chosen field.

The San Francisco Union Hall had as much character and history as the city itself, and while no one is ever really happy to see an East Coast carpetbagger wander into the hall with a killer card, this particular hall was more open to out of towners looking for work than most other halls. There was a 'Seaman's Hotel' nearby, which was really just a sort of Spartan Bed and Breakfast that one of the local Mariners operated for itinerant job-hunting Seamen. The union hall was close to the waterfront, and between job calls I would wander out to the dock and look out at the bay. This time of year I was the only one out there, the grey cold weather matched my state of mind perfectly.

I was listening, appropriately, to Otis Redding's "Sittin' on the Dock of the Bay", and imagined that maybe Otis had written this song just for me: "Watching the ships roll in, then I watch them roll away again." Every time a ship rolled in, there was a potential job to be called. I knew which ships were US flagged and which union crewed them. I knew the scuttlebutt of which ship might be re-crewing, or how long the Third Mate had been riding that ship, and how likely he or she was to be seeking relief. I had spent the past six months 'watching the ships roll in', and knew the disappointment of watching 'them roll away again'. His words cut through me deeper than the icy cold wind rolling off the bay. This was in fact that very same bay, and for all I knew, this was that very same dock.

The afternoon job call for my unlicensed union was coming up soon, so I wandered in. I still had a few days on my officers cards, so I wasn't ready to take a job just yet, but I wanted to get a look at the schedule of my target tanker, and play some poker with the boys before heading out for some seafood and blessed whiskey. It was a good card game, and an old shipmate of mine named Milo was there telling stories and entertaining everyone at the card table. Milo was old timer, and had started shipping just after WWII on passenger liners. He was a deck hand, like me, but had worked as a ships carpenter back in the days when there still were carpenters on ships. You could almost tell by looking at his hands how skilled he was. Every movement he made with them was careful and precise, down to the way he arranged the cards in his hands.

He was originally from New Orleans, and could make a Harmonica come to life. He would tell stories of how he had spent his youth 'Jamming' with some of the biggest names in Blues and Jazz. He was in a constant state of animation, and laughter followed him everywhere he went. He was an avid storyteller, and his sea stories were magnificently embellished, when they weren't complete fabrications.

He was telling just such a story now, about how the harmonica riff for 'Mannish Boy' was his, and how he and Muddy Waters had come up with that tune before Muddy headed up to Chicago and taught his riffs to Little Walter.

"That damn Little Walter was good, but he wasn't Milo Jefferson good, and them was my runs, my riffs. Damn Muddy warn't nothing but a country-assed farm boy who could play guitar, it was me taught him big city blues." Milo, drew one card and looked slyly over his hand across the table. Sea stories were a good diversion at a poker table, when you were always lying, it was tough to tell when you were bluffing. The best part was, how perfectly plausible his story was, it could very well have been true. I had heard Milo play harmonica, and he was right about one thing, Little Walter was good, but Milo was better. I had originally met Milo in New Orleans years before, and that was definitely his town. It is hard to imagine someone that good at the blues harp, who grew up in that era, in that town in the musical heart of the Mississippi Delta, not having played with the great Bluesmen.

Milo, held his head up, with his chin cocked, almost challenging anyone to display any doubt. He seemed satisfied that were all giving his story the proper respect. He raised the bet a fiver. I saw his five and raised him another. I knew his tell, Milo's stories got louder when he was bluffing.

The radio in the background started playing a Michael Bolton song, and someone went to change the channel, which infuriated Milo. "Why you wanna change the damn channel every time a black man start singing?" It took us a full hour to convince him that Michael Bolton was a white boy. Mile just kept repeating "You can't tell me that is a white boy," emphasizing the words 'can't' and 'tell' and enunciating each word, "You cain't, tayll me, that is a white boy, aint no white boy can sing like that, aint NO white boy can sing like that." We finally convinced him, by asking him to explain then why would a talented black man who could sing that well cover a Percy Sledge song, and not find some song to make his own. For some reason that made sense to him.

181

THERE I WAS

At one point, I started humming Otis Redding, and of course Milo had something to say.

"You know Otis was in this very union, and wrote that song while trying to find a job right here in this hall, mm hmm."

"The fuck you say?"

"Damn straight boy, right outside on that dock right there." What a great sea story, one so great, that I heard many times over the ensuing years as my career moved on. There was a legend in this union that Otis Redding was an alumni. Many people would tell of their friendship with Otis Redding, Merchant Mariner. It was extremely unlikely that Otis ever got near a ship, but when you write a song like that, that strums the heartstrings of a Merchant Marine, then they will bring you into their world and build a legend around you.

Milo was as great a storyteller as he was a poker player, and everyone walked away a little richer, though only Milo gained financially. Milo won our bet, leading me to believe that the volume was not him bluffing, but genuine anger at Little Walter for stealing his riffs.

My target tanker was due the next day, and again in a few weeks, so I decided to throw my card on it and see how it played out. I came back for the job call, Milo had found himself a ship, and presumably a new audience. Being so very senior in the union, I not only scored the job, but I got a 'steady berth', meaning that the job was mine till I gave it up. Steady work was a privilege only afforded to Group 1 book members, so there was more than a little bad blood when an out of town mercenary wandered into the local hall and scored one of the prime local jobs.

This ship was fairly new, double hulled, and ran up the coast from Long Beach to the Bay Area stopping several times along the way. Ships that run 'coastwise' go in and out of port a lot, this ship pulled in or out of port every 12–18 hours or so. Going in and out of port is a lot of work. It means hauling all the heavy lines out, preparing the equipment, maybe standing by the anchor or on lookout for a few hours as the ship ran along in a narrow channel or up a river.

The ships pull in when they arrive, regardless of the time of day or night, so you get dragged out of bed, and sent down on deck in the freezing cold every 12 to 18 hours. On this ship, the work days were 12 hours, plus any additional hours that the crazy schedule imposed. Lots of work, lots of hard dirty work in a harsh environment, and not a lot of sleep. In fact, it was rare to get a single full night's sleep in a full 30 day tour. That was the reasoning behind the brief 30 day rotation.

My brother unlicensed crewmen were a good bunch. Like most ships it was a richly diverse slice of humanity, about half of which were Philipino. I loved working with Philipino's, their food was fantastic, they were hard working and honest, and generally minded their own business. You were not likely to have a problem with a

182

THERE I WAS

Philipino shipmate, unless you caused a problem with him. They liked to laugh, and they were not prone to griping, even on miserable ships with horrible scab deck officers, and harsh working conditions. I had sailed with one of these Philipino deck seamen before, his name was probably Jun, and he invited me to the poker game.

He was small of stature, with heavily tattooed arms, and a mop of thick black hair as course and straight as broom bristles. He seemed serious to those who didn't know him, but if he liked you enough, he would share his wealth of jokes and funny stories with you. He constantly spoke of his family, including his two sons, one of whom was also an AB in the union, and the other who had recently been accepted to a Maritime Academy. He told me that this was why he was inviting me to the poker game, he needed my money for tuition.

This ship had a steady poker game that pretty much ran around the clock. It was a very serious game of straight seven card stud. The cards and chips flew around the table as fast as the good natured pokes and jabs, and on any given night one could walk away plus or minus a few hundred dollars. The game ran during breaks, at meals, and in the evenings and gave us all something to look forward to, something other than the meals.

The Steward on this ship was an enormous Creole whose name was probably Pierre. He was a magnificent cook, and the food on this ship was world class. He was as round as an egg, with pencil thin mustache, and he was passionate about food, wine and women. He had a fantastic sense of humor, with a sharp incisive wit, and the masterful ability to hide it. He loved to make sport of the dim witted Mates, and would cook difficult to pronounce foods or even intentionally miss-spell words on the menu to illicit ridiculous mis-pronunciations from the nearly brain dead Second and Third Mates. His Cordoon Bluey or Etoupee was as good as one would get at any of the finest French restaurants in Paris or New Orleans, and he loved to take care of his crew. The great food, and righteous poker game kept life tolerable on this ship.

As I mentioned previously this ship had 'scab' deck officers. Now, these Mates hadn't just recently crossed a picket line to get these jobs, it had been years since the tankers canned the union, but apparently the tensions hadn't subsided one tiny bit.

The union folk, that is, most of the rest of the crew, were none too fond of the non-union folk, who were half of the officers that ran the show, including the Captain, who was far and away the most miserable son of a bitch that I had ever met. That set the tone for his deck department.

The deck officers were a motley collection of mean, stupid, arrogant jackasses who were constantly striving to out 'dickhead' one another. The Chief Mate was less than five feet tall and spitefully arrogant. He was unclean and constantly reeked of black oil. His hair was black, but it was roundly believed that it would likely be a different color were he ever to wash it. The Second Mate was tall and broad

183

shouldered, and still yearned for his glory days of Division eight football at the Maritime Academy. He was constantly bragging of his glories overcoming some community college football team in Woonsocket RI, or Podunk State.

The third Mate was an enormous fat bully, who was amazingly stupid given his station in life and the role he played on an oil tanker. It was common knowledge that this corpulent buffoon took a full six years to graduate from a four year Maritime Academy, and didn't graduate with the license, taking another full year and a rumored dozen or more tries at the licensing exams to finally earn his license. He had been a third Mate for close to a decade, and the story was that he had been sitting for the Second Mate licensing exams every year for the past seven years, and still hadn't passed.

He was the worst kind of stupid, he had that special brand of idiocy where he firmly believed that he was brilliant, and everyone else was stupid. He was constantly over compensating for his own lack of even the most basic understanding of the world around him by insulting his intellectual betters and berating their 'stupidity'. He was abusive and mean, and relentlessly attacked everyone around him that was beneath him in rank.

This pathetic pack of miscreants were nasty by nature, under the best of circumstances, but when they learned that I had a license, they turned the volume up. Having obtained their jobs at the expense of others, they just presumed that anyone who could backstab them and steal their jobs, would do so. So aside from being in a deep dark funk, being sleep deprived, and spending most of my time in the freezing cold with icy spray from a 20 knot head wind cutting through my flesh to the bone, I had an entire pack of recalcitrant assholes going out of their way to make my life difficult. Worst of all, was the Third Mate. He understandably felt the most threatened by any competition, and made a point to seek me out and harass me. I in turn, had no qualms about telling him what a stupid fat pile of pig droppings I thought he was, and it just kept escalating.

My Philipino friends, would shake their heads and counsel me to just ignore him, not to pick a fight with him, because mean stupid people were not just a danger to themselves but to others. It was unwise to make myself the object of his mean stupid focus. They recommended, like my dad always used to, to "Knock it off before you get your ass in trouble." It was good advice, but my tolerance had been eroded by the relentless petty animosity, lack of sleep, and spending 8-12 hours each day, wet and cold.

It was on one particularly bitter, icy night, at about 2AM, after standing watch till midnight, and getting called out only two hours into my precious sleep time, that my Philipino friends saved my soul. We were pulling into a terminal in Seattle to offload, the wind was merciless and the air was frigidly cold.

THERE I WAS

We set about getting the mooring lines ready to tie up. On most ships, the lines would have been stowed below decks, but since this ship came in and out of port so much, we often left them on deck, carefully laid out and tied off. The cold weather and sea spray had coated most everything with a fine layer of ice and hoarfrost, and the lines were frozen stiff. This made them extremely hard to work with. The decks were covered with a slushy mix of wet ice and snow.

Tankers often run steam pipes into the cargo tanks to keep the cargo warm and to prevent it from solidifying, or becoming too viscous to pump. This meant that there were steam lines running along the deck which made steam available for other uses throughout the ship. In the old days, most ships were powered by steam, and there are still a few rare steamships out there. There were still many an old timer who remembered when 'them there fancy new-fangled noisy diesel ships' started to come out.

This ship was diesel, but still had a boiler plant which was easily as large as the propulsion plants of the recent past. Like the steamships of old, this ship had steam powered winches on deck. The winches were massive pieces of equipment used to tension the heavy lines while mooring, or heave the 30 ton anchor. They stood as tall as a man, and had a footprint of eight feet by 12 or more. Most ships had hydraulic winches nowadays, but this ship was a throwback.

This ship was designed for coastwise trade, and had some mooring lines kept wound up on spools attached to the winches, which made them easier and faster to break out and stow. We had spent an hour or so pulling these lines out, leading them carefully out across the deck and around the guides, called fairleads, to the openings in the gunwales, called chocks.

Steam would bleed from the winches every time you moved the lever to spin the mighty drum to play line out or in. This created a thick fog of steam all over the bow that gave the deck an eerie quality under the intense floodlights. The steam would then condense on everything, including the bedraggled deck seaman bustling about, who were consequently, in this weather, covered from head to toe in hoarfrost.

The thick miasma of steam fog cut down visibility shortening lines of sight, and caught and reflected the light making things seem overly bright. This affected one's depth perception in addition to adding a profoundly surreal quality to the night. We were working in a bubble of bright light that was bounded by a visually impenetrable wall of smoke, like a dream scene in a cheap Hollywood horror flick.

These old fashioned steam winches were touchy, and didn't feather slowly up to speed like modern hydraulic winches. The lever had a 'sweet spot' where the steam suddenly passed through the valve and the drum would startle to life abruptly. This made things somewhat dangerous. The winch could develop thousands of pound of force rapidly, and the lines when tugged so suddenly and forcefully would jump and come to tension quickly.

The fairleads were designed to guide the line from its drum, through the maze of equipment on the bow, and out the chock. The drum was at chest height, and the chock was an opening in the hull from deck level up to about knee height. The leads changed the direction of the line while also leading it down from the drum height to the chock height.

The leads themselves were grooved wheels, like a pulley sheave, a foot or two across, set horizontally on short pedestals 3-4 feet high. Since their function was to change the direction the line, they created a bend, or a loop in the line, called a bight. A bight is any loop or bend in a line, whether the 'hole' created in when line is coiled or looped, or the ever so slight area inside the gentle bend of line that is just mildly less than perfectly straight as it runs from one lead to another.

Bights are dangerous. Bights can kill. If one is unfortunate enough to stand in the bight of a line when it runs away, or comes to tension the consequences can be deadly. Indeed, bights formed by mooring lines, are often referred to as 'kill zones', and it is not uncommon for one to hear the angry shouts of a Bosun or Chief Mate chiding fools and greenhorns who are prone to wandering into the bight.

On this bow, on this cold windy night, amid the thick industrial haze of a mighty steam engine, a mooring line as thick as my arm, ran from the lead to the chock in a long looping bight. The line ran about 40 feet, and instead of leading perfectly straight, it carved a long gentle arc, like an over exaggerated letter 'c' from the lead to the chock, and then down to the dock where a surly longshoreman had looped its eye onto the bollard.

This was not uncommon, especially on an icy deck, with frozen lines, and experienced professional deck seamen who were accustomed to working with bights, and were smart enough to stay clear of them. Everyone knew that when that twitchy winch caught and that line snapped to tension, then the arc that defined that bight, would whip into a straight line instantly and with enough force to reap a man's legs right off, or at the very least, hit him like a wrecking ball.

Everyone knew that, except of course the obese obnoxious third Mate, who was signaling me to heave in on the line. He was shouting obscenities at me through a megaphone. I could only see his massive silhouette through the fog, and apparently he couldn't see me signaling him to get his fat ass out of the bight. The noise of the equipment, and his abusive application of the megaphone prevented him from hearing my shouts. My lifesaving advice:

"Get the fuck out of the bight you fat stupid fuck" went unheard, except of course by my Philipino friends most of whom had been trained from birth to stay clear of a bight, and hadn't even wandered near a kill zone in decades, much less

THERE I WAS

parked themselves square in the middle of one. The Mate's screams grew more hateful and intense the longer I spared his pathetic life by not moving that lever and heaving the line. As he moved closer, coming into view, his expletives grew louder and more personal and at one point he mentioned my mother.

So there I was... under the bright glare of industrial floodlights, awake these past 36 hours, standing on a freezing cold steel deck while powerful wind whipped the snow and steam around me with enough force that the windward side of me was literally encrusted in snow and ice, all while a useless, fat, stupid, lame excuse of a human being launched a hateful personal tirade of abuse at me because I was being kind enough to spare his meaningless life.

The darkness that had been eating my soul grew exponentially in that moment, taking over, and an odd twisted reasoning started to develop in my mind. I was being ordered, loudly and hatefully in front of a slew of witnesses to move that lever forward. I am sure that high above us on the Bridge, they could hear that bloated fools profane tirade, but could not see through the mist, and only had that partial audio portion of the spectacle. Visibility was low, and technically my job was to receive the orders of "heave away" or "slack down" from the officer in charge, and operate the winch accordingly.

Now I had been in some very heated moments in my life, and had, on countless occasions, fought for my life. In situations like that, the thought of killing a man as he tries to kill you rises like a fire from the most reptilian portion of your brain, in an instinctive heat of passion. Never in my life, till that moment, had I ever coolly and calmly considered willfully harming someone, but now my sleep deprived angst ridden mind was slowly convincing my sore and over-exposed body to just move that lever a few inches and rid the world of an oxygen wasting buffoon, while simultaneously creating a much needed vacancy in a third Mate berth.

My hand flexed on the lever, moving it just enough to cause the winch to hiss and burp steam, and give the drum a tiny twitch, another inch of movement on that lever and the drum would rocket back, snapping that line taut in an instant, reaping the oversized jackass in the process. My eyes narrowed as I prepared to divert the course of my life down the road to perdition, when the sea gods stepped in to save me.

Two of my Philipino card buddies and brothers in arms, both of them probably named Jun, took a strong departure from their cultural bias to not get involved in other people's conflicts, and risked the wrath of the giant, obnoxious screaming oaf, and they intervened. One came to me, and with his endearing accent, spoke the voice of reason.

"Clip", (in Philippine broken English, the letter 'f' is pronounced like a 'p'). The first time I had ever heard a Phillipino accent, was in boot camp, where a tiny

187

THERE I WAS

Phillipino drill instructor barely five feet tall, covered from head to toe in military decorations, and with the stone cold face of career military, stood defiantly before a towering Texan recruit. The Drill instructor, stood close, as drill instructors will, face to chest, chewing out the poor recruit in his distinctive accent.

"Puck you, you pilthy pucking recruit." He seethed slowly, his voice dripping with venom, savoring the obscenities. "Gib me pipty puchups, pucker." I had never heard that accent, and the odd combination of that accent emanating from that tiny badass chewing out that enormous cowboy was making it extremely difficult not to laugh. I knew that all those ribbons on his chest meant that he had likely seen combat, and being a Navy Corpsman, had likely seen that combat serving with Marines in some god forsaken jungle in Southeast Asia. He was a genuine war hero, and drill instructors are tough bastards no matter who they are, but to me, not laughing at the sight of a half sized person telling that oversized country boy to "puck off" may have been the hardest thing I have ever not done.

I had since learned to love the sound and cadence of that accent, associating it with ships, friends, good food and good times, and after that night on the bow... salvation. Jun had stepped in, hand on my arm.

"Clip, no, you hap to slip at night, (you have to sleep at night) don't let him take away your piss (peace) for the rest op your lipe (rest of your life)." His voice cut through my darkness like a beacon of light. He gently inserted his tiny frame between me and the winch control and carefully moved my hand from the lever, whilst another shipmate braved the fury of the imbecilic Mate, pointing at the bight and in almost comically over acted Pidgin English carefully effected to diffuse and distract. He pointed to the bight, while gently trying to steer the oafish clod away from the kill zone "You in bight, no good, danger Mate, danger, no good, no stand here, you get hurt, no stand here." as he gradually got the Mate to move aside.

This particular deck seaman actually spoke better English than the fool he was saving, but he was clever enough to effect the broken English to appear less threatening to the insecure ego maniac. Jun was now at the winch control and the very instant that our heroic deck seaman and the inane fool he was guiding, stepped clear of the kill zone, Jun slammed the lever back, dramatically snapping the line to tension. The wet line whipped up straight, throwing a cascade of water up into the air in a brilliant arcing rooster tail that caught the light in a dazzling visual display of the energy of the event.

Even through his densely thick skull, and his limited ape like capacity for thought, the Mate realized instantly that he had been standing in a kill zone, and had loudly and obnoxiously ordered me to perform an action that could have killed him, and then berated me for not following the order. We all watched as he slowly and stupidly re-processed the last few seconds, realizing that even as he screamed

188

THERE I WAS

and insulted me, I was sparing his life, and then the slow dawning of realization of what that familiar hiss of steam that always preceded the winch drum snapping the line to tension meant, and how only the moral strength of a few deck seamen that his bigoted brain likely never even acknowledged as human, saved his useless life.

He gawked at the man who had just saved his life, and then at me, and realized that I had nearly carried out his orders, and that not only had I nearly killed him in cold blood, but that he had used a megaphone to order that I do so, and I likely would have gotten away with it. I stared straight at him through narrowed eyes with the coldest, meanest stare I could conjure.

He sort of glazed over, and was jolted back to reality by the voice of the Captain on the walkie talkie, asking why he had suddenly stopped tying up the ship. The Mate snapped out of it, and told the Captain we were on it, and he quietly went back to work. He didn't scream, or yell, and he never spoke nor even looked me in the eye again. From then on, he took great care to avoid me. From that moment forward, I made sure to bet heavy on bad cards when it looked like Jun was going to win the pot. When he lost his deck knife, I took mine to the machine shop, engraved his name on it, with the words thank you, in his native Tagalog.

THE PASHTUN TRIBESMAN

Heroic strength of Character

> *The strongest man in the world is he who stands most alone. Henrik Ibsen*

In Dubai, like most Arab Cities, there is a shopping district dedicated to jewelry called the *Gold Souk* (112). It is *a destination for tourists, Mariners, and locals alike* (113).

I had visited the Souk in search of natural pearls, which are highly valued in the Persian Gulf, a former center of the pearl industry before oil exploration destroyed most of the oyster beds. Natural pearls are rare nowadays, as cultured pearls have taken over the market, but here in the heart of Araby, they are preferred, and in some of the Arab states, cultured pearls are even banned.

This made for a unique shopping opportunity, as natural pearls would be hard to find even on Fifth Avenue in NYC, that rarity driving the price higher, but in Dubai, every jeweler in an entire neighborhood full of jewelers, would have high quality natural pearls. It was heaven for a bargain hunting pearl enthusiast. I had located an exquisite strand of graduated pearls for a few thousand dollars that would easily sell in the US for three times what I paid for it. With my mission accomplished, I was ready to head back to the ship.

I found my way to a taxi stand in time to find an Arab storming away from a cab after brutally beating some poor cab driver, while shouting an endless tirade of what I can only assume was angry profanity. Either that or he was choking on a hairball, it is often difficult to tell in that part of the world. The cab driver, like all other menial labor in Dubai, was a foreigner. Most of the locals were either business people, merchants, worked for the government, finance, or occupied traditional Arabic roles in society. Low level labor and menial jobs were done by imported Sri Lankans, Pakistani's, Philipino's etc. Middle management and professional jobs were usually done by Indians or Westerners.

The dockworkers in the shipyards and cargo ports, like this poor cab driver, were indentured laborers with no status and no protection in this society that had only just officially ended slavery in the sixties. Slavery still existed, this cabbie was the perfect example, but it was cleverly masked by a web of bureaucratic rules and draconian protocols that left these 'visiting workers' with perhaps less status than a slave.

The workers were usually brought there by an 'agency' that would then take and hold their passport. The agency could keep them, or deport them at their will, and the workers had no power or choice in any of the most basic matters in their lives. They would often live in housing provided by the agency, dorms or barracks, and even their money was managed by the agency, which would charge exorbitant fees and commissions. They have little to no rights, nor protection, nor status, nor recourse and lived lives of indentured servitude.

The Arab that was abusing this poor soul need have no fear that mercilessly beating another human being in broad daylight might result in any legal consequence. It was normal. It was not the first time I had seen locals physically abusing the imported labor. There was little I could do, except to offer the cabbie my fare, and the respect he deserved.

He was slight of frame, but wiry with dark brown skin and a head of thick black hair so dense and shaggy that it looked like a hat. The cab was neat and clean, and smelled of incense, and curry. It was adorned, decorated and trimmed with pride, with pictures and cards that displayed Arabic writing, presumably Islamic wisdom. He had a thick mustache, and giant tufts of hair popping out of his ears. His accent was rich, so thick it was almost a caricature. His head bobbed from side to side in that classic 'sub-continental' way as he spoke.

It was a long ride from Dubai to the port at Jebel Ali, and I spent the time engaging the cabbie in conversation. His English was surprisingly good and I learned that he was originally from the hills in the hinterlands of Pakistan on the Afghanistan border. He had never intended to leave his home and family, and would have been content herding goats in the ancient tribal tradition of his family, but his five year old daughter had become ill. She had some rare disease that was almost always fatal, but doctors had told him of an experimental treatment that would have only a very small chance of curing her.

The treatment was expensive. More money than he might see in his lifetime of subsistence farming in the rugged hills of Pashtun. Even with such a small chance of success, and at the risk of going into a debt that may take generations to pay, he asked:

"What choice did I have? She was my daughter, my joy." He choked up a little in the telling. I listened politely, choking up a little myself, imagining myself in such position. The potency of his story transporting me to rough craggy hills of Pashtun, where traditions older than history still dictated the daily routines of these proud people. He said that, of course, the treatment failed, and he was left heartbroken and destitute with no option but to seek work overseas where he might be able to earn enough money to repay his debt with 5-10 years of near slavery at the hands of cruel masters.

He wasn't bitter, in fact most of the conversation was upbeat and cheerful. We laughed and discussed how people everywhere shared things in common, how everyone from rich Arab merchants to Pashtun tribesmen to American Merchant Marines were, as people, more similar than different.

THERE I WAS

It wasn't till an hour into the ride, as our rapport grew that he opened up about his daughter, and his home and family. He had not seen his wife in four years, and sent home what little was left over after paying the medical bills to his struggling family. His agency overlords had arbitrarily changed the terms of his contract, raising their fees, and his initial five year plan to pay his debt would now take at least an additional three more years.

I was amazed at how difficult this man's life was, and how unfair, and how fortunate I had been to have been born to the American suburbs instead of the Pashtun hills. Or was I? Did I have even a fraction of the intestinal fortitude of this man? Could I have endured the death of my daughter, soul crushing debt, separation from home and family, a life of near slavery at the hands of merciless overlords?

We approached the gates to the terminal, where he was required to pull over and enter the gatehouse to obtain a permit to enter. He parked the cab and explained that he would be back in just a few minutes. I knew that in the gatehouse, the uniformed security, like all positions of authority in this land, would be an Arab, and that he would be treated as less than human.

I watched as he stepped out of the cab, his back bent, and shoulders hunched from the unbearable burdens he carried. He looked like a man who carried the weight of the entire world on his shoulders. He stopped a moment after stepping out of the car, and slowly and carefully straightened his back, squared his shoulders, and raised his chin, assuming a proud unbroken posture that stated clearly, that whatever they took from him, they could not take his dignity. In that moment, as he stood tall, bearing the burden of the weight of the entire world, and walked proudly into the gatehouse, I learned more about the strength of human character than I had learned in 35 years of life, and more than 15 years of travelling the world.

He greeted me cheerfully as he re-entered the cab, and he drove along slowly as we enjoyed the last few minutes of our conversation. While he was in the gatehouse, I had decided to tip him $100. Even in the unlikely event that it had all been a sob-story ruse to illicit a fat tip from a foolish tourist, the story and performance had been worth $100. There was no doubt in my mind though, that he was telling the truth, the best Oscar winning actor in Hollywood could not have conveyed the amount of courage and dignity that I watched that man muster and don in that brief moment under the westering sun on the Jebel Ali waterfront. His name was definitely Darwesh, and he could not conceal the tear in his eye, nor the emotion in his voice when he saw the $100 bill.

He thanked me and nodded his head, and I shook his hand and thanked him for the ride, and for sharing his stories with me. I wished him the best of luck, and my hopes that he would see his family and beloved hills again soon. I watched him drive off into the brown haze of the Emirati sunset and wondered if his life would ever improve. To this day, whenever things go bad, or I am faced with some adversity, I think of my friend the Pashtun tribesman, and my problems seem to shrink away to nothing. I live each day hoping that I can be as tough, courageous, and dignified as Darwesh, and thank the sea gods for introducing him to me that I might understand what it means to be strong.

Part 7 – The Story Ends

"At sea, I learned how little a person needs, not how much." – Robin Lee Graham

Rescued

The adventure continues

> *Never in my life before have I experienced such beauty, and fear at the same time"— Ellen MacArthur*

"Art drove that boat straight at me, and I thought after all that, I am going get mowed down by a motor whale boat, but he flared out at the last minute and brought me right alongside. I was so cold, I couldn't hold on to the rope, or help rescue myself. They had to heave me back on the boat. I was finally out of the water, freezing my ass off, but delighted none the less to finally be on the right side of the water's edge again."

"The boat officer had been in communication with the ships, and they were all preparing helicopters, but after the Russian incident the week before, it was less comfort to me than it should have been. I couldn't shake the image of the night sky alight with searchlights, and helicopters, and the bustle of five warships searching for that poor Russian swab who had suffered the exact same misfortune as I, and didn't survive it. The Dutch were kind enough to lower some blankets, dry clothes and a shot of rum, and since the US Navy's ridiculous alcohol restriction only applied to 'commissioned' vessels, and only ships are commissioned not boats, no rules were broken when I thankfully took my tot o' rum like a good and proper sailor. I raised my glass (a small fuel sample bottle that still tasted vaguely and somehow appropriately of diesel) to my Dutch benefactors, and they cheered."

"Changing clothes in an open boat in the winter, in the angry north Atlantic was just as awkward and nipple hardening as you might imagine, Santo, and since I still couldn't move my arms and legs very well, my shipmates had to help undress and dress me, and that might be the strangest experience in a long history of strange experiences, but soon I was dry, dressed in an orange boiler suit, swaddled in blankets, sipping diesel flavored rum and headed back to my ship to a warm welcome and some hot soup."

"That day, I learned the lesson which followed me throughout my entire career, that anytime, in any weather, in any sea, on any vessel... the ocean can take you. That day she gave me back, but it is not something I ever take for granted, Santo, it is why I am going home tomorrow for the last time."

Santo, nodded, and raised his glass. "To the end of an era! Old shipmates never die."

"They just smell like they have!" I replied, giving the traditional response.

THE WICKED WHISPER

When to leave the ship

> *"There is one knows not what sweet mystery about this sea, whose gently awful stirrings seem to speak of some hidden soul beneath."*
> Herman Melville

Believe it or not, it is entirely possible to spend too much time on a ship. Shipboard life is a relentless mix of monotony, terror, excess, and extreme. You can spend days or weeks on end in heavy seas and rough weather, with no sleep, and only cold food. The floor bucking and slanting beneath you, is constantly conspiring to hurl you headfirst into some sharp deadly steel protuberance.

You can spend months confined with the most miserable collection of *cut throat* (114) bastards ever assembled outside of a penitentiary. Crews can have a predominant ethnic bias, and you may not be fortunate enough to be a member of that club, enduring day after day of people speaking about you in a language you don't understand. Staring at you with malice in their eyes, blathering on in their native tongue as their countrymen nod knowingly, while they eyeball you sideways.

Typical tours are four months. 120 straight workdays, often with not a single full day off. Imagine how long 120 days could be when the food is terrible. The same six tasteless dinner entrees served over and over again, meat boiled gray, canned veggies reduced to mush, frozen crap fried into oblivion. It can affect a person at their core. It isn't always that cut and dry. Ships, like real life, are usually a mix of good and bad, they just range across a broader spectrum of extremes. The terrible food might be tempered by *fantastic company* (115) or high pay.

There is a danger in staying on a ship for too long. You can easily become one of those miserable cut throat bastards and maybe there is no turning back. You can't un-stab someone. When the polish of civil society is abraded away, it may never grow back. In the older days of shipping, before women arrived and civilized things, there was a class of near criminals that resided on ships who were unfit for civilized society, but not quite criminal enough for incarceration.

Then there are the mentally ill. Now I am no expert on mental illness, so I am likely speaking out of school here, but most everyone who has sailed the ocean blue has stories of some very strange people. Every Mariner has a story or two of some poor swab who snapped under the pressure and did something crazy. Jumping overboard and trying to swim ashore, or breaking down completely to a gibbering mess.

THERE I WAS

Stories of Seamen reaching the breaking point and snatching a fire ax off the wall and attacking someone with it are so common that I have known captains that removed the fire axes off the walls when morale started to fall, in fact I was just such a captain. Most long time Mariners have a story or a shipmate with a story that involves insanity and a fire ax. I have met at least two Mariners who were nicknamed "Ax wound." Ships often bear the scars of ax wielding rampages with pride, preserving the ax damage as a reminder to all of the dangers of staying too long afloat.

How long is too long, you might ask? It varies from ship to ship and Mariner to Mariner. Some are hardier than others. Some ships are more prone to drive a man over the edge. The road to hell is a personal journey, some meander, others B-line. There is some ancient wisdom to assist the concerned Mariner in gauging their state of mind.

The first indication that you have been on the ship too long is that you start talking to the seagulls. It isn't uncommon, they are out there, they may perch themselves on some rising current of air coming off the hull and float there for days on end. Or they may come visit you each night when you go out on deck for a moment of solitude and a smoke. Talking to them means you need to consider leaving as soon as possible. It isn't too late yet, but the situation is becoming dire.

The second sign is that the seagulls start talking to you, and this is more than just a red flag, this is a screaming Klaxon bellowing "Run for your life!" Remove yourself at the first opportunity, while you still have time to recover what is left of your sanity, because from the third sign, there is no return.

The third sign is that you start listening to the seagulls. They are the ones who will convince you to pick up a fire ax. They are the ones that lead you to believe that you can swim to that coast just a few long miles away, at night in the winter. They never have anything nice to say, and the moment you let them in, the moment you take their advice, you are doomed and can never return to the life you once knew.

Under The Falls

Moments of truth

> *"Any damn fool can navigate the world sober. It takes a really good sailor to do it drunk." – Sir Francis Chichester*

I was home now, back from a long trip at sea, just sitting in a local waterfront dive bar enjoying some fine blessed whiskey when suddenly I felt a grip like an iron vice grasp my shoulder:

"Jesus, they will let anybody in here." I turned to see the grizzled scarred face of my old friend Sean O'Grady standing behind me.

"You old dog, you look ten years older since I saw you last year, is your life just one long binge drinking bar fight?"

"Fuck Yeah, what better way to live your life, good to see you, you ugly bastard."

"Same to you... I mean the ugly bastard part, it not really all that great to see you."

"HA! For that you owe me drink!" It was the first of many drinks. We were in South Boston, near the waterfront, and Sean had grown up in this neighborhood, scrapping and fighting along with his six brothers in a tiny three bedroom duplex. It was close enough to the waterfront and my union hall, and served such fine Whiskey, that I had grown quite fond of it over the years. I had been drinking here for more than 20 years now, but this being Boston, and me not having grown up within five blocks, I was the outsider. Mildly tolerated was good enough for me.

I hadn't been back in over a year, but it looked just same as it did every time I had walked through that door over the past 20 years. It smelled just the same too, and the same cast of characters were sitting in the same spots at the bar, Dicky, Martin, Paulie G, Patrick and Joey all in a row, ordering the same brand of beer (Guinness of course) from the same battered old bartender that had been serving there for more than 40 years now. They were having that same discussion they had every day, about the perpetually under-achieving Red Sox, and the corrupt local politicians and the goddamned traffic. Even the "Specials" on the menu never changed, it was Tuesday, and that meant Corned Beef. And Corned Beef and Blessed Whiskey was what I was thinking about at that moment.

Then something different did happen; I heard the soft pitchy pubescent voice of a boy who didn't look old enough to be in this bar ask me a question.

"Hey Mister, what is it like to be in the Merchant Marine, and live on a ship at sea?" I stopped and looked straight at the boy, sizing him up. Typical South Boston,

THERE I WAS

thin, wiry, red-headed, tough as nails. He was young, not a whisker on his freckled face, but his eyes were older and wiser, like they had already seen too much, and his face already bore the scars of the battles he had fought. He sat at a table in the middle of the barroom with a small crowd of his friends. I looked them over and decided that these young men needed a sea story. They needed to hear about the world beyond L-Street, a world that didn't know that the Red Sox even existed, much less that they were God's gift to baseball.

"The best I can describe it, is that it is 95% boredom and 5% sheer terror, and that 5% boys, is the measure of the man, it's what makes a Merchant Seaman a Merchant Seaman"

"Whaddya mean?" the boy pressed

"Yeah do tell Yoda, fuckin' enlighten us." came a different voice. Gus was a crusty, cantankerous old buzzard from the neighborhood, and was a mean as a snake. He loved to fight, and I had tangled with him before, as had anyone who frequented this bar, it was almost like the toll you had to pay drink here. Gus himself had likely never travelled farther from this neighborhood than across town to Fenway, and didn't like having his nightly binge drinking interrupted with stories of strange foreign lands.

"The opportunity to enlighten you is long past Augustus, I seek only to entertain, but I can give you an example." Sean just glared at Gus, which shut him up, even Gus rarely got drunk enough to brave getting on the bad side of Sean. I paused, staring around the room to read the crowd, I deemed them interested, and ready. I started slowly:

"It was one of my very first merchants, the Sally Sykes she was named, and she ran from Boston to Europe about twice a month, to ports in England and France." I spoke slowly, pausing between phrases as if savoring the recollection. "We were launching the lifeboat for a drill, to run the boat's engine a little, and do some work on the launching davits."

"Launching and recovering a small boat from a ship is harrowing in the calmest of seas, but in rough seas it is downright terrifying. The small boat has to maneuver close aboard to a giant steel ship in angry roiling seas ten or fifteen feet tall." I paused a moment and sipped my blessed whiskey, damn this was good Scotch. I continued slowly, thoughtfully:

"The boat was getting tossed about, rising and falling with the waves. The ship doesn't move as much, but she moves nonetheless, differently though, adding relative motion to the mix, just enough to make it interesting"

"To recover the boat, the ship lowers the 'davit hooks', to the just above the water."

"Whatsa davit hook?" The boy asked

200

THERE I WAS

"They are two large, steel, crane hooks mounted on giant steel block and tackle pullies, they hook to the boat to raise and lower it to the water," I spread my hands like a fisherman lying about a catch, to indicate the size of the hooks.

"The hooks are known as 'Boat Falls', or just 'The Falls'. They are lowered to just above the water so that the boat can maneuver under them and when the boats is in the right spot, they lower them some more, just enough so that the boat crew can hook them to the sling points and get the boat hoisted back home."

"This operation is dicey in calm seas, but when the seas are rough, the boat is rising and falling with waves, ten, fifteen or 20 feet high or more, up and down on the waves beneath a pair of 800 pound headhunting falls swaying at the end of 50 foot wires, it can be lethal." My voice rose up and quickened as I described the boat maneuvering under the falls, and cut off sharply at 'lethal'. I paused a moment slowing the tempo down again.

"We maneuvered the boat under the falls, which are elevated to a safer height just overhead, and a line called a painter that has one end tied to the fall and one end secured to the ship far ahead of the falls. The painter is removed from the fall and tied to the bow of the boat. Now the boat is tethered to the ship.

Then the Coxswain, who is driving the boat, slows it down nice and easy until... BAM! The painter takes the strain, and the boat is in tow."

"This matches the speed of the boat to that of the ship exactly, and makes maneuvering somewhat simpler for the coxswain, just right or left. Provided of course, that the ship isn't moving too fast, which is like holding a tiger by the tail. So there I was, with the ship towing us along, we are slamming into waves, there is spray and water all over, or we run up a big wave fast, and back down the other side, and the painter slacks for a moment, then SNAPS tight again, jerking the boat and crew around like rag dolls" The young man who had originally asked the question, like everyone else in the bar, was rapt and focused on the story. He was there in the boat with me, covered in salt water, with the wind screaming in his ears. I continued:

"The falls are then lowered carefully so the boat crew can attach them. You have to time it just right to get the falls connected as the boat climbs a wave directly under the man-killing falls. The falls have to be lowered close enough to get the hooks into the metal rings at the hoisting padeyes but not close enough that the hooks smash the fiberglass boat to smithereens."

"You have to time it precisely so that the rising boat peaks and stops rising just before the falls slam into the boat, which would wreak havoc on the boat and boat crew alike. There is just a brief moment near the top of the wave peak, where the boat is located correctly and holds still long enough to provide an extremely brief opportunity for the crewman to grab the hooks and manhandle them into the padeyes before the boat starts to fall away." I pantomimed snatching an enormous steel rig, and manhandling it into place.

"If that weren't hard enough, both the bow and the stern must do this at the exact same time, so that when the boat starts to fall back down the wave, both of the hooks catch the weight of the boat, hopefully without so much velocity as to jar the equipment, rip out the eyes, part the wire or shear some piece of equipment off the ship causing it to tumble down onto the boat below like raining engine blocks." I let that visual sink in, as I sipped my whiskey contemplatively.

"If one hook gets connected, and the other doesn't... one end of the boat can end up suspended out of the water while the other falls, leaving you hanging like a giant orange trophy fish. If the davit operator, 50 feet above looking down, lowers the falls too low and the boat rises on a wave into the falls, it leaves the giant tackle slack and loose in the boat, with loops of un-tensioned wire strewn about the deck like snares grabbing at your feet. It's either the giant unconnected hooks swinging about at head level or dragging about the deck of the boat like a dredge."

"That day," I continued, "under the falls... in rough seas, as the boat was climbing a wave, I was there on the bow. I was the bow hook and it was my job to catch and wrestle that fall hook into the boats padeye. The Coxswain would maneuver the boat on the painter right and left under the falls, which were being lowered to that dangerous height, to that exact point where the hook was suspended at padeye level, not less where it would come to rest on the boat and require 800 pounds of force to handle, not more where it wouldn't reach, but just so... all in a few eternally brief seconds."

"The fall was swaying, the boat was heaving, and slamming in the pounding seas..." I had one hand pantomiming the swinging fall, and the other moving up and down beneath it like a small boat in a heavy sea

"...and this giant dangling hook was whipping back and forth as if it wanted to remove my head," I started whipping my hand back and forth at head level, and I knew the crowd could almost see the giant steel hook and pulley whipping past my head.

"And even if it came to the correct height, and I could manage to hold myself steady enough to grab and manhandle it onto the padeye, the odds of doing so without losing a finger or two were long at best. I realized that at any moment, I could be reduced to hamburger. I was facing death, or dismemberment, and that realization hit me like a brick in the face, this moment is just as likely to be my last moment on earth, as not." The entire bar was watching, silent, and imagining themselves at age 20, wrestling a massive block and tackle and facing death in high seas on the North Atlantic, you could almost feel and smell the salt spray.

202

THERE I WAS

"And I tell you boys that was the first time that fear opened up the door to my soul enough for me to see in and take a measure. In the span of just a few microseconds I went from paralyzed with the fear of the realization that I could die at any minute, then passed through that fear to the most focused clarity and heightened awareness that I had ever imagined. The fear became exhilaration, the hesitation and paralysis were gone and replaced with a laser like attention to the task at hand, and a scary clear awareness of everything going on around me. If I was going to die, then I would die doing a dangerous job that I loved, and I would die living life, not fearing it."

"The fall came down to the correct height, as the boat rose rapidly to meet it, and I seized those few seconds of opportunity, lunged in, slammed the hook into the padeye, snatched my hands back in the nick of time out of harm's way. No time to count fingers, I spun my attention back to the stern to see how the stern hook was faring, and stood ready to remove my connected fall if I saw that the stern hook would not be connected in time. All went well, and we got the boat hooked on. When they started hoisting the boat, it was like floating up to heaven. No finer feeling have I ever experienced."

"That moment served me well for the rest of my life. I knew that there would be moments when I was facing danger or death, and that I could choose to let go of the fear, and pass through it, and that on the other side of that fear was an amazing and heightened state of being... a place that..." I stopped, searching for the words, "a place that is nearly impossible to describe."

"Everyone will face danger one day... death, dismemberment, marriage... or some other heinous catastrophe, but Mariners face it more often. Every Mariner will stare death in the face and be forced to account. How a man reacts to fear is character defining. In the face of danger, the course of your entire life can change. Me... I got hooked on that feeling, just like Gus here got hooked on cheap beer."

Gus scowled but kept his mouth shut. He was a mean and scrappy old bastard, but he generally wasn't moved to violence until his eighth or ninth beer, which didn't typically happen until sometime after 10PM

"It's the most amazing feeling you could ever imagine." I looked pointedly straight at the kid who had asked the question, then back to the audience. "It's better than sex I tell you. It the kind of feeling that makes you want to climb to the top of the mast laughing like a madman, shake your fist, curse God and shout, "You call this a storm!" That is the best example of that feeling I can compare. That is where you end up when you pass through the fear, and you can live entirely in the moment, revel in it, drink it in, respond to it, and be a part of it."

THERE I WAS

"A small boat in a big sea will teach you that at any moment, in any weather, in any sea, it can all end abruptly, you can wind up in the water... under the water. Nothing can put a person more profoundly in the present than that realization."

"Going to that place not only affects the person feeling it, but those around him, infecting them with courage. In a street fight, nothing is more frightening to the bastard you are about to pound on, than watching you accept that it might be your time to die, and that a glorious death in battle is something you are prepared to accept, they sense it, and it scares the living shit out of most people, not here in Southie, of course, but most everywhere else." Now I was staring right at Gus, my right eye twitching slightly. I was feeling scrappy, and never cared much for Gus, and I was hoping for a little sport, but Gus was not rising to the bait.

"So that my boy," I finished, turning to the mesmerized barfly who had initiated this story, "is what it is like to be in the Merchant Marine."

I took one last sip of my drink, gazed around the room at my audience, satisfied that I had satiated their need for a good story, and turned back to the bar. Sean had ordered me another drink and slid it over to me. "It almost makes me want go and join the Merchant Marine"

"Frankly, I don't think that you quite have the nuts for it." Sean chuckled. Sean had been sailing for a lot longer than I, and he was possibly the toughest, bravest person I had ever met. Like many a fine lad from Southie, he graduated high school and joined the US Marine Corps, following in the footsteps of brothers and father. He was either brave or foolish enough to do this during the height of the Vietnam War, and had spent two tours as a force recon, and was an expert in unarmed combat. Fighting was as natural to him as walking, and even now, in his fifties, he was easily a match for any two people in this bar. Which is how exactly how many he matched that night.

Sean suddenly got a serious look on his face.

"Actually, I have decided that next year is my last. I'm retiring."

"You? Get the fuck outta here."

"No Shit brother, it's been over 30 years, and I am just tired, I just don't love it anymore, it's time to find something else."

"Wow, when did you decide this?"

"Just last night, sitting right at this bar, in this very fucking spot, there, which is the same spot I was sitting in when I decided to join the Merchant Marine."

"No shit, how did that go down?"

"I was six months back from 'Nam, had a good job at the shipyard, and one day my fiancé just up and left me. She left a fucking note for me when I got home from work." Sean paused a minute, clenching his jaw, he took a hard swig of his whiskey and slammed the glass down. It seemed that time had not fully healed that wound.

THERE I WAS

He signaled the bartender for another. O'Brien, the wizened old barkeep came over and started pouring the next round. It was a few minutes before he continued. I had never seen Sean show anything resembling human emotion and it was unnerving.

"I found my way here of course, still had the note in my hand..." He paused, remembering.

"Obie here poured me a shot of the very same whiskey he is pouring me now. He was a lot younger then, but just as ugly and mean."

"Go fuck yourself O'Grady," he replied good naturedly.

"I got a quarter for change, and dropped it in the jukebox. Obie didn't like the music of the day, all the songs were 10 years out of date, fifties music, which was ok with me, that was the music I had grown up with. You got three plays for a quarter in those days, so I picked 'Runaway', by Del Shannon, 'PT109' which was a song about JFK in World War two, and the 'Wanderer' by Dion." He slammed down the entire drink and took a deep breath.

"Fucking Maggie just ran off, just flat out left town without a word. We were going to be married, I had a good job at the shipyard in Southie, and we had our whole fucking life planned out. That song, Runaway, was Dell singing about some girl that ran off, so between that and the fine, fine blessed whiskey that they serve here, I was getting into a certain state of mind."

"I was starting to ask myself, what now? Then PT109 comes on, and JFK was my hero in those days, hell he still is. Irish boy from Boston in the White house, young, good looking, new ideas, and that kid had giant balls. Not afraid of Nixon, not afraid of Khrushchev, didn't take crap from anyone. PT109 was a song about how in World War two, Kennedy was Captain of a small torpedo boat that the Japs sank, and how he saved his crew."

"That day in the yard, we had just finished work on an old freighter and the union sent over a bus full of crew to man the ship and John Clark, the patrolman, tried to recruit me, he said that they needed riggers and welders and he could get me into the union, and get me a job... I remember watching the ship pull away from the dock, sound a long blast on the horn, and I thought 'that is no life for a married man'. He paused again, staring off into space for a while.

"That van had been coming and going to the yard couple times a week since the day I started and Johnny never said boo to me before, I tell you the sea gods moved him to talk to me, and put all the other pieces together that day." Another pause.

"I was just sitting right here, thinking about what it would be like to be Captain of a torpedo boat, in the dark, with Japanese destroyers prowling about. Then The Wanderer came on, and I thought, I too, am the kind of guy that likes to roam around, and what the fuck was left to stop me? Not Maggie, that bitch panicked and took off. So I walked right out that door, and called Johnny, and two weeks later I

205

THERE I WAS

had my Z-card, joined the union and went to sea in the Merchant Marine. The rest is history and sea stories."

He finished his story and we sat together quietly enjoying the fine liquor, and admiring the curvy cocktail waitress. But in the meantime, old Gus had been drinking up his courage. His balls got bigger with every bottle, and when some of his thick skulled drinking buddies showed up, they seemed to feel that their numerical advantage evened the playing field up. Sean decided that Gus, as the instigator, and a miserable fuck in general, needed a special lesson, and a mere beating was not enough.

Gus was afraid of just such special attention, so he managed to get some poor strapping young lad who was blissfully unaware of the magnitude of his opponent, to lead the charge. Sean, who was getting on in years, was impatient, and was in no mood to gently school this young bull and turned the volume up to 'Southeast Asia' immediately. The boy tried to tackle Sean, who moved ever so slightly towards the young fool, closing the distance, messing up the boys timing, and delivering a vicious elbow to the boy's face, breaking his nose, and standing him up on his heels.

Sean was pretty focused on getting to Gus, and this young buck was still, unfortunately for him, between Sean and his prey, and foolish enough not to quit while he still had the choice. Sean's left hand hooked up at the boys head, open handed, cuffing his ear, which by itself is an effective blow, concussing the ear can mess a person's balance, but Sean didn't stop there, he closed his hand, grabbing the ear and snatched his hand back quickly taking the ear with it.

This was actually a signature move of his. It is only a tiny bit of skin that holds the ear onto the head and it is remarkably easy to snatch someone's ear right off. Sean would then hold the ear up in the palm of his hand right in the persons face, showing his victim, which had quite a bit of shock value, and tended to capture the full attention of the poor fool who would be too focused on the mayhem of his separated body part to see Sean's right hand drop way down low for the well-practiced knockout punch from downtown.

The fracas in the bar wasn't loud enough to mask the whimpering sound that escaped the young tough when he realized that he had just lost his ear, that sound was followed immediately by the resounding smack of a perfectly delivered one step, full body weight haymaker, and the ensuing crash of a young fool flying through the air and crashing into a table. Two of Gus's posse came flying at me, one after the other. I had my back to the bar and no time to find a better place but I had been here before, and had a signature move of my own.

The first one to come at me was a bit too aggressive, and gave me all kinds of his own momentum to use against him. I stepped towards him, turning sideways and bringing my hand up alongside his face getting it behind his head and drove his head

THERE I WAS

down across the front of my body, slamming his face into the bar. My Martial Arts instructor would call that 'control the head for an inside takedown', but I rarely did it in the open where it would become a takedown, I called it "Bar Face". The best part came right after their face hit the bar and their natural instinct and Newton's Law of equal and opposite reaction came into play. The victims, if still conscious would whip themselves backwards, which even without my help would result in them landing flat on their ass, but with a well-timed shove on my part ended up launching them across the room, in this case driving his head right into the face of his idiot friend, knocking him out.

That bought me enough time to look over to see how Sean was faring, and he had just launched his earless attacker across the room, but didn't see the bastard coming at him from behind with a pool cue raised up over his head like a sledge hammer, just as I opened my mouth to shout a warning, the young red-head who had inspired a sea-story launched himself at Sean's attacker, delivering a furious rain of blows from the oversized fists at the end of his long lanky arms. The attacker managed to get a few weak shots in with the pool cue, which barely seemed to even register with the boy's fierce attack, which simply intensified until the pool cue was broken to splinters and the man wielding it was reduced to a moaning pile of hamburger on the floor.

Sean was as this point systematically dismantling Gus, ensuring that teeth would be lost, and ribs broken, and his beer inflated balls would be sore for a long time. The bartender, also a USMC Veteran, was used to such Shenanigans, and barked an order at Sean:

"ENOUGH!" Sean stopped, looked around, nodded and raised his head victoriously, thumped one hand to his chest

"Time for a victory drink!"

"Not here champ, you know the drill, you have to leave now, go raise hell somewhere else."

"Your loss Sgt. O'Brien, but Aye Aye sir," he turned to the young boy that had saved his skull from the pool cue, and said "You coming along boy? There is whiskey just waiting for us, and I have a present for you. What's your name?"

"Patrick."

"Well alright Patrick, since we are in God's own country here, there is another bar just down the block, so let's get ourselves there and get the festivities started." We adjourned to the next place for the post victory celebrations. Sean sat the boy down at the bar, bought him a drink, and pulled his belt off, handing it to the boy.

"I made this myself, and while it may look like an ordinary belt, it is really a survival tool." The boy looked intrigued. The belt was made from three pieces of

THERE I WAS

leather, one at each end housing the buckle hardware, and one in the back, all held together by several braids of black nylon Para-cord.

"There is a couple hundred feet of sturdy nylon rope in these braids, and each side has two braids, so you can pluck some rope off, and it still functions as a belt. The buckle is a T-grip knife, you can snatch it right off like this." He grabbed the buckle in his fist and a short dangerous looking blade emerged, protruding from the knuckles of his fist. "The blade is black so it is almost invisible at night. Back here, on the leather part in the back." He held the belt up so the boy could see.

"This strap is two pieces of leather laminated together, and there is a secret pouch here, with the opening side up, and some Velcro to hold it closed, and look what is inside there, see, a small gold coin, and a handcuff key. That key is accessible to a man with his hands unjustly cuffed behind his back. The gold coin is currency everywhere on planet earth, and is almost always enough money to get you back to the ship, if you are going to be in the Merchant Marine, you will need that." The boy's eyes opened wide.

"Me? In the Merchant Marine?"

"If you want to boy, you fight and drink well enough, and I owe you one for watching my back, I can get you in if you have a mind."

"Hell Yeah!" The boy shouted. Sean smiled, and patted the boy on the back, and bought us all another round. Sean seemed pleased with himself, as if he had passed the torch and personally seen to it that the traditions would survive to the next generation.

THE ODYSSEY ENDS

Finished with Engines

> *"All of us have in our veins the exact same percentage of salt in our blood that exists in the ocean, and, therefore, we have salt in our blood, in our sweat, in our tears. We are tied to the ocean. And when we go back to the sea – whether it is to sail or to watch it – we are going back from whence we came." – John F. Kennedy*

At that place where the Sahara desert meets the Mediterranean Sea, just outside Bizerte Tunisia, five people from five different corners of planet earth stood against the backdrop of the desert twilight enjoying the moment.

We were gathered at the gate of the oil terminal outside the city proper. As we faced the ocean, to our right, across a towering span of bridge, was the city of Bizerte. The road ran from Bizerte, across that bridge that spanned the shipping channel, out to the oil terminal where we were moored. Beyond the terminal, to our left, was an ocean of sand, the mighty Sahara. The road continued past the gate a few hundred yards and then just ended abruptly in the dust.

A small van that transported Mariners from the ships to the gate had just dropped us off, and we stood at the gatehouse chatting with the guard as we waited for the bus to town. The guard was Tunisian, an Arab of the Fez wearing variety, whose name was probably Achmed. Like most Africans, he sported a giant smile and was perpetually joking around.

I had gone ashore with a Cajun shipmate and the van had picked up a Phillipino Mariner from a Greek tanker, a giant Norwegian from a car carrier, and we all stood there together, enjoying the cool Mediterranean breeze and a lively discussion about how similar we all were, the world around. The five of us, each from different worlds, different cultures, all shared the same joy of the African desert twilight.

As we all watched the sun paint the desert an astonishing array of pinks, purples and reds as it settled into the west, a small cloud of dust began to grow on the horizon. Soon a vague silhouette appeared beneath the cloud, and as the moments passed, it became clear that a caravan was emerging from the desert. Like something out of an Arabian Nights storybook, a long train of camels, complete with chunks of salt strapped to their backs, slowly trudged out of the desert. Dust encrusted Bedouins draped in robes and head dresses rode or walked alongside. Pans, bags and the various Bedouin necessaries dangled and clanged as the camels and travelers stomped by, bringing their dust cloud with them.

THERE I WAS

The Tunisian guard smiled and waved at the travelers, and gave us a knowing nod, acknowledging that we were all together watching the past and present meet where the ancient desert sand meets the modern pavement. As they walked past, barely acknowledging us, I looked back out over the desert they had just crossed and wondered if Timbuktu had been their port of origin.

The dust settled as the sun grew massive and landed on the desert. The profound silence that we were all drinking in was interrupted by the loud click of a loudspeaker microphone being keyed and echoing across the water and under the bridge, followed immediately by the Muezzins call to prayer. I had been hearing that call in various countries for decades, and prior to this evening, I always speculated that it was the ritual strangling of a cat, but there on the edge of the Sahara, the dust from a Bedouin caravan still settling, a cool breeze blowing off the mother Mediterranean, and my new friend laying prostate on his prayer rug facing Mecca, I heard the music.

Even though I had heard that sound a thousand times before, I heard it in its proper context for the first time that very moment, we all just bowed our heads, facing in the same direction as Achmed, and enjoyed the power of the moment. The prayers ended, we said goodbye to our new friend, and rode the bus to town. I enjoyed kebobs, bought a Fez, went to an open air market, and then headed back to the ship, taking a better understanding of the world with me as I left.

The ship was on its very last journey, bound for the shipbreaking port in Alang India, where we would deliver it, and fly on to our next adventure. This meant that the next leg of the journey was a trip through the ditch. Next stop, Port Said (pronounced Sa-eed) at the northern end of the Suez Canal. The Canal isn't big enough for two way traffic, so each day they run one northbound and two southbound convoys, the first two of which are timed to pass at a point along the way called the Great Bitter Lake.

We anchored at Said with the rest of the Southbound Convoy and prepared for the transit. There were special lights that needed rigging and various other details, but the Canal Authority arranged all that, in fact, you had to use their electricians, line-handlers, and various other workers while in the Canal. Not that most of them worked, they just came for the tribute.

The Captain would personally receive each worker, up to and including the Pilot and issue them cartons of cigarettes in quantities appropriate to their rank. Line Handlers got one, Customs Officer and Pilot got something between 5-10. More skilled trades and petty bureaucrats and inspectors got something in between. They were each escorted into the Captain's office, in a long greedy parade, some maintained the pretense of legitimacy by issuing their permits or other various forms of paperwork after receiving their graft. Many were escorted right back to the gangway and left on the same boat upon which they arrived, moving on to the next boat to conduct a 'lighting inspection' that in no way involved lights.

The 'line handlers' and 'electricians' didn't have many real functions, they rigged a light or two, did some minimal line handling, but not even enough work to keep one person busy for more than a few minutes, much less the half dozen or so that were required. It was all about the tribute, and to pay the salary of these well connected locals. They were generally corralled into a single area, which they inevitably converted into a bazaar, laying out blankets and selling trinkets, Arab head dresses, and tourist junk.

By this time, I had been transiting the Canal for decades, and had at least a few dozen transits under my belt. My first trip through was in the early eighties while I was still in the Navy. At that time, you could still see the occasional pillbox, or burnt out building, bearing the scars of the battles of the Suez War, fought back in the fifties. The bullet hole riddled shells of burnt out buildings and scorched fortifications were slowly removed over the years until now little to no evidence of the conflict was visible.

Transiting is a lot of work for the Captain, who needs to be on the Bridge for the entire event. He or she is ultimately responsible for the safety of the ship and crew, but is in the awkward position of having to defer entirely to the Pilot, who is directing the Helmsman. The southbound convoy would often have to anchor in the Great Bitter Lake while the northbound cleared the southern reaches. The run takes about 12 hours, depending on how long you spend at anchor. Preparations, the cigarette tribute, leaving the anchorage, forming the convoy, all take about 2-3 hours, and the navigation at the southern end is incredibly complex and busy for another 2-3 hours, which means a long day for both the Captain and the Navigator.

Our convoy started bright an early in the AM, and on this occasion involved several Naval ships from various Navies. This meant higher security, so as we steamed through the canal, a column of military vehicles flanked the canal on either side rolling along with us. The transit ends when you and dozens of other ships spill into the crowded confines of the Gulf of Suez at the northern end of the Red Sea.

Ships are leaving and arriving by the dozen, in the dark, going to anchor as they arrive, or all heading south as they leave. It is like leaving a rock concert, while simultaneously, thousands are arriving for the next concert, only all the traffic is massive, and explosive. South we steamed into the Red Sea, a slender reach extending a few hundred miles between the Arabian Peninsula and Africa.

The Red Sea meets the Gulf of Aden at its southern end, above the Horn of Africa in a *narrow strait* (116) called the Bab-al-Mandab. There is a small island there, owned and occupied by Yemen, where they traditionally maintain a tank that patrols the beach, running along with the shipping traffic, training its gun at you. It has

THERE I WAS

been rumored to have taken a few potshots at ships from time to time. As you leave the Red Sea, you enter the pirate infested waters of the Gulf of Aden north of the Horn of Africa.

From there it was just few days run to the shipbreaking yards in Alang India. A lot of shipbreaking was done in India in those days. India had more lenient environmental laws, and cheaper labor. Things have tightened up a bit with the US passing some laws restricting on how US Flagged ships can be disposed of, but the US is no longer a large fleet, and only owns a small fraction of the world's ships. So the gesture, while noble, had little effect.

The ships in the port of Alang are not docked. There are so many of them, and the port is so primitive, that they are just run up onto the beach and boats and barges full of workers- come alongside to perform the work. As a Navigator, you spend your entire career learning how to keep the ship off of the beach. Letting the ground hit the hull is the cardinal sin, and perhaps the worst mistake a Navigator can make.

So there I was... my bow pointed straight at the beach, with the Indian Pilot explaining in his deeply accented, but perfect English the proper speed to achieve, to run it up on the beach properly. The Captain couldn't bring himself to beach his beloved ship, and so he let me do the honors.

I ordered the engine ahead to ramming speed, against every instinct I had so carefully honed over the years, and drove the ship up onto the beach. We had pumped out every bit of ballast so she floated up as high as she could, and timed the entire event so that we would be hitting the top of the tide right as the bottom hit the hull.

The feel of the sand hitting the hull was sickening, having been experienced before in many a nightmare. We carved a slot into the sand as everything eventually grinded to a halt. The Pilot seemed pleased. We were settled in nicely, no list nor lean. The shipbreakers wasted no time swarming the ship, and we all gathered our bags to head to the airport.

There was a bit of a hullabaloo on the way out when the Indian official receiving the ship saw me carrying my sextant, and decided that I was stealing the ships equipment, which was now rightfully theirs. He didn't seem to believe that the sextant was mine. I told him that Navigators don't assume that a ship will have a working sextant, so they bring their own.

He asked me if I had a receipt, I told him I didn't carry the receipt around with me, there was no earthly reason to do so. He persisted, I asked him if he carried a receipt for his fancy hat. This argument actually got him thinking. Indian officials are inherently reasonable and polite. As reasonable as he was, there is an ingrained habit of law and order in the commonwealth traditions, and he would require more

THERE I WAS

than a reasonable explanation. He tracked down the manifest and sent out an agent with a much less fancy hat to confirm that the requisite number of sextants were still on board.

By now I had missed my flight, but given that the fault was theirs, they put me up in a nice hotel, and re-arranged my travel schedule. I took the opportunity to request a route via Singapore, with the connections back to the states open ended. He was happy to comply, and by now we were getting to be old friends. I asked him where he would recommend I seek some fine authentic Indian cuisine and he didn't just tell me, he showed me. He invited me to join him and several of his colleagues for dinner that night at a local function where they would be serving Tandoori. My meander towards the US was off to an auspicious start. Nothing like a good curry to launch an adventure.

Singapore is an old friend. It is located almost directly on the equator, at the eastern end of the busiest waterway on earth, the Straits of Malacca. The Straits of Malacca were pirate infested long before the Somali's took to ocean pillaging. The Somali's just seemed to get more press.

I planned on staying in Singapore long enough to decompress, and then ride a train that dubbed itself the "Orient Express" to Chengmai Thailand and visit some friends.

Chengmai is home to the 'underground' jade market, an open black market that trades in rare gems from Burma. All of the world's imperial jade, and most of the world's finest rubies and sapphires come from Burma, now officially Myanmar, and many of them are smuggled into Thailand where they are sold in this somewhat tolerated and open "Black" market.

It is also close to the bridge over River Kwai, which I was hoping to visit. I had a Merchant Mariner friend who lived in Chengmai and ran tours and excursions to these various attractions and also owned a bar with rooms to rent upstairs. It was at this bar, which was a favorite haunt of expats and the community of Merchant Marine from all over the world who lived here, that I bumped into my old shipmate Santo.

Santo and I were enjoying some fine San Miguel beer, another dear old Philipino friend, and listening to the fantastic Philipino cover band that, like the thousands of other Philipino cover bands throughout Asia, was playing covers that sounded precisely like the originals. It was is if Michael Jackson and Lionel Ritchie were playing the bar. Santo was telling me stories of his days in the police department on the Island of Mindanao, where there was an ancient tradition of head hunting, now adopted by the local Muslim terrorists.

Santo had a wife here in Chengmai, and invited me to dinner the following night. He also had a wife in Manila and invited me also to come visit his homeland. Santo

THERE I WAS

had many wives, a practice not unheard of in the Maritime trades. Many Philipino Mariners work long contracts, leaving for years on end, and that was Santo's story. He came home to Manila about every two years. He and his wife owned a small beach resort just west of Manila that rented "Nipa Huts" a tourist version of the traditional Philipino bamboo and grass abode, and he wanted to introduce me to his family.

So there I was, a week later, in tiny but luxurious Nipa hut, on a gorgeous tropical beach, with a fantastic Tiki bar and restaurant, and all the San Miguel and Blessed Whiskey a reprobate Mariner could ask for. His entire family lived and worked at the resort, his brothers and sisters, mother, aunts and uncles, his wife's family, and I was the guest of honor. He introduced me to the Bar Manager, a gorgeous brown eyed Filipina named Lucy from a good Manila family who had just graduated from college.

Santo was looking for some help in his endeavor. He wanted to find a partner to help look over the place in his absences. He had no plans yet for abandoning his polygamist ways, and he wanted to sell the bar and restaurant to expand the Nipa hut portion of the resort.

Many a Mariner is tempted to 'go native' and it had been something that I had been thinking about a lot lately. My trips home were becoming more like dutiful chores than joyous returns. Every attempt at romance in the West ended up failing. No matter how clear, open and honest I was about my chosen calling and how going to sea was a part of me that would never change. Inevitably, once a relationship became serious, they would ask.

"When are you going to stop?", or "When we get married, are you going to keep doing this?" That was always the end. A misunderstanding that profound was not reconcilable. Merchant Marine is not what I do, it is who I am. I had recently come to the conclusion that some people were meant to go through life alone.

The world needed soldiers and sailors to keep the world safe, and the cargo moving, fueling the engines of trade. Pushing forty now and never married, I was thinking that I had a damn good life, and should just reconcile the fact that I was not normal and never would be, and thank God for that. I loved adventuring and to die fighting in a bar on some God forsaken waterfront was a glorious end. Certainly preparing to die fighting prior to engaging in violence in a dark alley generally scared the shit out of whoever was suddenly realizing that a glorious death might be what you were seeking. It gave me quite an edge in that respect. Valhalla was awaiting, and it is a fantastic battle cry.

Santo sprung his idea on me the day I was leaving, telling me to "tink about it." So off I went back to the States, to my stressed out family and friends, in their fast paced insulated bubble of a country, focused on OJ Simpson or whatever tripe the

214

media was feeding them, oblivious to the harsh tragic history that was constantly unfolding around them.

Back in Boston, I went through the motions, visiting family, looking up my boys, telling sea stories. All the while my mind was on that beach in Manila. I knew that taking the first step down the road to going native was like taking that first shot of heroin, my future would forever be shaped by the decision. Stepping through Far Eastern looking glass would be the beginning and the end. I was getting bored at home, but not yet nearly ready to return to sea, so I decided to visit some family in upstate NY. Take a nice drive through the middle of nowhere, far from the Siren's song.

It's when you stop looking that you find what you seek. The sea gods, of course, guided me to Ithaca, as sea gods will do. There I met my match, and found a home and hearth. I continued my travels for several years, but for the first time, had a reason to come home. I had finally paused long enough for roots to take hold. All voyages end. Mine was not the first Odyssey to end in Ithaca, and likely won't be the last, but the adventures live on in the stories.

"We shall not cease from exploration
And the end of all our exploring
Will be to arrive where we started
And know that place for the first time"
T.S Elliot

Appendix A – Life at Sea
An overview of all things maritime

Anthropologists who study different human cultures have acknowledged that shipboard life is indeed its own distinct culture. The stories in this book take place in environments that are bafflingly foreign to most people, so a little background is in order.

The pointy end is the bow, the end from whence comes the wake, the stern. If something is closer to the bow than it is to you, then it is forward of you, if you are moving towards the bow, you are moving forward. If something is closer to the stern than it is to you, then it is aft, after, or abaft of you, if you are moving towards the stern you are moving aft.

If you draw a straight line down the center of the ship from the bow to the stern longitudinally, that is the centerline. If you are facing the bow anything to the right of the centerline is starboard, anything to the left is port. If something is between you and the port or starboard side, it is outboard of you, if something is between you and the centerline, it is inboard of you.

The backbone of the ship is the keel, which is a structural member that runs the length of the ship from bow to stern, dead center at the base of the hull. The hull is the skin of the ship and keeps the ocean out. It is the part of the ship whose enclosed volume creates the buoyancy that keeps the ship on the correct side of the water's edge. The hull runs up from the keel to the main deck, which is the highest deck that intersects the hull. Any structure above the main deck is the superstructure.

Each 'floor' or 'story' below the main deck is called a 'deck' and numbered starting at the Main deck, One, increasing as you proceed down to the bilges. Any 'floor' or 'story' above the main deck is referred to as a 'level' and numbered upwards from the main deck. The first nine levels are preceded by a zero, so the first level above the main deck is the 01 level. The first deck below the main deck is second deck.

Ships are powered in various ways nowadays. Classic propulsion was via steam turbines that spin the propeller, or more correctly 'the screw'. Imagine a tea kettle the size of a small apartment building creating steam at pressures high enough that a pinhole in a pipe would neatly slice a man in half. On the plus side, steam that hot is invisible so the poor Engineer would never see it coming. Old school steam Engineers were known to carry a broom stick and wave it about before them to check for leaks.

THERE I WAS

Steam is far less common these days, and gave way to diesel propulsion back in the sixties and seventies. Non-engineers can tell that they are on a diesel ship by the constant vibration. If you feel as if you are living inside of a lawn mower, it is most likely a diesel.

A new trend in propulsion is the 'diesel electric' where the diesel is connected to a generator which makes electricity for electric motor propulsion. These ships often have 'azimuthing' pods instead of rudders, where the motor itself spins about and the ship is maneuvered using 'vectored thrust'. These ships are a pure joy to drive and depending on how many thrusters they have, can maneuver as gracefully as a ballet dancer pirouetting in tight confines on the stage of the inner harbor, mocking the vestigial tugboats as you leave them behind, departing the harbor unescorted.

Rarer still is the gas turbine propulsion. These are literally jet engines that spin a shaft that is reduced through a giant gear train to turn the screw. Life on board these ships is like living on board a vacuum cleaner as large as a skyscraper. They are far more common in the Navy than anywhere else, as they are fast, quick to ramp up to speed, and can be easily replaced. They are also quite finicky and require a small army of technicians constantly tweaking, tuning and occasionally singing a sweet lullaby softly, to keep them running properly

You may ask, 'what is the difference between a boat and a ship?', and there is no simple answer. There is no clear threshold that defines when a boat becomes a ship. One simple working definition is that a boat can be carried on a ship but not vice versa. Regardless of the boat/ship semantic debate, all vessels are categorized by their size, measured in tonnage. Tonnage is a complex measurement that is intended to equate to the volume of water displaced by the vessel. The largest ships, those above 1500 Gross Registered Tons, are in the highest "unlimited tonnage" class. To give an example a tugboats run from a few hundred to a few thousand tons, the largest yachts are just a few hundred tons, a destroyer is a few thousand tons, an aircraft carrier 50-60 thousand tons, and supertankers can run from 100,000-500,000 tons.

Ships come in a nearly endless variety of shapes and sizes, and are peopled by the most varied slice of humanity imaginable. There is the 'brown water' environment, harbors and rivers and near coastal regions in sight of land, which bustle with the full range and scope of maritime diversity: Fishing boats, pleasure craft, commercial vessels of every tonnage and category; ferry's, freighters, tankers, tugs, barges, workboats, pleasure boats, passenger vessels, fishermen, and warships alike all tooling about in narrow buoyed channels, in and around reefs and obstructions, under bridges, and just offshore, all within sight of humanity.

Then there is the blue water environment. Deep blue, the big open... the watery part of the world. Blue water environs are far less crowded, and far less forgiving.

THERE I WAS

The restless souls who willingly lose sight of land and leave the hard mountains for a hard life amid mountainous waves are a special breed of Mariner. Those lonely tracts of endless wind and surf are the sacred haunts of the big ships, professional Mariners, brave fishermen, rare intrepid pleasure boaters and of course the occasional south Pacific Islander in a canoe wearing nothing but a smile and a loin cloth.

Among the large ships, in the realm of the unlimited tonnage, there are two primary communities; the Navy, and the Merchant Marine. The Navy is a branch of the military and mans the warships that are the property of the state. Naval Mariners are enlisted sailors and commissioned officers from every walk of life, serving their country to man the frigates, destroyers, cruisers, patrol boats, Amphibious Landing ships, Aircraft carriers and other "Capital ships of war". Their ships are gray, their clothing is uniform, their discipline is strict, their service is admirable and their food is just awful.

Navy ships are sleek, fast and dangerous, and are tightly honeycombed to withstand the damage of combat at sea. They are crowded to capacity with sailors, dozens of people for each single job. The manning scheme is premised on the concept that when the bullets start flying you need extra people. People to step over the body of the Helmsman and take the wheel, people to fight the fires, people to shoot the guns, man the phones, get the equipment to continue functioning after the explosions. People are needed to keep fighting and then get the ship patched up to fight again (you should be imagining that Anchors Aweigh is playing loudly in the background).

The Bridge of a Navy ship is manned with a dozen or so people on a slow watch, but while navigating in tight confines, or during some complex naval operation, a ball park crowd crams itself into the pilothouse, each sailor yelling into a phone, or walkie talkie, or screaming orders and acknowledgements. Rapid fire staccato protocols being shouted as fast as humanly possible through the intercoms:

Engineering Officer: "Ensure-the-shaft-brake-engage/disengage-pushbutton-indicator-is-the-disengage-position-and-the-shaft-brake-disengage-indicator-is-illuminated"

Junior Officer of the Deck: "The-shaft-brake-engage/disengage-push-button-IS-in-the-disengage-position-and-the-disengage-indicator-IS-illuminated"

This song and dance plays out in a crowd among a dozen or so other such interactions all at equally high volumes amid the background noise of a half dozen or so active harbor and tactical radio stations chattering away incessantly. Each comment is repeated by some phone talker passing along the status to some remote station letting everyone know that the

THERE I WAS

ShaftBrakeEngageDisengagePushButtonIndicatorIs…indeed…
InTheDisengagePosition.

People scribbling furiously in the logbooks describing the event in crisp prose with capital block letters.   Quartermasters, Boatswains Mates, Signalmen and lookouts with binoculars, telescopes and alidades roaming about the bridgewings, taking bearings and identifying and scanning the movements of nearby vessels. RADAR operators taking ranges and plotting the vessel traffic. Radio operators talking with harbor control, the naval squadron commander, the naval tactical commander, the base operations, every other naval vessel within a thousand miles, and to the great naval gods at the Pentagon.

The Combat control center below will be just as busy, but less frenetic, the engine control room will be in similar state, dozens of people working, communicating, shouting, pushing buttons, reading gauges. The bow and stern will be covered with dozens or even scores of deck seaman, scurrying about like ants. Ten to a line, heaving and tugging, and coiling while vapid boatswains scream at the top of their lungs.   Hundreds of people working at full bore to achieve the gargantuan feat of getting the ship off the dock and out to sea.

At the next pier down, a Merchant ship ten times as large will have 3-5 people on the Bridge, the Captain, who may or may not be taking an active role, the Navigator, and a Helmsman, sometimes an additional lookout will quietly join the routine, and usually a harbor Pilot if the port authority requires it. A quiet phone conversation between the Navigator and the Engineer below decks brings control of the engine to the Bridge, the Navigator takes a moment to log the event using a brief, universal shorthand, then makes a quick call on the VHF to the port control authority. He then tells the Helmsman to conduct the appropriate tests before peeking into the RADAR to see any traffic of note, and then to the bridgewing to visually assess said traffic. When the 'gator' has finished his checklist, and is ready to get underway, the Capt. will give the order to 'let go the lines' and three people on the bow, and three on the stern will recover the lines with massive capstan winches and windlasses, and no small measure of maritime skill. A small crew of a few dozen professionals working together to achieve the routine task of putting to sea.

The Merchant Marine is the commercial/industrial side of the Maritime coin, filled with the giant privately owned ships upon which the trade that powers the world economy is built. Their ships come in every size shape and color from rusty freighters filled with finished goods, to bulk carriers full of rare dirt, to shiny white cruise ships filled with old people and honeymooners (the nearly dead and the newly wed) to specialized cable layers and survey ships. Their crews range from the tattooed dregs of society, in full pirate regalia singing sea chanteys, to no nonsense tankermen in hardhats and khakis' barking crisply into a walkie-talkie.

THERE I WAS

There are similarities between the Navy and Merchant Marine, plenty of common ground and a mostly cordial relationship, but there are some fundamental divergences, and differences of opinion are not unheard of. Like many in the trade, I have done both. I spent my youth planning to go to sea, and started that journey in the service of my country. I was a Sailor in my youth, but now, I am a Professional Mariner. I have nothing but respect for Sailors, and the fondest memories of my days of sailoring, but there are some very basic differences between a Sailor and Mariner.

Anyone can walk to the recruiter, raise their right hand, and if they survive boot camp, they can be a sailor. A farm boy from Iowa, who has never seen the ocean, or smelled the tide can report to his ship, discover a propensity for seasickness and spend the next four years of his life green and puking. God bless them all for what they do, for their service and their dedication, and their youthful vigor, but the average sailor is about 19 and only recently salted.

Even the grizzled old veteran Navy swabs, 'rotate' from ship to shore duty, spending several years ashore between ships three ashore, four asea. A typical rotation for a Mariner is 4/4, four months on, four months off year after year. Navy ships spend about 60% of their time at sea, and the other 40% at the dock, training and polishing brass. Merchant ships spend more than 90% of their time at sea (time is money, and a ship at dock is costing money, not earning it). When a Navy sailor applies his experience for a Mariners license, only 60% of his or her sea time is counted as actual sea time.

A person can span an entire career as a sailor and never handle a line, rig a ladder or boom, launch a boat or even tie a bowline, and there is nothing wrong with that, the Navy is huge and they need barbers, disbursing clerks and storekeepers to run their show, but one can retire as a sailor having only spent a few years at sea, and never having practiced any seamanship.

Mariners live at sea, working in Maritime trades. Everyone on a Merchant ship is a Mariner, from the lowest bilge in the Engine Room to the top of the Mast. The average age of professional Mariner is about 40. I once sat at dinner with a several officers of both services, and the subject came up, and the Merchant Captain at the table summarized the difference in experience perfectly when he asked the seasoned Naval Captain how much total sea time he had in his career. This particular Naval Captain was a man whose career had risen above the mere commanding of ships, had spent 25 years in the navy, 17 of them aboard ships, the last two tours, or six years, as Captain. The Merchant Captain simply replied, I have more than 17 year's sea time as a Master.

The term "Master" is a more accurate title for a Merchant Marine ship's Captain. In the Navy, Captain is both a title and a rank, that is, anyone who commands a ship is that ship's Captain, but smaller ships may have lower ranking officers as

220

THERE I WAS

'Captains'. The rank of Naval Captain is equal in rank to a full Colonel in the lesser (non-naval) services. Professional Mariners must be licensed, and those licenses are based on experience in the class (size) of ship, like the Navy, anyone who commands a vessel is that vessels Captain. In the unlimited tonnage class, the highest level, the most senior license is that of Master of Ocean steam or motor vessels of any gross tonnage, any waters: or simply Master Mariner.

For all their differences, that gap in experience is generally acknowledged, and most Naval personnel are amazed that such huge ships have so few people, and your typical Merchant Marine, like most people, watch Naval ships doing Naval exercises such as landing and launching aircraft or offshore bombardment with awe, and grudgingly given mutual respect is the norm.

All ships have similar organization and routines. There is the Deck Department, and the Engine Department, and some version of the 'Stewards Department'. Some ships, especially Navy ships in all their glorious complexity, will have other departments, Aviation, Combat information, Gunnery, etc. but all ships have deck-apes, engineering snipes, and cooks. All ships personnel have rank as well, there are officers and non-officers.

In the Navy, there are commissioned officers and enlisted personnel, in the Merchant Marine, there are licensed officers and non-licensed personnel. That distinction exists on all large ships, and generally on small ones as well. In the Navy, it is a more formal and serious distinction, with both the classic distinctions of military rank in addition to the naval traditions of officers and crew. On merchant ships, it is generally much less formal, but no less real. They are distinctions rooted in hundreds of years of tradition, abuse and privilege.

I climbed through the ranks from the lowest level to the highest, starting as an ordinary deck seaman and rising to the rank of Unlimited Ocean Master, a Master Mariner, and I learned all of the subtle, but very real differences. I watched as the thickness of my mattresses and the width of my rack (bed) grew with each promotion. I went from sharing a room and/or a head (bathroom) to having a suite of rooms of my very own. The line between officers and non-officers still separates two worlds.

Merchant ships are mostly just the three departments. There are generally, on modern ships, eight licensed officers and a handful of non-licensed officers and crew. The Captain is the senior officer of the deck department and ship overall, and is equal in rank to the Chief Engineer. The Captain typically has three mates, The Chief Mate who is usually the cargo officer, the Second Mate, who is the Navigator, and the third Mate, who is possibly young and inexperienced. Older ships, or certain types of ships can have more deck officers, but four is typical. The Chief Engineer will also have three 'Assistant Engineers'. The First, Second, and Third assistants.

THERE I WAS

Unlicensed people in the deck department at the entry level are Ordinary Seaman, skilled journeymen are Able Bodied Seamen or AB's. The senior unlicensed member of the deck department is usually the Boatswain. AB's come in various flavors, and there are various 'deck trades' and job titles, but Able Bodied seaman is the credential they all carry. There are Quartermasters, Boatswains Mates, Coxswains, and even a few Ships carpenters and sailmakers are left, but they all hold credentials as Able Bodied Seamen.

The engine department is more complex, at the entry level there are Wipers, above that there are many different trades and titles, Firemen, Oilers, Water tenders, Qualified Member of the Engine Department (QMED), Deck Engine Mechanics (DeMechs), Pumpmen, refrigeration engineers, junior engineers, Electricians, and more still I am sure. The senior unlicensed member of the engine Department, can be have various titles, but typically is an Electrician on Freighters, or a Pumpman on tankers.

Before the days of automation, when labor costs were low, crews were larger. There would be two Third Mates, and two Third Assistant Engineers, and the Chief Mate and First Assistant Engineer would not have to stand a watch. Ships would have Pursers to deal with paperwork and administrative chores that are now handled by the Captain and Chiefs. Before the days of the autopilot, a Bridge watch would have a Mate, two AB's and an Ordinary seaman (OS). Modern ships have a Mate, and one or maybe two AB's.

Back in the 80's and 90's as ships became more automated, crews were shrinking at alarming rate. This trend in shrinking crews was quite alarming to the Merchant Marine Labor community, already in a long state of decline since WWII. The demise of passenger liners in the sixties, and the increasing size and efficiency of cargo ships had caused a steady decline in the size of Merchant Fleets the world around.

The trend was mercifully arrested in the late 90's by an international accord originated by a group called the International Maritime Organization, a sub-branch of the United Nations crime family that set standards in the maritime industry. A rule was created that was adopted by all nations' party to the treaty; it was called the Standards of Training, Certification and Watchstanding, or STCW. It had a broad impact on how ships were crewed, and how crews were trained and certified. It sent the entire industry into a frenzy to get crews trained and certified up to the new rigorous standards.

Most aspects of shipboard life, the daily routine, the departmental organization, even the meals are rooted in traditions and history. Both the US Navy and US Flag Merchant Marine are proud scion of the British Maritime tradition. The sharp distinctions between officers and crew, licensed and unlicensed are vestiges of

THERE I WAS

European elitist class distinctions. British built ships, even in the modern day, have the privileges of the upper crust engineered into them. Officer's accommodations are larger, more ornate and opulent. The table from which officers dine, would be fine carved mahogany versus the more utilitarian ship fitted steel or aluminum of the unlicensed mess.

The Glorious British nautical tradition has spawned many a Maritime culture, and Canadian, Australian, New Zealand, and Indian officers are often referred to as "Commonwealth" officers. The days of Admiral Nelson are long gone, but the echoes of that proud tradition ring down through the generations to the maritime of today, though without the funny hats. Many of the mundane, ordinary details of everyday shipboard life are rooted in the history of the British Navy.

Ships never sleep, they operate constantly, moving cargo, or patrolling the seaways, fishing, transiting, surveying, or working their specific trade. At any time of day or night, Mariners and Sailors are awake, steering, navigating, tending the engines, baking bread, or staring endlessly at the RADAR sweeping across the screen. The days are divided into watches and while there are various ways to set up a watch schedule, by far the most common is the traditional six four hour watches per day.

It is normal for a Merchant Marine to work 10-12 hours/day or more, every day for 120 days straight. It is a grueling schedule, working a 12 hour shift every single day for four months straight, except on the days when you are called out every day for a week in the middle of the night to extend your work days to 16 hours or more, while conveniently interrupting your already insufferably brief sleep intervals.

With sleep such a privileged rarity, one can imagine the importance of coffee. Ships all have emergency generators large enough to power the primary needs of a ship in the event the big generators fail. The rudder will always have power, the fuel pumps and ventilation fans. On the Bridge, when the ship loses power, the RADARS, the GPS and other electronic navigation equipment all go dark. All the communication gear except the bridge to bridge VHF and the distress signaling equipment are silent, the lights go off, the engine controls revert to the Engine Room, and the helm, the VHF radio, and the coffee machine are the only functioning pieces of equipment on the Bridge. The coffee machine is required by law, to be on the emergency circuit, you can navigate and avoid collision by seaman's eye, but those eyes must be open.

When the ship is in port, the watches, which are much less involved, are usually adjusted to be eight hours long, with odd rotations to allow longer intervals for the off-watch people to go ashore and get into trouble. Not that one needs much time to get into trouble on a Merchant ship as those places where they affix themselves to the land, tend to be criminal wastelands.

223

THERE I WAS

The industrial waterfront is generally acres and acres of cargo yards, warehouses and industrial facilities in a thick band between the water and the civilized world (or not so civilized depending on where you tie up). These areas are generally fenced in securely, and are technically private property, so the police are a very rare site. Security is generally some private enterprise engaged by the owner. The owners and/or the private enterprises they engage are often simply the local crime lord. Now not all waterfronts are the same, there are shipyards, cargo yards, oil terminals, public docks, etc. Many of them are perfectly, well run, marginally crime free places, with professionals running the operations, but those ordinary places, by their very nature exclude themselves from these stories. Most of my experience has been on waterfronts at the margins of the civilized world, or worse, the less than civilized world, and are often peopled by less than savory individuals.

Ships are loaded and unloaded by Stevedores and Longshoremen. Stevedoring and Longshoring has a long proud tradition of criminality. These same longshoremen that provide the local 'security' for the waterfront, are generally in the direct employ of the local organized crime lord and see Merchant Marines as a source of income and sport. To get from the ship to the real world, and more importantly, back to the ship, is often an adventure in itself. This often requires a long walk across a half mile of industrial gulag while being actively hunted by professional thugs who know that you have money, exactly what time you will be returning, where you are going, and precisely what route you will be taking.

In Bayonne NJ, the crime is so institutionalized, that when the cops were notified, they made it clear that the local thugs were working in their authorized area, and that no local crime lord ordinances were being violated. The constable seemed genuinely amazed that anyone would complain of being attacked on the waterfront, explaining to us: "That's their dock, what were you doing there anyway?" It was a series of these adventures in some of the rougher waterfronts of the world that led me to a lifetime of studying the Martial Arts. In theory, longshoremen and Merchant Marines are brothers in the maritime trades, oppressed workers of shipper barons in tall top hats and long limousines. In reality there is very little love, and often a vibrant hatred and profound disrespect. Longshore unions have long been openly affiliated with organized criminal enterprises, a practice also not unheard of in the Merchant Marine.

All ships eventually come into port, and this is typically a very happy event for the crew. I, like many (but not all) Mariners, refer to land as the "the beach". Not just sandy bathing suit, Pina colada beaches, any incarnation of dry earth is simply "the beach". Going ashore, to me, was always "storming the beach", probably my Naval background. The various activities that I would seek out when storming the beach varied throughout my career, but it often involved fermented beverages,

224

including of course blessed whiskey, and occasionally there were violent adventures. Swashbuckling was a frequent and revered diversion. There were times, when I, like so many of my maritime brethren would seek more peaceful pursuits, ones that involved feminine companionship, though even those peaceful pursuits often led to adventures less gentle than desired.

When going ashore, I developed a useful set of skills and practices over the years that were instrumental in my survival. There are three things you should always learn how to say in the local language: first and foremost - "Don't Shoot! "This one is very important. In many places in the world, the machine gun toting cops are only four feet tall, and when confronted by seemingly giant western drunken sailors, tend to shoot first and ask questions later. It is my belief, that shooting an American is career enhancing for many of these foreign law enforcement officers. It is worth noting, that as I travelled the world asking people how to say "Don't Shoot" in their native tongue, they universally and without fail state the phrase and hold both hands up palms out. Apparently there is a universal international hand signal that means 'keep your bullets to yourself'. The other two phrases crucial to survival are "Take me to the big boat" and "Cold Beer Please". I have uttered these words in over 30 languages and they have saved my ass or slaked my thirst dozens of times.

I also believe that arresting Merchant Mariners is considered a for-profit enterprise in many lands. It is literally part of a Chief Mates job description to round up jailed crewmen prior to leaving port. The fines paid in green cash are likely a great source of revenue for these underpaid public servants. That is why I would always make or modify my own belts and hide a handcuff key in a small hidden pouch at the very back of the belt, accessible by a man with his hands unjustly cuffed behind his back.

Another important accessory for any traveler is the small gold coin. Gold is money everywhere on earth. You could be lost in the Amazon or the deepest jungles of Borneo and stumble across some lost primitive tribe adorned in loin cloths, with jewelry fashioned from the bones of their enemies. Even a tribe that has never been exposed to the modern world, and even though you hold none of the beads or bone fragments or goat meat that serves as currency in their economy, a gold coin will buy you your way out of there.

Utter your memorized "Take me to the big boat" in the local patois, offer up the precious metal, and be they Basque, Arab, Mandarin Chinese, Bostonian, African Pygmy or Dirty Frenchman, the gold pays the fare home. That is the root of the traditional gold earring of Maritime lore, and while many a Merchant Marine still sports a gold hoop, I found it prudent to keep my gold less public. In the third world the average annual pay is about $300-$500 per year... they will kill you for your boots, and that gold earring looks like a bull's-eye to them.

THERE I WAS

This is also why I always carried both the local currency, as well as some standard American green, which is nearly as universal a currency as gold. I kept little bits and stashes of cash and coin all over my body. A C-note tucked in my boot, gold coin and handcuff key in the secret compartment of my belt, a few bills in each pocket, a money belt under the clothes. Even the most thorough search by the most skilled local cops or criminals was likely to miss something and leave me just enough to get back to the ship.

Arriving back to the ship safely was always a pleasant surprise. Now penniless, bruised and painfully hungover, leaving the dock for the peaceful solitude of big skies and endless oceans was a welcome event. In the early days of my career, before email, and cell phones, leaving the dock meant leaving the entire world behind. News was rare on ocean voyages, and only the occasional ship would have a radio officer caring or sober enough to copy a news telex and post it on a bulletin board somewhere. I always travelled with a short wave radio and would rig a wire antenna up the mast in some convenient place early in the tour, and connect every day at the top of the hour to tune into the BBC news. In those days, ship to shore telephone conversations cost $5/minute, and telexes were twenty five cents a word. Being at sea meant being, at best, only marginally connected.

Arriving to a ship for the first time was always an ordeal. In my youth for the first few tours, before I learned the finer points of managing a maritime career, like many of my ilk, I would return to the union hall looking for work only after the money from the previous tour had run dry. Job hunting in the Merchant Marine has many nuances. In some maritime fields such as Able Seamen and certain Engine Room positions, there are vast personnel shortages, and work is easy to find. In other jobs, such as cook, or junior deck officer, there are dozens of people chasing every job and landing a job usually involves membership in some secret fraternity, or bribing a union official.

I started as a deck seaman with an AB card, and never had to wait long to find work. But I eventually earned my license as a deck officer, and spent years trying to break into the closed confines of the officer's mess. I was told early on to pack your bag prior to starting a job search, and I developed the habit of having my seabag packed and ready to go at a moment's notice, in case an opportunity arose on short notice. Ships can't sail without a full crew, and shipping companies often need people on short notice. I made it a point to let every crewing agent on earth know that I was available on short notice and prior to holidays for the right position.

Walking into a union hall could mean months of waiting, or it could be a brief momentary stop at the beginning of the long trip to meet a ship. As I was ambitious, adventurous, young and single for most of these stories, I did mostly what is known as 'relief' work. Many Mariners would seek 'steady' work with a single company, or

THERE I WAS

on a single ship. Returning every four months to the same berth. I rarely sailed the same ship twice, and had a desire to see everything and learn every skill that the Merchant Marine had to offer. I am self-educated, and each ship and the industry it served was a research project in my autodidactic maritime adventure. Steady Mariner work rang too similar to the 9-5 routine that I was so stringently avoiding.

So at the end of each shore leave, with bags packed I would find a new ship, in a new trade, in an as yet unexplored part of the world: Black oil tankers and pump theory in the Valdez trade, or a tramp freighter and advanced heavy rigging in the southern extremes, car carriers and the rise of post WWII Japan, or maybe military cargo on commercial charters in Europe, touring the grand architecture of Italy, the hearty beer and drinking songs of Germany, the fine art and cultural extremities of the Netherlands, and the pure history of Greece. It was rarely planned, each ship an opportunity to work, learn and seek adventure and fortune, and it usually started with an odyssey.

Relief workers, especially those from Boston, a port which fewer and fewer ships service every year, do a lot of "fly outs". The relentless 120 days of solid 12 hour or greater shifts, sleep deprivation and back breaking physical labor in the harshest environments, would usually begin with a grueling 2-3 day exodus that involved lugging your seabag (filled with everything you might need to work and survive indefinitely for months on end in every environment from the arctic to the tropics) through airports, trains, taxi's, perhaps a small pack animal, small boats and finally up the steep gangway. At the top of the gangway, the person who has been anxiously awaiting relief for days or weeks, would greet you and inform you that the ship was heaving anchor, or letting go lines in just three hours, and you had the first watch... be alert, traffic is heavy here in Port Suez at night, and a storm is expected. He would then bring you, groggy and stumbling with your entire kit strapped to your shoulders up the six flights of stairs to the Captain's office where you would sign Articles.

Articles are the legal agreement between a Captain and the crew. They bond the crew to the ship, especially a ship in foreign trade, and give the Captain ruthless authority over your life. Foreign articles can only be broken by returning to the US, or by the choice of the Captain. The Captain holds your passport, and it is by his/her authority that you are granted the Seaman's Visa. By law, foreign articles must be broken upon entering a US Port, and US Mariners have the right to leave the ship with full payment in cash. I learned early on to be wary of ships that tried to scramble you to the Captain's office too quickly after arriving, and I developed the habit of insisting on stowing my gear, visiting a restroom, and grabbing a drink prior to signing on. This would give me an opportunity to do a quick roam about the ship and get a fair idea of seaworthiness and the crew's state of mind.

THERE I WAS

Cracked welds, plate patches on the main deck, buckled hull plates, rusted through hatches or coamings, or a miserable crew were huge red flags and I had no qualms about turning around and leaving a ship if I felt it was more sink worthy than seaworthy. Insisting on stowing my gear and getting a drink first also allowed me a quick opportunity to assess the cleanliness of my room and the mess, another good indication of the caliber of ship and crew. More often than not, I would sign aboard and begin settling in.

Staterooms in the Merchant Marine are slightly smaller than a hotel room, having a bunk, a desk, and a "settee' or couch, and some space to stow your gear. The rooms get bigger the higher up you are on the food chain, and the newer the ship is. Older ships, and larger crews, often required unlicensed people to share a room, or a head. I never had to share a room during my unlicensed years, though shared heads were still very common.

Once I found my room, dropped off my bags, and met the Captain, it was time to find the Steward. The Steward is usually the senior person the Stewards Department in charge of hotel services on the ship. On typical merchant ships, it is an unlicensed officer, but on passenger ships, they are very senior officers with enough corporate clout to get a Captain fired.

On the scrappy freighters and tankers that I was inclined to ride, the steward was usually an older ethnic gentleman who had been around the world more times than he could count. In the older days, but not so long past that the crustier old salts couldn't remember, the Stewards Department was the only shipboard opportunity for people of color, or Philipino's or other various ethnic groups. Those days had passed, but there remains still several ethnic traditions in the stewards department, and it was not uncommon to find the entire Department crewed by Philipino's or Creoles, or Puerto Ricans, and it was always exciting to see a spicy ethnic bias in the galley and know that you would be enjoying some exotic delicious cuisine on a daily basis for the next four months.

I once sailed a ship where the Captain would brave the dangers of violating the law and union rules upon returning from Europe and not break articles in Jacksonville, the first US port of entry, but wait till New Orleans to re-crew, thus ensuring the hiring of Cajun cooks. Crew morale and food are directly linked, and I believe that bad food is more conducive to mutinous behavior than frequent flogging.

In the decades following WWII, the primary means of transportation across the oceans was via passenger liners. These ships were slowly and painfully replaced by aviation in the fifties and sixties and by the seventies only a few liners remained. These ships were famous for the quality of their cuisine, and many of these world class chefs still remain in the Merchant Marine, feeding small crews of thugs, pirates and fugitives in simple mess rooms, instead of the crème de la crème of society in grand ballrooms. But the Merchant Marine pays very well, and even the best chef will make far better money working a cargo ship, than in the finest restaurant in Manhattan, LA or Boston. I would always seek out the steward in my first few hours aboard ship, introduce myself and tip him handsomely. You never know when you might want an additional towel or some extra fries with your burger.

It usually takes about two weeks to settle in, re-capture your sea legs, and get past the culture shock of a new ship, new time zone, latitude, diet and routine. The first month of the typical four month tour was always the fastest, rushing past in a haze of new stimuli, new sleep schedule and the cascade of thoughts, ponderings and soul searching that always seem to accompany the upheaval of leaving hearth and home for parts unknown. Four months was the normal tour since four months was about the limit of a typical person's endurance. 120 days is about as long as one can be sleep deprived, and continue without a day off. The last month always dragged on slowly, through a fog of exhaustion and sore joints, anticipating with joy the four month recovery till the next tour.

Appendix B – The full 1000 words

1. Pussy
2. Piece of cake
3. Piece of ass
4. Sacred Object of desire
5. Consummation devoutly to be wished
6. Promised land
7. Alter of Venus
8. Amazon Forest
9. Ode to the love garden
10. Pink turtleneck
11. Pink Muffin
12. Baby cannon
13. Baby cave
14. Melting pot
15. Buckwheat in a headlock
16. The Philosopher
17. Bear trappers hat
18. Joyous Occasion
19. Lavish Tropical adventure
20. Old friend
21. Treasured friend
22. Life of a Mariner
23. Main fuel transfer station
24. Hole in the deck
25. Bed of seaweed
26. Fire pit
27. Recruit in-processing facility
28. Foggy darkness
29. Gorgeous flowers
30. Object of our every desire
31. Pink Flamingo

THERE I WAS

THERE I WAS

67. Strait transit
68. Pie
69. Remote reaches
70. Far southern reaches
71. Pocket Monster
72. Epic Adventures
73. Primitive pavilion
74. Life ring
75. Iron Jaw
76. Coolie hat
77. The red sea
78. My mission
79. Beloved Homeland
80. Sheltered Harbor
81. Magnificent bay
82. Grand harbor
83. A wonderful dinner
84. The Wildcat
85. Rats nest
86. Final Masterpiece
87. Grand tribute
88. Piece de resistance
89. Ja Booty
90. Dusty Brown Landscape
91. Scrub
92. Specially Modified Cargo hold
93. Dark smelly hold
94. Acoustical Chambers
95. Gaping Crack
96. Port of Call
97. Guard shack
98. The Cat
99. The Major league
100. The target
101. The Punching Bag

THERE I WAS

102. Necessaries
103. Piece
104. Equipment
105. Oblivion
106. The areas that are forbidden
107. The Pirates cove
108. Holes and Cracks
109. Golden Gate
110. Glorious Landscapes
111. The adventure
112. The gold souk
113. Destination for Tourists, Mariners and locals alike
114. Cut throat
115. Fantastic company
116. Narrow Straight
117. Puki
118. Fotze
119. Snooch
120. Punani
121. Mouse's ear
122. Baloney Flaps
123. Love junction
124. Tampon tube
125. Pok pok
126. Hot Tamaki Wok
127. 'gina128. Penis Place
129. Flange
130. Landing Strip
131. The inlet
132. Pink bits
133. Grotto
134. Fish taco
135. Button
136. Twitchet
137. Penis glove

THERE I WAS

138. Birth chute

139. Squeeze box140. The den

141. Gizmo

142. Crotch waffle

143. Bunny tuft

144. The big casino

145. Dogs mouth

146. Red sea

147. Cuntzilla

148. Ass

149. Flesh tuxedo

150. Snuggery

151. Saloon doors

152. Pie

153. Python siphon

154. Bologna flower

155. Slice of heaven

156. Rooster Jaws

157. Cubby hole

158. Whim wham

159. Oyster

160. Triangular target

161. Harbor

162. Homebase

163. Tongue roll

164. The deflower patch

165. Love crack

166. Taco town

167. Birds nest

168. Lick n stick

169. Tuchas

170. Fuzz bucket

171. Love Donut

172. Arby's with fur

173. Cranny

174. Fur pie
175. Cut up
176. Open wound
177. Cunt
178. Welcome mat
179. Bang hole
180. Cherry pop tart
181. Queef
182. Love blossom
183. Lunch meat
184. Chango
185. The unmentionable
186. Pud pocket
187. Ass neighbor
188. Lady garden
189. Pudenda
190. Bald biscuit
191. Whiskers
192. Pole hole
193. Anchorage
194. Deep pink
195. Clunge (Scottish)
196. Bearded Oyster
197. Piss flaps
198. Furrogi (polish)
199. Passion fruit
200. Stinky speedway
201. Republic of Labia
202. Tuna
203. Canyon
204. Cock Silo
205. Cock Sleeve
206. Beef Crevasse
207. Pink fortress
208. Rack of clam

THERE I WAS

209. Tuna town
210. Carpet
211. Basin
212. Dong purse
213. Cat's Paw
214. Laps
215. Baby zipper
216. Love muffin
217. Coose canal
218. Cock hotel
219. Consummation devoutly to be wished
220. Fish canyon
221. Head catcher
222. Wonder bread
223. Courtney cocksleeve
224. Bacon hole
225. Chicken tongue
226. Temperamental ring piece
227. Rat
228. Jaws of life
229. Fuck donut
230. Bitter and twisted burger bar
231. Cold cut combo
232. Sheath
233. Flesh dent
234. Punta
235. Pink panther
236. Vagsicle
237. Stink Crevasse
238. Bone polisher
239. Biscuit of love
240. Hairy potter
241. French Fry dip
242. Pooty poot
243. Fly catcher

244. The vegan store
245. The easy bake oven
246. Fuzz box
247. Belly entrance
248. The schlong sucker
249. Clam canal
250. Hair pie
251. The great divide
252. Tuna salad
253. Love tunnel
254. Jewel box
255. Coo
256. Mule nose
257. Fur burger
258. Mans charity bash
259. Spitball bullseye
260. Golden valley
261. Lobster pot
262. Jane
263. Nana
264. Love Mop
265. Cooch
266. Love Pocket
267. The death of Adam
268. Bread
269. Lock up
270. Bobs bungalow
271. Gowl
272. Where Uncle Doodle goes
273. Strawberry
274. Bread box
275. Goodie basket
276. Bag pipe
277. Meat wagon
278. Cock toupee

279. Bacon sandwich
280. Bald Cupcake
281. Twotch
282. Fat rabbit
283. Interstice
284. Kitty kat
285. Dick dungeon
286. Vajayjay
287. The vegetarian's temptation
288. The orifice
289. Triangular Destination
290. Fuck tunnel
291. Dick Hotel
292. Scrubby pad
293. Heater
294. Kitty cage
295. Nest
296. Pastrami Flaps
297. Boy in the canoe
298. Cocktease
299. Fly bait
300. Mound
301. Pink Donut
302. Bubble gum by the bum
303. Niche
304. Panty hamster
305. Petticoat lane
306. Velcro love
307. Chatte
308. La pepita
309. Panty rat
310. Tweeny
311. Snake lake
312. Pound cake
313. Clam Candy

314. Lagoon
315. Chin chin
316. Hair treat
317. Lotus blossom
318. Home plate
319. The helmet hideaway
320. Jizz receptacle
321. The fish flap
322. Vault
323. Dicks Dock
324. Cum dumpster
325. Love crease
326. Mop
327. Fish sandwich
328. Shmekel Sheath
329. Hairy heaven
330. Sugar walls
331. Wizards sleeve
332. Nappy roots
333. Mossy Jaw
334. Garage
335. Lair
336. Slit
337. Tickled pink
338. Mystical fold
339. Bikini Treasure
340. Devils hideaway
341. Cock socket
342. Putang
343. Sanctum
344. Sideways sloppy joe
345. Babby
346. Pork pie
347. Mumble pants
348. Pink mink

349. Hairy donut
350. Split dick
351. Red river gorge
352. Love canal
353. Gap
354. Bologna Curtains
355. Lip tip
356. Papaya
357. Cock canal
358. Pocket
359. Monkeys chin
360. Cooze
361. Candy kiss
362. Cat flaps
363. Cream pie
364. Snatch
365. Mumbler
366. Elephant ears
367. Devils doorway
368. Toolshed
369. One eyed worm hole
370. Bologna flap over
371. Doodle sack
372. Glistening blossom
373. Georgia's flower
374. Vertical bacon sandwich
375. Pudding
376. Richard's house
377. Bergina
378. Peach
379. Apple pie
380. Baby bear
381. Saluud
382. Perforation
383. Soggy Box

384. Hairy clam
385. Furry delight
386. Vertical smile
387. Genny
388. Pink truffle
389. Clam
390. The furry cup
391. Baby exit
392. Coochie pop
393. Crack
394. Cherry pop
395. Prison purse
396. Cat's meow
397. Pachinko
398. Nappy dugout
399. Sperm bottle
400. Girl grommet
401. Slurpy
402. Love dimple
403. Donut
404. Cooter muffin
405. Old catcher's mitt
406. Cock sock
407. Cachucha
408. Meat cleavage
409. Crotch Carpet
410. Indiana bones and the temple of poon
411. Sperm dumpster
412. Fatty
413. Hooded lady
414. Fandango
415. Penis warmer
416. Beaver
417. Precious
418. Mount pleasant

THERE I WAS

419. Bits
420. Penis Fly Trap
421. Smush mitten
422. Sea food six pack
423. Pickle
424. Cock berth
425. Wuss
426. Fishamajig
427. Mary
428. Valva
429. South mouth
430. Man in the boat
431. Fissure
432. Coffee house
433. Spunk pot
434. Curly curtains
435. The shrine
436. Pink velvet
437. Pissy froth hole
438. Joy hole
439. Kitty
440. Peehole
441. The plowshare
442. Chasm
443. Nice slice
444. Hairy canary
445. Cock sheath
446. The indoor picnic
447. Dick mitten
448. Pearl hotel
449. Sweatbox
450. Happy place
451. Dick rack
452. Baby factory
453. Deer hoof

454. Fruit cup
455. Hairy Gap
456. Service
457. Mr. Vagoo
458. Purple people penis eater
459. Silk funnel
460. The Underground Railroad
461. Displabia
462. Vacuum Vulva
463. Baby tent
464. Cunt hole
465. See You Next Tuesday
466. Crack of heaven
467. Dog lips
468. Meat counter
469. Missile silo
470. The Keep
471. Fish buffet
472. Pek pek
473. Tuna taco
474. Devils hole
475. Flower
476. Fuck pocket
477. Beef Crease
478. Beef curtains
479. Goop chute
480. Rosebud
481. Pink portal
482. Dick Warmer
483. Male slot
484. Fanny (Australian)
485. Naughty bits
486. Tail
487. Lotus
488. Blue waffle

489. Stench-trench
490. Sweet briar
491. Bikini Muffin
492. Moose knuckle
493. Meat flower
494. Gauntlet
495. Mammal hole
496. Slash
497. Lulu
498. Eyelet
499. Love glove
500. Little Debbie
501. Faith
502. Red lane
503. Baloney flower
504. Toto
505. Heaven's gate
506. Cuntry pie
507. Poonani
508. Bone burnisher
509. Fuck hole
510. Dick eater
511. Pussy
512. Bermuda triangle
513. Love Flaps
514. Tabernacle
515. Beef flower
516. Pink sausage wallet
517. Arroyo
518. Scrambled eggs between the legs
519. Conch shell
520. Pole magnet
521. The chamber
522. Stop n pop
523. The pump protector

524. Hair burger

525. Hot spot

526. Banana box

527. Pocket pie

528. Mission objective

529. One eyed python trail

530. Love gulch

531. Count Flapula

532. Penis purse

533. Sausage silo

534. Horse collar

535. Queef quarters

536. Concavity

537. Pink velvet sausage wallet

538. Beav

539. Ham wallet

540. Knish

541. Clown pocket

542. Cookie

543. Beef silo

544. Pancake fold

545. Cock curator

546. Love target

547. Sperm bank

548. Happy Harbor

549. Whispering eye

550. Honey pot

551. Pink circle

552. The pink happy

553. Pootie tang

554. Cock HQ

555. Crack of doom

556. The red zone

557. The virginator

558. Panty prize

559. Skins
560. Furry Feast
561. Triangle
562. Cupids cupboard
563. Horn of plenty
564. Cockring
565. Mums glovebox
566. Cavern
567. Hump hole
568. Crevasse
569. Unobtainium
570. Golden Palace
571. Beaver teeth
572. Furry 8 ball rack
573. Wet mark
574. Happy pie
575. The abyss
576. Camel toe
577. Natures treasury
578. Wookie
579. The welcome opponent
580. Brake Pads
581. Meat sleeve
582. Cunt punt
583. Cock squeezer
584. Hairy Muffin
585. Meat crease
586. Cleft
587. Plum
588. Black oak
589. Slop hole
590. Serpent socket
591. Haven
592. Rusty brillo pad
593. Poo tang

THERE I WAS

594. Venus butterfly
595. Mouse
596. Black hole
597. Box of assorted creams
598. Vagoo
599. Juice box
600. The indoor barbeque
601. Fuzzy wuzzy
602. Phoenix nest
603. Bone hider
604. Cock mitten
605. Blow hole
606. Yeast pocket
607. Mound of Venus
608. Bear trap
609. Sperm Depository
610. Panty Muffin
611. Mommy parts
612. Mud flaps
613. Fun hatch
614. Cummer
615. Cock Quarters
616. Fox hole
617. Poody-tat
618. C – word
619. Bush tucker
620. Aphrosiacal tennis court
621. DNA dumpster
622. The blind alley
623. Puncture wound
624. Receptacle
625. Snizz
626. The bone collector
627. Theme park
628. Lawrence of Alabia

629. Mini
630. Baby slot
631. Women's weapon
632. Baby gate
633. Tackle box
634. HQ
635. Penis pothole
636. Hungry Minge
637. Baloney Drapes
638. Douche luge
639. Furry taco
640. Ruby
641. Shaft shelter
642. Cock cave
643. Lady parts
644. The house in pooh corner
645. Snap
646. Beef sheath
647. Love button
648. Crash pad
649. Snapper organ
650. Coochie
651. Peter vise
652. Bits and pieces
653. Ham flap
654. Mangina
655. Smuggler
656. Gravy bowl
657. Love taco
658. Fish mitten
659. Happy flappy
660. Trench
661. Hairy goblet
662. Cock holster
663. Meat locker

664. Down there

665. Privy counsel

666. Glory hole

667. Vadge of honor

668. Jewel

669. Peter's grove

670. Brazilian caterpillar

671. Lap flounder

672. Private parts

673. Cock Cove

674. The beard below

675. Birth tunnel

676. Beetle hood

677. Mossy cleft

678. Tuna spread

679. Peter parking

680. Brojocola

681. Morning Glory

682. Tuna pot pie

683. It

684. Dinner roll

685. Bone collector

686. Vajizzle

687. Southern belle

688. La Rossa

689. Downtown dining and entertainment district

690. Beef box

691. Cush

692. Ax wound

693. Pee jaws

694. Baby flaps

695. Quim

696. My lady

697. Front bottom

698. Bald man in a boat

699. Love crater

700. Bearded cave

701. Cutty

702. Penalty box

703. Grommet

704. Cathedral

705. Panty candy

706. Egg drop box

707. Urine pump

708. Poochicka

709. The beard down under

710. Muffin

711. Wunder down under

712. Bluntfront

713. Hollyhock

714. Downstairs

715. Hot pocket

716. Holy grail

717. Skin canoe

718. Beef tomato

719. Davey jones locker

720. Vag

721. Sperm shack

722. Hand warmer

723. The toothless blow job

724. The study

725. Sweet potato pie

726. Trough

727. Flesh cavern

728. Slot Pocket

729. The objective

730. Sausage slot

731. Dick holster

732. Poontang

733. Buffalo gums

734. Cock warmer
735. Baby foundry
736. Pushpin cushion
737. Birth cannon
738. Tuppence
739. Jelly roll
740. Chaude veg
741. Blossom
742. Mossy Garden of Delight
743. Celestial gate
744. Sausage wallet
745. Cock pocket
746. Quif
747. Big bud
748. Bitch ditch
749. Bearded clam
750. Fruit salad
751. Snake charmer
752. Moneymaker
753. Thresher
754. Whisker biscuit
755. Tomahawk chop
756. Wilt Chamberlain's daily glove
757. Round mound of beehound
758. Hatchet wound
759. Wand waxer
760. Incision
761. Launch pad
762. Joyful garden
763. Manhole
764. Juicy cooter
765. Bacon Biscuit
766. Pickle stinker
767. Mans ambition
768. Jelly donut

769. Hush puppy
770. Cooter
771. Goo guzzler
772. Hippos yawn
773. Jen Italia
774. Cooley hopper
775. Buffalo lips
776. Silk igloo
777. Calamari
778. Dugout
779. Love silo
780. Snail tracker
781. Crotch Cleavage
782. The nether beard
783. Ground zero
784. Musty thicket of wonders
785. Cunny
786. V
787. Man Trap
788. Bone tunnel
789. Notch
790. Muff
791. Nookie
792. Chia hole
793. Meat cave
794. Meat lips
795. Trim
796. Cavity
797. Sugar basin
798. Cloister
799. Poonaner
800. Girl parts
801. Fortune nookie
802. Taco
803. Happy hole

THERE I WAS

804. Tongue depressor
805. The breach
806. Fetus flaps
807. Tabby
808. Lip jeans
809. Flap biscuit
810. Fuck slot
811. Sugar hole
812. Crack of delights
813. Fish dish
814. Fuck canal
815. The red carpet
816. Cock chafer
817. Salami salon
818. Cockpit
819. Love Triangle
820. Indentation
821. Netherlands
822. Bone chute
823. Hairy Love muffin
824. Hamper of goodies
825. The condo downstate
826. Flesh mitten
827. Tinker bell
828. Birth canal
829. Temporary lodgings
830. Axe gash
831. Pasta shell
832. Furry clam
833. Baby hole
834. Pikachu
835. Gorge
836. Dove Breast
837. Bikini biscuit
838. Cock nest

THERE I WAS

839. Thatched cottage
840. Depository
841. Baloney crease
842. Clap trap
843. Oven
844. Gash
845. Dry mouthed widow
846. Happy valley
847. Map of Tassie
848. Fourth base
849. Breakfast of champions
850. Stinky cooler
851. Cucumber canal
852. Furry cupcake
853. Shaft sheath
854. Bait
855. Bone cave
856. Slurpee machine
857. Weiner wrap
858. Squish mitten
859. Girly bits
860. Bonefish
861. Packin shack
862. Shark fin
863. Hole
864. Pineapple
865. Spunk dump
866. Power Center
867. Fish lips
868. Camels foot
869. Cock curtain
870. Split tail
871. Mommy's pie
872. Mail slot
873. Fish Flaps

THERE I WAS

874. Penis parking
875. Holiest of Holies
876. Baby oven
877. Furry Enchilada of love
878. Grandest canyon
879. Clit
880. Innie
881. Hairy dale
882. Flapped nap
883. Box hot box
884. Tinkle
885. Richard's companion
886. Crave cave
887. Bean
888. Camel lips
889. Hair farm
890. Triangular temptation
891. Meat curtains
892. Erie canal
893. Tongue magnet
894. Hairy ax wound
895. The Promised Land
896. Woo hoo
897. The burrow
898. Ravine
899. Cream canal
900. Cherry
901. The nettle bed
902. The alter
903. Peter warmer
904. Nether regions
905. Pink Cookie
906. Fuck Furnace
907. South of the border
908. Bat cave

909. Moustache
910. The apple of One Eye
911. Love rug
912. The pink
913. Peephole
914. Watermelon
915. JJ
916. Dick driver
917. Slot
918. Cupcake
919. Love Garden
920. Salami garage
921. Baby Condo
922. Privates
923. Dildo hotel
924. Meat canal
925. Wet seal
926. Baby tunnel
927. Coosie
928. Baloney curtains
929. Bearded Taco
930. Bowl
931. Fuck freeway
932. Lady's low toupee
933. Hairy cupcake
934. Ass mate
935. Big Montana
936. Grassy knoll
937. Precious Petunia
938. The peace maker
939. Love biscuit
940. Stink rink
941. Aperture
942. Bologna drapes
943. Cave

THERE I WAS

944. Finger hut
945. Biscuit
946. Key hole
947. Spasm chasm
948. Field of dreams
949. Everlasting cum stopper
950. Flesh Pocket
951. Notorious V.A.G
952. Ham sandwich
953. Tampon tunnel
954. Coozie
955. Happy clam
956. Grumble
957. Golden arches
958. Catfish
959. Poon
960. Willy's haven
961. Nether lips
962. Crotch Cleft
963. The big split
964. Poon tang pie
965. Wagon ruts
966. Clamarama
967. Pandora's box
968. Wee wee
969. Mysterious lady parts
970. Furrow
971. Jezebels smell
972. Treasure
973. Red bread
974. Furry furnace
975. Love tomato
976. Dick deposit
977. Midnight dip
978. Precious Gem

979. Bikini Treat
980. Sperm sucker
981. Bone Sleeve
982. Sausage bun
983. Love cave
984. Hoo Hoo
985. Bucket
986. The wombsday book
987. Baby launcher
988. Pink Pineapple
989. Sperm chute
990. Piss fenders
991. Love sheath
992. Bologna Crease
993. Bone garage
994. Mans ruin
995. Snapper
996. Kebab
997. Kooch
998. Pflaume
999. Minge
1000. Puki

Last lift. Cargo operations secured/

Manufactured by Amazon.ca
Bolton, ON